A SEASON IN THE ABYSS
SPORTS GAMBLING VS. THE NFL's INTEGRITY

BRIAN TUOHY

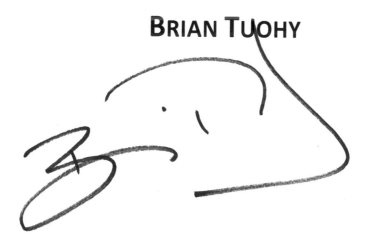

SUPER BOWL LIII 3/3

ISBN: 0988901129
ISBN-13: 978-0-9889011-2-4

Library of Congress Control Number: 2015914162
Mofo Press LLC, Kenosha, WI

SCHEDULE

A SEASON IN THE ABYSS

ACKNOWLEDGMENTS

First and foremost, I must thank my beautiful, caring wife Sarah for all her support and encouragement over the past 20 years. None of this would be possible without her. Also a big thank you to my family and friends for their constant support.

I would also like to thank Patrick Hruby, Ryan Rodenberg, Lance Williams and the Center for Investigative Reporting, Larry Burke, Michael Ravnitzky, Dan Moldea, Scott Schettler, Benjamin Best and crew, Jay Kornegay, Lauren McGuinn & all the FBI FOIA specialists, Charles Farrell, David Meggyesy, Pete Korner, Heather Wardle, Keith Whyte, Howard Schlossberg & all at Columbia College, Jerry Tapp, Sam Bourquin, Ian Punnett, Chris Boros at Coast to Coast AM, Steve Solomon & Steve Czaban, everyone at the Tony Basilio Show, Erskine, Kathleen Dervin, the Gamblers' Book Club, the Society of Former Special Agents of the FBI, everyone at Feral House, all the radio show producers & hosts who were brave enough to give me a little air time, and those who assisted me with this book who were not, cannot, or refused to be named.

A big hat tip to all my fans and followers who have helped spread the word, sent in tips, and offered advice over the years. And a final word of thanks to you, the reader, for taking the time to read this book (while ignoring the poor grammar and typos).

PRESEASON

"I, Roger Goodell, under penalty of perjury, declare as follows:

"...As Commissioner of the NFL, my most important responsibility is maintaining the integrity of professional football, and preserving public confidence in the NFL.

"The NFL is the most popular and widely recognized professional football league in the United States. The great popularity of NFL football, and the goodwill it has achieved with its fans and the public as a whole, is rooted in the integrity of the game itself. NFL football stands for clean, healthy competition, and rewards hard work, dedication, and honest effort. Maintaining these values and the highest integrity of the game of professional football is a critical aspect of preserving the NFL's goodwill. For these reasons, NFL owners and players have worked diligently since the league's inception nearly ninety years ago to protect the NFL's integrity and maintain the public's confidence in the league.

"The spread of sports betting, including the introduction of sports betting as proposed by the state of New Jersey, threatens to damage irreparably the integrity of, and public confidence in, NFL football. An increase in state-promoted sports betting would wrongly and unfairly engender suspicion and cynicism toward every on-the-field NFL event that affects the betting line. If gambling is freely permitted on sporting events, normal incidents of the game such as bad snaps, dropped passes, turnovers, penalties, and play calling inevitably will fuel speculation, distrust and accusations of point-shaving or game-fixing. I am aware that in the past, betting scandals related to legal sports betting have occurred both in the United States and in foreign countries.

"The new sports gambling scheme that New Jersey proposes would also greatly increase the likelihood that the allegiance of certain fans will be turned from teams, players and high-level athletic competition, toward an interest first and foremost in winning a bet. The core entertainment value of fair and honest competition between teams and athletes that is reflected in NFL games will be replaced by the bettor's interest, based not on team or player performance, but on the potential financial impact of each on-the-field event.

"State-sponsorship of sports gambling also trades unfairly on the property and goodwill of the NFL. For example, casinos and other gambling institutions that permit betting on sports are often viewed unfavorably by a significant portion of the public. The NFL, on the other hand, strives to preserve and promote an image of fairness, and has invested mightily in maintaining this image. State-sponsorship of sports gambling threatens to confuse fans into believing that the NFL supports sports gambling, thereby allowing casino operators and other sports-betting operations to trade unfairly on the NFL's goodwill and image of fairness.

"The NFL cannot be compensated in damages for the harm that sports gambling poses to the goodwill, character and integrity of NFL football, and to the fundamental bonds of loyalty and devotion between fans and teams that the league seeks to maintain. Once the character and integrity of NFL football have been compromised, and the bonds of loyalty and devotion between fans and teams have been broken, NFL football will have been irreparably injured in a manner that cannot adequately be calculated in dollars."

-- Declaration of NFL Commissioner Roger Goodell, filed August 10, 2012 to the US District Court, District of New Jersey.

BRIAN TUOHY

WEEK 1
vs. NEW JERSEY

Integrity. That word seems to mean a lot to the powers that be in the National Football League. Commissioner Roger Goodell invoked "integrity" seven times within the first six paragraphs of his official Declaration submitted to the US District Court when the state of New Jersey attempted to legalize sports gambling in 2012. By way of comparison, he used the word "football" nine times.

My hope is that by the end of this book you will realize that the word "integrity" is actually meaningless to the NFL. Oh, the *appearance* of integrity matters to the league. It's part of their sales pitch. Integrity is supposedly what puts fans in the stands and keeps them glued to their television sets. But abiding by the true definition of the word—the quality of being honest and having strong moral principles—isn't really the NFL's thing.

Because if you believe the league's owners and their crony Goodell, nothing strikes at the heart of the NFL's integrity more than people gambling upon its sport. Not performance-enhancing drugs, not criminals filing the rosters, not athletes suffering from brain damage resulting from playing the game, not any of the lies or half-truths the league has spun through its

5

media partners; nothing will cost the sport its soul like you betting $50 on the Seahawks to beat the Patriots in the Super Bowl.

Do you believe that?

Now I do agree with the NFL on one thing: I don't think you should gamble on football. In fact, I don't think you should gamble on any sports, play the lottery, or partake in the table games and slot machines casinos offer either. Why? Because you are going to lose money in the long run. It's inevitable. The odds are not in your favor. Worse yet, you may become addicted to what it is gambling offers and spiral far out of control, losing not just money, but family, friends, jobs—anything of value in your life.

With that said, I have no problem if you're the wagering type either. Nothing should prevent you from gambling if that's what you choose to do with your money. If you find the endeavor entertaining and the environment exciting, then by all means, place your bets. Who am I to judge? I have been known to gamble on occasion. In fact, as you will see throughout the course of this book, I gambled *a lot* on the NFL in 2014-15. Not just to thumb my nose at the league (though that is implied), but to see in how many ways I could bet the NFL despite the league's anti-gambling stance. I wanted to know how far down this rabbit hole went, who lurked behind what doors, and what it truly encompassed.

As gambling has transformed from a taboo into a socially acceptable form of entertainment, slowly but surely states have been easing their prohibition on gaming in all its varieties. Lotteries are available in 44 states, 35 states have casinos, 31 states offer horse racing, and so far, three states have legalized some form of intrastate internet gambling with others lining up to follow suit. But only in the state of Nevada can you legally bet on sports in all its incarnations.

It is the sports leagues—the NFL, MLB, NBA, NHL,

and NCAA—that have enforced this status quo. Congress, in its infinite wisdom, deputized the leagues to maintain the moratorium on the spread of sports wagering with the passage of the Professional and Amateur Sports Protection Act (PASPA) in 1992. It's a very basic law which reads:

"It shall be unlawful for—

"(1) a governmental entity to sponsor, operate, advertise, promote, license, or authorize by law or compact, or

"(2) a person to sponsor, operate, advertise, or promote, pursuant to the law or compact of a governmental entity,

"a lottery, sweepstakes, or other betting, gambling, or wagering scheme based, directly or indirectly (through the use of geographical references or otherwise), on one or more competitive games in which amateur or professional athletes participate, or are intended to participate, or on one or more performances of such athletes in such games."

PASPA carved out an exemption for four states—Nevada, Delaware, Oregon, and Montana—all of which offered some form of sports wagering in the past. These states were allowed to continue (or reinstate) the sports betting options they possessed between January 1, 1976 and August 31, 1990, but they could not expand upon their sports gambling "schemes" (as the law labeled them). This ensured Nevada would be the lone state in America to offer single game wagering as Delaware, Oregon, and Montana never allowed such bets.

Written into the law was a gift to the state of New Jersey. PASPA gave the state a one year window in which to enact legislature to legalize sports gambling exclusively in its casinos. The state promptly fumbled away this opportunity. If it hadn't, it's likely that everyone would quote the "Atlantic City line" as opposed to the "Vegas line" when it comes to today's sports wagering stories.

Nearly twenty years later, as Atlantic City's casinos began filing bankruptcy and shuttering their doors one by one, the state decided to give sports gambling a second go. State Senator Raymond Lesniak filed a lawsuit in 2009 challenging the constitutionality of PASPA and hoping to pave the way for New Jersey casinos (and race tracks) to offer sports wagering. Was Senator Lesniak concerned about his constituents' inability to legally bet on a Broncos game? No. What he saw was a potential $100 million a year tax revenue increase for the state.

The voters of New Jersey took a shine to that financial boon as well, passing a statewide referendum to allow sports gambling in November 2011 with 64 percent of the vote (648,760 "yes" to 367,283 "no"). The following day Lesniak introduced a bill to decriminalize sports wagering in the state. Though New Jersey governor Chris Christie seemed hesitant to back the law, in January 2012 he signed the Sports Wagering Law into being. The law's only caveat was that wagering would not be allowed on New Jersey teams or sporting events that took place within the state (a similar in-state sports wagering ban existed for 40 years in Nevada, but was lifted in 2001).

Then came the lawsuits. The four major sports leagues in conjunction with the NCAA took New Jersey to court and promptly won, striking down the Sports Wagering Law. Then they won on appeal. Then they won when a second appeal was denied. Then, just when it appeared New Jersey would defy the odds and have the case heard before the Supreme Court, its dreams dropped like a brick trying to fly. The Justices refused to hear it.

Many believed New Jersey's case had the merits necessary to be heard before the Supreme Court even though the court hears less than one percent of all the cases for which it is petitioned. Most likely, the deciding factor against the state was that time and again PASPA had been ruled by lower courts to be constitutional. There simply was no argument for the Justices to decide. Despite claims that PASPA granted Nevada a monopoly on legalized sports gambling and violated the 10th Amendment (which declares, "The powers not delegated to the United States by the Constitution, nor prohibited by it to the States, are reserved to the States respectively, or to the people."), no court seemed to believe this was the case.

The interesting part, though, is when defending its position, the leagues—as represented by their respective commissioners—wouldn't argue or quibble over the legalities of PASPA. Instead, they worried about the "harm" legalized gambling would bring to their product. This notion was best laid out by the commissioners themselves in their respective Declarations.

NHL Commissioner Gary Bettman: "Instead of enjoying the NHL for the skill of our athletes and to root for their team to win the game, many fans will feel cheated and disappointed when they do not win their bets, regardless of whether their team wins or loses. By making sports gambling a widespread institution tied to the outcomes of NHL games, the very nature of the sport is likely to change for the worse."

(Former) MLB Commissioner Bud Selig: "Another likely result of sports gambling is that fan loyalty would diminish as many fans would focus less on their allegiance to certain teams, players, or cities and instead focus more on the outcomes of individual bets. The inevitable shifting 'loyalties' that would result from sports gambling could forever alter the relationship between teams and their fans. Players would not be viewed by fans as exceptionally skilled and talented competitors, but as mere assets to be exploited for 'fast money.'"

(Former) NBA Commissioner David Stern: "The NBA cannot be compensated in damages for the harm that sports gambling poses to the fundamental bonds of loyalty and devotion between fans and teams. Once that special relationship has been compromised, the NBA will have been irreparably injured in a manner that cannot adequately be calculated in dollars."

Remarkably, the courts have found that the leagues can prove this "harm" brought about by fans gambling. Writing the majority decision in New Jersey's 2-1 loss in the United States Court of Appeals for the Third Circuit (one judge did take the state's side), Judge Julio Fuentes wrote, "They [the leagues] are harmed by their unwanted association with an activity they (and large portions of the public) disapprove of—gambling....Here, the reputational harm that results from increasingly associating the Leagues' games with gambling is fairly intuitive.

"For one, the conclusion that there is a link between legalizing sports gambling and harm to the integrity of the Leagues' games has been reached by several Congresses that have passed laws addressing gambling and sports....It is, indeed, the specific conclusion reached by the Congress that enacted PASPA, as reflected by the statutory cause of action conferred to the Leagues to enforce the law when their individual games are the target of state-licensed sports wagering....And, presumably, it has also been at least part of the conclusions of the various state legislatures that have blocked the practice throughout our history....

"The record is replete with evidence showing that being associated with gambling is stigmatizing, regardless of whether the gambling is legal or illegal. Before the District Court were studies showing that: (1) some fans from each League viewed gambling as a problem area for the Leagues, and some fans expressed their belief that game fixing most threatened the Leagues' integrity; (2) some fans did not want a professional sports franchise to open in Las Vegas, and some fans would be less likely to spend money on the Leagues if that occurred; and (3) a large number of fans oppose the expansion of legalized sports betting. This more than suffices to meet the Leagues' evidentiary burden...[that] being associated with gambling is undesirable and harmful to one's reputation."

Now, I'm no lawyer, but there are a few things to take

issue with here. For starters, why do we need a "Protection Act" for sports in the first place? It's not like sports are an endangered species. Congress has enacted four laws—the 1961 Wire Act, the 1964 Sports Bribery Act, the 1970 Illegal Gambling Business Act, and the 2006 Unlawful Interact Gambling Enforcement Act—which are supposed to prevent both illegal gambling and game fixing from occurring. The leagues themselves possess rules, regulations, and contractual stipulations designed to stop players, coaches, and referees from gambling on their own sport as well as punishments for those who fail to do so. Isn't all of that enough to protect sports from the criminal gambling element?

There are also a couple of statements Judge Fuentes made that aren't seemingly based in reality. He wrote that "large portions of the public" disprove of gambling. Later he added, "A large number of fans oppose the expansion of legalized sports betting." What are either of these claims based upon? If such a large number of Americans are so anti-gambling, why does every state with the exception of Utah and Hawaii offer some form of legalized gambling? It's estimated that as many as 80 percent of Americans gambled in 2013 and lost nearly $120 billion dollars doing so.[1] The notion that many sports fans are opposed to legalized sports betting originates from studies conducted by and provided to the court by the sports leagues themselves. These surveys and studies have not been made available for the public to review which, in my view, makes such claims dubious.

But remember, gambling by fans is going to cause irrevocable "harm." The commissioners said so, and Congress swallowed their argument.

One dissenting voice, however, came in the form of new NBA Commissioner Adam Silver. Having held a variety of positions in the NBA since 1992, Silver was handpicked for the top spot by departing Commissioner David Stern in February

2014. Nine months later, Silver not only wrote an op-ed piece for the *New York Times* titled "Legalize and Regulate Sports Betting," but was quoted as saying, "If you have a gentleman's bet or a small wager on any kind of sports contest, it makes you that much more engaged in it. That's where we're going to see it pay dividends. If people are watching a game and clicking to bet on their smartphones, which is what people are doing in the United Kingdom right now, then it's much more likely you're going to stay tuned for a long time."[2]

That doesn't sound harmful at all. It sounds downright profitable.

Of course, the NBA is not the king of sports in the US. That title belongs to the NFL. So, despite what Adam Silver writes and says, according to NFL spokesman Brian McCarthy it "doesn't change our stance that has been articulated for decades: no gambling on NFL games."[3]

There are just a couple of problems with the NFL's steadfast position. "What we know is, sports gaming is going on every day in New Jersey in the shadows," Governor Christie said during an appearance on the 94WIP Morning Show in November 2014. "I find it very funny that [the Leagues] are just not in touch with the reality of what's going on every day. The idea that they have shows on every Sunday to talk about the point spread. What relevance does the point spread have to an NFL game if it's not about gambling? I think their argument about the harm that comes to their leagues is really kind of ridiculous...."[4]

You may not like the guy, but Christie is right. Illegal sports gambling is a multi-billion dollar industry. Estimates range that $80 to $500 billion—that's billion with a B—is wagered illegally on sports every year in the US. The high end of that range may be a gross exaggeration[5], but when Las Vegas admits it accounts for only one percent of all the sports gambling in the US—and in 2014 Nevada booked nearly $4 billion in sports bets[6]—it might not be that crazy of a number. The

American Gambling Association reported that "Americans will make $3.8 billion worth of illegal bets on this year's Super Bowl between the New England Patriots and Seattle Seahawks. That figure stands in stark contrast to the approximately $100 million bet legally on the Super Bowl each year. In fact, the illegal market is 38 times greater than the legal one."[7]

What's worse is that the underground sports gambling world is controlled by organized crime. I've been told by more than one former FBI agent that sports gambling is the mob's top money maker. With hundreds of billions being tossed around, you can understand why.

So which is the greater harm: funding organized crime by keeping sports gambling illegal to protect these leagues/businesses, or defunding the mob and having fan bases that are more engaged in their sport of choice via legal, regulated wagering?

If it's not actual harm that's preventing the NFL and its brethren from assisting and participating in the legalization process, then what is the hold up? Senator Lesniak believed the answer was simple. "They [the sports leagues] have their heads in the sand. They know they are not being honest and truthful. They're playing out the string, until they can get a piece of the action from sports betting."

"It's hard to buy that argument [irreparable harm]," he continued, "when they just added another NFL game at Wembley Stadium [in the UK where sports gambling is legal], where people are betting right across the street. Look, until the NFL feels that it can profit from it, they'll be opposed to it. I believe we could cut a deal with the NFL and the sports leagues tomorrow to give them some kind of franchise fee for using their official statistics. Problem is that, though, we'd have to get an act through Congress to do that. And they [sports leagues] are not going to openly support that."[8]

NFL spokesman Brian McCarthy disagreed, "[Revenue]

has nothing to do with it and never has."[9] Considering that the NFL has sold itself out in nearly every possible way, it's hard to believe a business like this wouldn't add another major revenue stream if presented the opportunity. But the NFL booking its own bets might not be the best decision it could make. I would surmise, however, that offering betting windows at stadiums or perhaps via NFL.com through a third party might be deemed okay some day if—and that's a big if—the NFL getting a little taste of the action didn't raise any eyebrows.

Yet doing so would be a 180 degree about-face. The NFL has been publicly anti-gambling for so long, it cannot change course at this point. And why should it? At the moment, the league holds the moral high ground. If some sort of gambling or game fixing scandal should ever hit the league it can easily state, "We never wanted people to gamble on football. We feared this would happen. What more could we have done to protect our sport?"

What the league needs is an out. A loss. It needs New Jersey to win its court battle. Then the legalization decision would be out of the NFL's control, and any move to embrace that new legal standing wouldn't seem as disingenuous.

New Jersey's latest legal maneuver might just do the trick. After the Supreme Court turned down the case, Christie issued a directive in September 2014 proclaiming the state would not prosecute a casino or race track that offered sports wagering. In essence, New Jersey was going to allow unregulated sports gambling. The move caught nearly everyone by surprise. But the state argued that the Third Circuit Court's ruling left New Jersey with an all or nothing decision, one "with so little flexibility that they [the states] must either prohibit sports wagering entirely or allow wagering by children on the doorsteps of their elementary schools."

This deregulation idea might be just want the NFL ordered. Way back in 1972, the NFL issued a "policy paper" which I obtained in an FBI file in which the league asked itself 12 somewhat rhetorical questions regarding legalizing sports gambling. The seventh question was, "What is the difference between betting on a game and betting on a horse race?" Within its own answer, the NFL revealed one of its greatest fears. It wrote, "In racing, a State Commission sets dates and sites of meetings, licenses trainers, owners, jockeys and drivers. It hands down suspensions, assesses fines and takes a generous slice of the betting action. This tight supervision has become necessary to guard against drugging, fixing of races and false identification of horses. Any similar governmental obligation to control team sports would involve far-reaching changes in their present structure of operations and place a costly and staggering burden to not only oversee sporting events in its own state but also presumably everywhere a sporting event is held, if legalized bets are accepted on that event."

In other words, legalization naturally brings with it oversight. *Outside* oversight that the NFL isn't keen on engaging. The autonomy the league currently enjoys (and in some opinions, abuses) when handing out suspensions, fines, etc. might vanish due to the spread of sports gambling regulations. The league wants to remain its own kingdom, and legalized sports betting with its licensing may interfere with the business the NFL is used to conducting.

NBA Commissioner Silver doesn't see it that way. He seemed to embrace such oversight, writing in his *New York Times* op-ed piece, "Congress should adopt a federal framework that allows states to authorize betting on professional sports, subject to strict regulatory requirements and technological safeguards. These requirements would include: mandatory monitoring and reporting of unusual betting-line movements; a licensing protocol to ensure betting operators are legitimate; minimum-age verification measures; geo-blocking technology to ensure betting is available only where it is legal; mechanisms to identify and exclude people with gambling problems; and education about responsible gaming."[10]

Even so, Silver was against New Jersey's move to deregulate the industry. Of course, so was the NFL. Christie's crafty maneuver was quickly blocked by U.S. District Judge Michael Shipp (who, coincidently, is the brother of former NFL player Marcel Shipp) who issued the leagues a temporary restraining order. Despite cutting a deal with English bookmaking company William Hill to run the unlicensed sports betting operations at Monmouth Park race track in New Jersey and more promises by Christie, not a single bet has been legally booked in the state as of August 2015. The state's last hope may ride with a bill presented to Congress by New Jersey Representatives Frank LoBiondo and Frank Pallone, Jr. which would open a four year window to allow states to enact sports wagering laws.

But I wouldn't bet on its passage. Not yet anyway.

WEEK 2
@ FANTASY FOOTBALL

Quick. Think of the last boring story you heard. Did it involve a beer snob pontificating about the hoppiness of some microbrew they imbibed? Or was it a proud parent gushing over the fact that their protégée 5-year old can squeak out an E note on a violin? Or did a coworker have to describe in minute detail the last team meeting and how much so-and-so is a bitch and how this guy doesn't get it and that guy is too demanding and...zzzzzzzzzzzzzzz.

None of that compares to how boring it is to listen to someone talk about their fantasy football team. Steals in the draft, unlikely injuries, last-second wins, crushing defeats...no one wants to hear it, even though they may be smiling and nodding as you talk. As Nick, a sales rep I work with, complained, "Do you know how ridiculous it is to hear grown men arguing over something with the word 'fantasy' in its name?" It's hard to argue. But a growing number of people would take umbrage at such a statement.

According to the Fantasy Sports Trade Association (FSTA)—and yes, that is a real organization—14 percent of the US population aged 12 and over play fantasy sports. The typical player is an unmarried 34-year old Caucasian male with a college degree[1] though FSTA studies show 22 percent of all American men and six percent of women compete in this endeavor. Overall, 41 million people played some form of fantasy sports in 2013[2] with at least 30 million engaging in fantasy football.

As the participation level increases, so, too, does the amount of money spent on this "hobby." The FSTA reports that in a 12 month period players will spend $1.71 billion on fantasy league fees, another $262 million in transaction fees within those leagues, nearly $300 million for websites to host leagues, and $656 million on informational materials like fantasy sports magazines.[3] All in all, fantasy sports has a $4 billion annual economic impact on the sports industry.[4] That nearly equates to the yearly revenue of the NHL. To go along with all of that money, players are spending an enormous amount of time on fantasy. Seventy four percent of players will visit four or more sports news websites, and the average enthusiast will spend nearly 18 hours a week consuming sports with another nine hours related directly to fantasy.[5]

Businesses of all sizes recognize the importance of these numbers. ESPN, NBC Sports, CBS Sports, DirecTV, Microsoft, and Yahoo were among the 130 different companies in attendance at the 2014 FSTA Summer Conference. According to George Leimer, ESPN's head of fantasy sports, during the NFL season fantasy players "drive 17 percent of traffic to the company's websites, which average around 90 million unique visitors each month. 'Which is amazing when you think about it. We could stop right there, full stop, period. That's proof of how important it is.'"[6]

With all of that said, you might be asking yourself, what exactly is fantasy football? In short, it's a game in which players create fictional teams comprised of real NFL players, translating their weekly game stats into points. Typically, teams consist of a quarterback, two running backs, two wide receivers, a tight end, a kicker and a team defense, but every league has its own roster format. Rushing, receiving, and passing yards are worth a predetermined amount of points, and like the actual sport, field goals are often worth three points and touchdowns six. Players match their teams against each other head-to-head with the highest scoring team being victorious.

A version of fantasy football has been around since the 1960s, but today there are two main variations. The traditional game usually features 10 or more teams in a league, and lasts for the majority of the NFL regular season. Players draft or acquire their rosters via an auction prior to the season's start and utilize this squad for the duration, making transactions along the way if necessarily. Today, however, "daily" fantasy leagues are the rage. These operate with a similar design, but offer much more instant gratification. Often advertised as "one week seasons," in daily fantasy games, players build a roster by purchasing players against an enforced salary cap. This team is then used for a single week of the NFL season. Daily fantasy players can then play that roster against not just another single competitor, but thousands of players all at once.

The uninitiated may be asking, why is all this time, money, and effort spent on such a silly game? The answer is simple: money is at stake. Perhaps as much as a million dollars. That's right. Fantasy sports' dirty secret is that it is gambling. And it's legal.

The FSTA and its members are adamant that this is *not* gambling, going so far as to devote an entire webpage on the FSTA website to explain why. "It's bad for the industry for this to be seen as gambling," Rotowire founder and FSTA Chairman Peter Schoenke explained to me, "because gambling in the US is perceived to be bad. Most forms of gambling are banned. Fantasy sports isn't gambling because the first thing is, it's a game of skill. Unlike craps which is all random, this is more like golf where there's a certain skill involved. There is a lot of luck, but at the same time, you look at these national competitions like the [National Fantasy Football Championship] or the [Fantasy Football Players Championship] and the same guys win a lot. There's a big divergence between the guys at the top and the rest of the field. It's not random. So that shows it's a game of skill. And that's an important distinction in the law of what gambling is."

Schoenke's argument was fantasy sports' lynchpin to success. In 2006, Congress passed the Unlawful Internet Gambling Enforcement Act (UIGEA). The law was designed to defund gambling websites, especially poker sites, by making it illegal for banks, credit card companies and the like from transferring money between the sites and the players. It effectively killed online poker. The UIGEA defined poker as a game of luck (read: gambling), meaning it was no different from playing a slot machine. Fantasy sports, however, was determined to be a game of skill which meant participants were not gambling when they engaged in the activity. This four sentence carve-out in the UIGEA birthed a multi-billion dollar industry.

The ironic part of the UIGEA exemption is that lobbyists from the major sports leagues, led by NFL lobbyist Marty Gold (who authored of a book on Senate procedure), were the cause for its inclusion. The leagues wanted—strike that, *needed*— fantasy to not be seen as gambling because they recognized its importance to their well-being.

"Fantasy sports has had a huge impact on viewership and interest," Schoenke said. "One of the things to happen to fantasy sports was in the 1990s, the leagues—the NFL in particular—didn't like fantasy. They thought it was geeky and they didn't want to be associated with it, or they thought it was gambling and therefore bad for the sport. Then in the early 2000s, around 2003 or 2004, the NFL did its own data and found out that the fantasy football player was their best consumer because they went to more games, they watched more television, bought more jerseys, all that kind of stuff. And the key for them was that they watch more television because [with fantasy football] people have a reason to watch more than their hometown team. So the light bulb went off and the league completely switched directions."

So much so, the NFL now offers its own fantasy football leagues on NFL.com. Not all are free. Entry fees ranged from $4.99 to $124.99 for the 2014 season. For the winner of each of these leagues, the NFL would award prizes ranging from an authentic game-used penalty flag to a football signed by members of the 2013 Pro Bowl (which the league called "the ultimate collector's dream"). These were 10-player leagues and filled up *fast*. I attempted to enter a $30.99 league, the winner of which would receive an authentic autographed football (second place and below got bunk). There were three slots available, but by the time I completed the sign-up process, the league was filled and I became the first member of another new league. Despite an attempt to contact the NFL about its fantasy football offerings and the number players who joined, the league did not respond to my questions.

I also was a member of two other traditional fantasy football leagues—one draft-based, the other an auction league—both of which had 12 participants as well as an entry fee. Yes, we played for money. In fact, I've never played in a league where the champion didn't win money. I haven't even *met* another fantasy player that played in a league without cash at stake. And when I asked my fellow owners at each football draft if they would label what we were doing as gambling, they unanimously declared "yes" despite the UIGEA's and FSTA's assurance it wasn't.

Now, I was going to chronicle my weekly experiences in these three leagues, but as I mentioned at the beginning of this chapter...zzzzzzzzzzzzz. However, for illustrative purposes on this notion of skill vs. luck, let me briefly review my fantasy season(s).

Each league begins with the highly anticipated draft. "Experts" write articles on how to prepare, sometimes getting into the nitty gritty of not just which players to target, but reminding you to "get a good night's sleep" and "not to get drunk" if you want to have a good draft. Having finished last in my draft-based league in 2013 (which might show you the amount of "skill" I possessed) I had the luxury of selecting the number one overall pick. The question was who should I take?

If I wanted a quarterback, the experts—that is the fantasy football writers for ESPN.com, CBSSports.com, FFToday.com, and NFL.com—all predicted that Peyton Manning would be the highest scoring QB. All four sites also concurred that Drew Brees and Aaron Rodgers would be a close second and third. If I wanted a running back, my best bets were Adrian Peterson, Jamaal Charles, or LeSean McCoy. At wide receiver, the consensus top choices were Calvin Johnson or DeMaryius Thomas with Dez Bryant and Julio Jones rounding out the field. Considering RB is traditionally a thin position fantasy-wise, I took the Chiefs Jamaal Charles in the top slot. I also wound up with Charles in my NFL-hosted league. Who I did *not* have in any league was Cowboys' running back DeMarco Murray. This, as we shall see, was a fatal mistake.

The expert advice I and many millions of other fantasy players relied upon from these and other websites was flawed. At times, extremely flawed. By season's end, the top three scoring quarterbacks in fantasy football—using a traditional scoring system—were Andrew Luck, Aaron Rodgers, and Russell Wilson. The consensus number one QB, Peyton Manning, ended up fourth. The experts were correct with Rodgers, and Luck was usually listed as a top five QB (though in 2014 he was actually the highest scoring fantasy player, period). But Wilson? CBS Sports had him ranked 17th for quarterbacks. In fact, out of the four sites I visited in the preseason, only ESPN rated Wilson as a top 10 scoring quarterback.

For wide receivers, the Steelers' Antonio Brown was the runaway top scorer at his position. The experts at these sites had him at best fourth overall (at ESPN), at worst eighth (CBS and the NFL). They were on target with Dez Bryant and DeMaryius Thomas, both of whom finished in the top four, but none had the Giants rookie sensation Odell Beckham Jr. on their radar. Beckham finished fifth overall at his position, yet not one of these fantasy experts put him in their top 25, much less top 40 wide receivers.

As for running back, DeMarco Murray *blew up*. No one saw him rushing for over 1,800 yards with 13 touchdowns as he did in 2014. No site I tracked listed Murray as a top five running back. Fantasy Football Today listed him sixth, behind the Jaguars' Toby Gerhart (who finished the season as the 55th best RB). Don't laugh. ESPN ranked Murray eighth, behind the Buccaneers' Doug Martin (who finished 48th). The NFL was wise enough to list Murray ahead of Martin—by one slot—at 11th overall. The other class of the running back position was the Steelers' Le'Veon Bell and the Seahawks' Marshawn Lynch. Both were usually considered top 10 backs, but easily outperformed their predicted numbers.

Still, it was DeMarco Murray that was the bane of my fantasy football existence. In my auction league, I put together a league best 11-1 season and was the highest scoring team. I earned a bye in the playoffs, but lost in the second round to the eventual league champion due to DeMarco Murray's 28.8 point day. No matter. In my draft league, I tied with three others for the best record in the league at 8-4 and reached our league's Super Bowl. I lost by half a point (seriously) in large part because of DeMarco Murray's 20.9 point performance. Ah, but in the NFL-hosted fantasy league, my team put up the second best record at 9-5, reached the Super Bowl against the number one overall team and…got creamed, thanks to DeMarco Murray. Catch the trend here?

Was having DeMarco Murray on your team a matter of skill or was it a bit of luck? I know playing against him in two fantasy Super Bowls was a big ol' bag of bad luck, but in the course of a full-length fantasy season, luck plays a huge factor in the final results. Injuries are impossible to predict (heck, I lost five starting pitchers *and a catcher* to Tommy John surgery in my 2014 fantasy baseball season) as are situations like that of Adrian Peterson who missed all but one game under allegations of child abuse. Players start hot and fade. Others come on strong as the season winds down. Some are consistently sporadic. It's a minefield to traverse. Skill can only get you so far. It's often the roster-filling picks made in the 14th round like that of Odell Beckham Jr. that can truly be the difference between last place and a championship.

But the FSTA wouldn't see it this way. Nor would they see these leagues in which I participated as gambling, despite the fact that I walked away—as a "loser"—up over $300. As for the NFL league with the autographed football on the line? That was a *prize* league. See, I paid a $30.99 entry fee to the NFL so it could run the league and award a prize to whoever won (I wonder which player's signature our league champion "Blue Blood" received. It was supposed to have a retail value of $250). That's not gambling. It's just more profit for the NFL. In the case of my other two leagues, well, FSTA studies show that the reason I likely participated in these was due to camaraderie and friendship, not money.

"The behavior of the people that gamble as opposed to the people that play fantasy are very different," Schoenke explained. "If you're gambling, it's pretty much all about the money. It's about the buzz you get when you're going to win money or lose money. When you do fantasy sports, the money is really secondary. It's all about competing with your buddies and rubbing it in their face by taking your sports knowledge and showing off what you know. The prize money is nice, but for the most part, the prize money is just to keep everybody honest. You're not going to get the same negatives you get with gambling. A person with a gambling problem is less likely to play in a million fantasy football leagues to get their gambling buzz as opposed to heading to the nearest casino. So it's just a very different recreation."

According to the FSTA website, "The vast majority of fantasy sports players participate in free contests that have no cash or material prizes (over 74 percent of the 30.6 million fantasy sports players in 2010 entered a contest or used league software that included no cash or material prize, according to an IPSOS research report). The only enjoyment is winning and competing against other sports fans. In fact, frequent surveys of fantasy sports players show that the top reasons for playing include 'competing with friends,' 'enhance my sports experience' and 'to be in a league with friends' [two of those responses seem redundant, but anyways...]. A 2008 survey of fantasy sports users from the Fantasy Sports Trade Association showed winning money or prizes wasn't in the top five reasons for playing fantasy sports and winning a prize was a motivating factor for less than 20 percent of players."[7]

This competing-with-friends-so-it's-not-*really*-gambling excuse does hold a wee bit of water. If I'm honest with myself, playing against my friends is the motivating factor for me to continue with the leagues I've been involved in for the past 20+ years. As for the NFL-sponsored league I joined, well...not so much. For me, these were nine strangers and they remained that way. Not one offered me a trade, sent me an email (even to talk smack), and in fact, no in-league communication appeared to exist once the draft ended. So was that about "competing with friends," "enhancing my sports experience," or winning that autographed football? Myself, I wanted the freakin' football...damn you, DeMarco Murray.

"I think FSTA is being a little disingenuous," said Keith S. Whyte, Executive Director for the National Council on Problem Gambling (NCPG). "Money may well not be the most prominent reason why people play traditional fantasy sports, but it almost certainly has to be a primary motivator for daily fantasy sports." And daily fantasy sports (DFS) is the growth industry. According to the FSTA only one percent of fantasy players play daily games, yet they account for 26 percent of money spent in the industry. And though some of the "this isn't gambling" argument may hold for the traditional game, it splatters on the pavement like Humpty Dumpty when discussing DFS.

Perhaps you've seen the ads or read the stories surrounding DFS. The two current leaders in the field, FanDuel and DraftKings, have certainly been promoting themselves. Part of their sales pitch involves hailing the conquering heroes of the game. For example, there's Ipsalante, MI postal worker Chris "Beermakersfan" Prince who was featured on ESPN's *Outside the Lines* in August 2014. Prince was the face of FanDuel which paid him to endorse the company. According to FanDuel's marketing material, Prince has won over $650,000 playing daily fantasy sports, although according to OTL, Prince "doesn't know his net earnings, but says he's made a profit in each of his five seasons."[8] In some years, he claimed to have made more from fantasy than working for the USPS. During the MLB season, Prince stated he has about $1,000 on the line "on a given day" which may rise to $5,000 for each NFL week. Prince records a daily video podcast for the website Rotogrinders (with which NBC Sports recently partnered) in which he provides expert advice on DFS.

DraftKings has its own success stories. Drew Dinkmeyer quit his job in finance to play DFS for a living. Two years after making that life choice, he boasted to the *Wall Street Journal* that he was making more in fantasy sports than he had been at his normal job.[9] Then in mid-December 2014, Dinkmeyer spent $1,323 to enter 49 separate line-ups in DraftKing's "Millionaire Maker" football tournament. Thanks to a meaningless Jay Culter to Marquess Wilson touchdown pass in the fourth quarter of the Chicago Bears 31-15 loss to the New Orleans Saints, Dinkmeyer is now a millionaire.

Prince and Dinkmeyer are by no means the only rags-to-riches stories in the DFS world. One of the more interesting instant millionaire tales took the form of Matt Smith. He, too, won a DraftKings "Millionaire Maker" contest in October 2014 by outscoring 92,400 other players. [10] The intriguing aspect to Smith's victory was his background as a professional poker player. When the UIGEA killed the poker websites, those "unskilled" poker players sought out a new avenue in which to dabble and quickly discovered daily fantasy sports—and its large, legal, easy to obtain payouts. Now many of those same poker players are filling up both the DraftKings and FanDuel lobbies. As one former poker play told the *New York Times*, "It's [daily fantasy sports] become an extended poker room."[11]

"I completely believe the leagues were only thinking about and seeing a lucrative market for traditional fantasy [when they sought the UIGEA exemption]," the NCPG's Whyte told me. "They had no idea that it would take off or that it would become daily fantasy sports. It is quite ironic that the leagues may have created the monster that led to daily fantasy sports."

FanDuel might send its lawyers after me for what I'm about to write, but let me explain some of the eerie similarities I found between the non-gambling activity of DFS as I experienced it and that of real-world casinos.

I chose to join FanDuel in part because I heard a radio commercial—on SiriusXM's NFL Network—in which the site offered a matching bonus for any initial deposit up to $200. Many casinos will offer "match plays" as well, especially when new members sign up for a casino's "Players Card." In fact, when I visited Las Vegas in September 2014 and stayed at the Encore, merely signing up for the Wynn's "Red Card" earned me $25 in free, matched play. FanDuel essentially had a similar "promotional offer." All that was required was a special code for my deposit to be doubled. As the 2014 NFL season wore on, I came to realize this "promotional offer" was always available to new players; the only variation was a weekly change in the code word. I transferred $50 into my newly created account via Paypal, but that money didn't magically transform into $100. No, the "deposit bonus is released as real cash at a rate of 4 percent of the entry fee of the contest you enter" so FanDuel "prevents fraud and discourages multi-accounting."[12] Five months later, I had $0.96 remaining in my account with a "pending bonus" of $46.06 which I am unable to access—unless I deposit more cash into my account and play in more contests.

After engaging in a few daily fantasy leagues, I came to recognize parallels between it and slot machines. One of the draws of penny slots is that for seemingly betting one cent, a player could walk away with a $10,000 jackpot. This is mostly an illusion; however, jackpots are quite real. Walk through enough casinos and you're bound to see Polaroids of past winners, joyfully holding up oversized checks on which is written the tens of thousands of dollars they've won. The casinos want you to see those photos because they want you to think that those people are a lot like you. Maybe your picture could be on that wall. FanDuel and DraftKings do the same thing in promoting Prince, Dinkmeyer and other past instant millionaires—and for the very same reasons. That's the allure. FanDuel does offer free contests in which you could win $1,000. Not a bad payday for a filling a roster. From there, however, one can enter multi-player contests for $1, $2, $5, $10, or more per line-up. Come in first (i.e. hit the jackpot) with your roster, and you'd win $10,000, $25,000, or much, much more. Dinkmeyer won $1 million on a $27 entry.

You don't have to finish in first place to make a profit. In the popular multi-player contests, the lower half pays the top half. So, when tens of thousands are won by the "skilled" players, the same amount is often being lost by the "unskilled." *Outside the Lines* noted, "FanDuel does not disclose how many players are ultimately winners over time."[13] It matters not to them, nor to DraftKings. Both sites make their profit by taking a nine or 10 percent rake off the top of all entry fees paid (by the way, FSTA member websites are not allowed to use gambling-related terms such as "wager," "rake," "parlay," and "spread"). FanDuel and DraftKings are printing money each and every night there's a game—be it college or pro—just by being the conduit for these "leagues." They only lose money if multi-player contests fail to fill to capacity because by law they have to pay out all promoted prize money. It does occur, but rarely. Because there's only one day of the year without a sporting event taking place (the day after the MLB All-Star Game), neither the websites nor its players have to wait very long to scratch that money-loving itch.

Slot machines are fueled in part by the psychology of the "near win" experience. Navigating modern slot machines aren't the same as trying to hit the triple 7s of yesteryear, but even the newest machines constantly put a player one symbol away from a win. "Oh, if Kristen Wiig was just on *this* line of the *Bridesmaids* machine, I would've hit *big*." Another loss mentally absorbed as a near win. "Oh, I had two of the three Seeing Stones to trigger the *Lord of the Rings* bonus. This machine is *due*." A foolish assumption built on an "almost." It's this type of false thinking that keeps slot players pumping cash into machines and making slots Las Vegas's biggest moneymakers.

With DFS, there are plenty of near wins as well. "Had I taken Kelvin Benjamin instead of Mike Evans, I would've score 15 more points and finished in the money." Missed it by *that* much. But thanks to daily fantasy, a new game is always starting.

A willing daily NFL player can begin a contest with the Thursday Night game, Sunday's 1 p.m. kickoff, the 4 p.m. kickoff, the Sunday Night game, or even just the Monday Night game. For example, I entered a contest starting with the Sunday 1 p.m. games, saw my players in that round fail miserably, wrote off that line-up as a loser, and entered a new contest with a new roster starting with the 4 p.m. games. And if this happened to me, I'm sure many other daily players have done the same.

Could DFS be addictive? The FSTA counters such a question by stating, "Surveys continue to show fantasy sports players do not show the negative/compulsive behaviors associated with gambling, where the motivation to gamble is overwhelmingly focused on winning money or prizes."[14] Even if this is true, as ESPN's *Outside the Lines* noted, electronic gambling is known as the "crack cocaine" gaming. The only way to play DFS is electronically, that is, online. With handy smartphone apps available, daily fantasy sports websites are captivating a new audience that's skewing ever younger. "FanDuel executives acknowledge that its typical players are in their mid-20s, and likely more drawn to the instant gratification of daily fantasy."[15] Yet, "fantasy sports players younger than 18 represent the industry's fastest growing segment, according to [FSTA president Paul] Charchian. More women are also playing fantasy sports, especially football. 'People who start playing fantasy usually don't stop,' Charchian said. 'Eighty percent of today's fantasy players plan to play for another decade.'"[16]

Should teenagers competing in fantasy be concerning? John Kindt, an emeritus professor of business and legal policy at the University of Illinois, is a leading national gambling critic. He claimed, "Young people like sports, and they like to take risks. If you combine the two, that leads sports enthusiasts into some problematic areas. The younger generation—the generation that has always had access to the Internet—is showing nearly double the gambling addiction rate of the next oldest generation. That is, about 6 to 8 percent of the youth population—including teens, the college-age and young adults—could be considered addicted or problem gamblers." He added, "In fact, something like fantasy sports may be the ultimate gateway drug to gambling."[17]

But this isn't gambling. It's fantasy sports, remember? As far as the NFL goes, it's open season. So it was no surprise to find an email in my inbox from the NFL promoting the NFLRush Fantasy Game. The marketing material prominently featured a smiling 10 to 12-year old, wearing a Seahawks jersey and raising his arms in the air as if in victory. The ad copy read, "Introduce the excitement of NFL Fantasy Football to your kids this season with NFLRush.com, the official NFL fantasy football game for kids! Your child could win a weekly prize of a $500 scholarship or even the Grand Prize of a $10,000 scholarship and tickets to a 2015 NFL regular season game! Many will participate, few will win." The fine print was quick to note, "This game may not be used to conduct, advertise or promote any form of gambling."

The NFL is literally altering itself for the benefit of fantasy football. The league offers fantasy football strategy programs on both its radio and television networks. It created *NFL Red Zone*, a channel which comes alive only on Sundays to instantly switch from one scoring play to the next throughout the league. *Red Zone* is broadcast in many NFL stadiums as well. In fact, both the San Francisco 49ers and the Minnesota Vikings designed their new billion dollar stadiums with the fantasy player in mind. The NFL's broadcast partners have been happy to play along as well, adding more and more crawls and updates—all for the benefit of people playing fantasy football. They all realize what NFL Commissioner Goodell recently stated, "Even if your team isn't playing well, you're still following your fantasy league or you're following the *Red Zone* or your mobile device."[18] In other words, you're consuming the

NFL product non-stop.

Despite all of the corporate sponsors and money being made, Kindt warned, "Fantasy sports has got a target on it. It has a target on it from Congress, and it has a target on it from the legal community." Why? For starters, there is *no* government monitoring or traditional gaming tax levied on these fantasy websites—because it's not gambling. Oversight is nonexistent. Five states—Arizona, Iowa, Louisiana, Montana and Washington—prohibit daily fantasy sports because those states *do* consider it gambling. Meanwhile, the federal government is currently reexamining its anti-gambling legislation which has the FSTA concerned.

To counter both the states and Congress, the FSTA ramped up its lobbying efforts. I received an emailed "advocacy alert" from the FSTA through RTSports.com urging me to help "fully legalize fantasy sports in Louisiana" (despite the fact I don't live in LA). The email also reminded me, "Please visit FantasySportsFreedom.com to help the FSTA keep fantasy sports legal in your state and throughout the country. We need to urge the governor of Kansas to sign a bill into law that would keep fantasy sports legal. We need Iowans to contact their legislators to pass a bill that would fully legalize fantasy sports. There's also active legislation in Illinois, Washington, Montana and other stats [sic]. Get active and help us keep fantasy sports fully legal." Apparently, not everyone buys the FSTA's snake-oil.

Though it sticks by its non-gambling guns, FanDuel quietly joined the membership of the National Council on Problem Gambling. Executive Director Keith Whyte sees that as a "good thing." He added, "It may seem incongruous, but at least they are taking a small step. More than any other fantasy sports company that I know of. While companies join NCPG for a variety of reasons, including cynical and/or enlightened self-interest, I'd rather see it as a positive than a negative."

WEEK 3
@ LEGAL SPORTS BOOKS

It didn't strike me until the plane lifted off. Here I was, a full-grown man able to drink, drive, vote, join the Army, sign a binding contract, see an R rated movie, and rent a car, yet I had to travel 1,500 miles from Milwaukee to Las Vegas in order to legally bet on a football game. There's something not quite right about that. If I lived in the United Kingdom, I'd have over 9,100 legal, licensed bookmakers[1] spread throughout the countryside from which to choose. But in America, land of the free? I had to take a four hour flight to arrive in a city where I could legally bet the Bengals -6.5 over the Titans.

I was on that flight for reasons other than just gambling. I had been in contact with Benjamin Best, a German filmmaker, who was shooting a documentary about my forte: game fixing in sports. Best and his small crew had traversed much of the world—Italy, England, Brazil, Turkey and elsewhere—documenting sports corruption prior to coming to America's gambling capital, Las Vegas. Seeing as how I'm one of the few US researchers/writers focusing on the subject of game fixing, Best wished to include me in his project. Although I have a (largely unused) degree in film, I've never actually been in a movie. So, I was happy to fly to Vegas and participate.

I was even more excited when I entered my panoramic suite on the 53rd floor of the Wynn Encore. These Germans were first class all the way. Well, not completely. After meeting in the morning and swapping stories and information, we decided to go to lunch prior to filming my interview. Though they had a significant budget, lunch was to be had at the food court above the Fashion Show Mall. Upon entering, the twenty-something cameraman Yannick took a deep breath and excitedly proclaimed, "Ah, this smells like America!" I supposed it did, what with the mixture of Asian, Mexican, and Wendy's cuisines filling the air. And who was I to complain? They footed the bill.

Filming was an interesting experience. We shot my scene from one of the Encore's suites so that the Strip would be my backdrop. I wasn't nervous, merely uncomfortable. When I've been on radio shows, I'm pretty free to do what I want: walk around, have a cocktail, talk in my underwear…what does it matter? It's radio. But in this instance, I had to be seated and remain in one place. I couldn't walk off any nervous energy. I had a pair of cameras focused on me, the afternoon Vegas sun shining through the window heating my back, a small bank of super-bright LEDs about an arm's length away from my left eye acting as a fill light, and four people staring at me while I spoke, during which time I had to try to remember not to look into either camera and ignore the rumbling coming from my stomach thanks to that Sbarro lunch special. Ah, the magic of filmmaking. I felt just like Jennifer Lawrence.

Afterwards, they asked me what else might be worth capturing for their film. I said, "Did you go to any of the sports books?" Of course they had. "But," I countered, "were you ever in one on an NFL Sunday?" They shook their heads. I smiled, "That's something you have to experience."

We met the next morning, piled into a cab, and headed for the "World's Biggest Race and Sports Book." Where's that?

Ever hear of the Westgate Resort and Casino? It was formerly the Las Vegas Hilton (or LVH) which was originally known as the International. It's Elvis Presley's old stomping grounds. An off-the-Strip place best accessible by the monorail, the Westgate is home to the SuperBook. Upon entering, the Germans stopped in their tracks to soak it in. "What do you think?" I asked. Best nodded and simply said, "It's big."

That's a bit of an under-sell. The SuperBook is 30,000 square feet of "football heaven" as one patron said to me. There are 19 betting windows, 28 large screen TVs, and seating for over 400. But on NFL Sunday the Westgate opens up its 1,500-seat theater for its popular Football Central promotion. There, gamblers can catch all the day's action on a dozen large hi-def televisions with the featured game shown on a mammoth 18' x 22' HD screen. As the Germans found a table from which to watch the pre-game spectacle (and clandestinely shoot a little B-reel footage), I made my first bets of the NFL season. Since I had to catch a plane home later that afternoon, I was limited in my play selection to strictly the 1 pm EST games. Yet the room's vibe quickly compelled me to over-bet. Smart plays? Money management? Any such thoughts left my brain as I stepped to a window. I rattled off the numbers to five games and threw a pair of three-team parlays on top of it. Then I sat back to watch some football.

When the NFL season kicked off two weeks earlier, I lived many a married man's dream: my wife was out of town and I had Sunday completely free and clear. Although the NFL beckoned me to my television, it was 75 degrees and sunny outside—a rarity for Wisconsin. How was I supposed to watch 12 hours of football on such a picturesque day? Here, in the darkened bowels of a casino, there was no such deal with the devil that needed to be made. Instead I was confronted with free raffles, drink specials, and a lot of gamblers yelling at a lot of football.

Case in point, the Cowboys-Rams game. It was reminiscent of the Bud Light commercial from the year before in which a football fan at home with friends laments, "I hate watching with Ramsey. All he does is yell. *They can't hear you, Ramsey.*" These Cowboys faithful verbally decimated poor Tony Romo as the Rams jumped out to a 21-10 halftime lead. "Romo, you homo!" was a favored cry, perhaps due to the rhyming nature of the insult. It was certainly cathartic because as Romo righted the ship and led the Cowboys to a come-from-behind 34-31 victory, those same fans were singing him praises.

I won't lie. About four hours after arriving, I left Football Central a winner. I hit on four of the five games and one of the parlays. During the course of the action, though, I lost track of the Germans. I don't think the reality of the Westgate's SuperBook lived up to its hype for them. Yannick seemed more interested in following a soccer game on his smartphone than watching a minute of the NFL. "I don't understand these rules," he complained. "They're nonsense." It was hard to argue with him. Sometimes no one understands the ruling on the field, but that's for another chapter.

As I chomped on a lonely, overpriced, but quite delicious sushi lunch paid for with my NFL winnings, I wondered about the connection between this city and the NFL. Did Vegas need the NFL? Does the NFL need Vegas? Could the two be in cahoots?

Not too long ago, there was no such thing as a casino with a sports book. It wouldn't be until 1975 when the Union Plaza opened one under the watchful eye of legendary oddsmaker Bob Martin that a Las Vegas hotel/casino offered their patrons such a service. Prior to then, sports books were independent, stand-alone operations often named after famous race tracks. Yet even those joints didn't come into being until the 1960s. Before then, NFL betting in Vegas was not to be found. There was no going to Vegas for the Super Bowl. Only illegal bookies offered what was known as the "outlaw line" on games. This originated from Minneapolis (of all places) and was disseminated throughout the country by a man named Leo Hirschfield. Over the course of the 1950s, organized crime in New York City took control of the outlaw line. It soon came under the guidance of Frank "Lefty" Rosenthal who the mob saw as a gambling genius (and whose life story made for the book and movie *Casino*). Rosenthal did have a sharp mind, but he was also known to influence a game or twelve. In fact, it was said Rosenthal would have the college basketball players he bribed to shave points practice *missing* lay-ups so that those attempts looked more realistic. He was a stickler for detail.

In 1974, there were only nine sports books in Las Vegas. This was largely due to the 10 percent tax levied on sports wagers. Nevada Senator Howard Cannon pushed legislation through Congress in 1974 slashing it down to just two percent. Nine years later, it would drop to its current 0.25 percent. On the heels of this change, Rosenthal ushered big time sports gambling into Las Vegas. Though the Union Plaza's opened first, Lefty's pride and joy at the Stardust was spectacular: a 9,000 square foot race and sports book with seating for 600 gamblers. "[Lefty] built a mammoth race and sports book with ceilings three stories high. The race and sports boards were a couple stories high themselves, reaching almost to the ceiling. They were big enough to require catwalks and ladders behind them, so odds and results could be put in by hand, much like the Fenway Park or Wrigley Field scoreboards. He installed a state-of-the-art satellite TV system with a monster theater screen and a compliment of smaller screens to bring in games and races other books didn't even acknowledge as existing. He had a maintenance crew assigned exclusively to take care of the satellite system and TVs."[2] Though common today, this was a never-seen-before attraction in 1975.

Despite its notoriety, Lefty and the Stardust relied on

their competitor for their betting lines. Of course, they couldn't be blamed. "Time was, between 1967 and 1980, when The Line on all sports contests was set by one man, Bob Martin. He was truly *the* nation's odds-maker. Any sportswriter who wanted to know by how much Notre Dame was favored over Southern Cal called Bob Martin, and what he got was *fact*—it was *The* Line, and no one disputed it."[3] Martin was a savant. Few questioned his expertise, and fewer still knew how he did it. He was quoted as saying that he knew the right number on a game because it "fit like a glove." That was it. But Martin was pinched by the feds and convicted for transmitting wagering information to mob bookies in and around Boston. He spent over a year in prison.

Even without Martin's numbers, the Stardust continued to be the nation's de facto sports book. In 1983, Scott Schettler was put in charge, and under his stewardship, the Stardust line became the number every bookie—legal or illegal—quoted. "A lot of the other places were timid, but we weren't," Schettler told me. "It was our line. We crunched the numbers ourselves, put up a virgin line, and opened up every morning like a bank at 8 o'clock. And there would be a mob of people. Money from all over the country, through their beards in Las Vegas, would bet that line." During the Stardust's heyday, sharp bettors would actually participate in a lottery just for the privilege to have a crack at the Stardust's opening numbers. "They were looking for weak spots in our line, of course. If they found a weak spot—so what?—they still had to win the game. If they won the game—so what?—they'd be back in the morning for new openers. Look at it like this. We were all passing the same $20 bill back and forth. Only we held it for twenty days, and the players held it for ten."[4]

Like all dynasties, the Stardust's reign as top sports books came to an end as the 80's faded into the 90's. As Vegas legitimized itself by turning corporate, the old school bookies like Martin and Schettler were imploded along with their former haunts. It's something Schettler laments. "In my day, individuals owned the books and they were all gamblers. You could just take whatever you wanted. But nowadays it's corporate run. The guys wear suits and ties and shake their heads up and down, yes and no. They don't take much money and they're scared to death to lose. It's a little different atmosphere now. If you tried to come out now and bet a few hundred thousand on a game, automatically you alert somebody. Back in my day, it was just a routine thing. Guys would bet that much every day. We had guys that would bet a hundred thousand a day. It just kind of blended in."

Today, Nevada is home to 187 sports books, many of which are operated by corporations like CG Technology, William Hill, or Boyd Gaming. In 2014, Nevada's sports books set a record, winning over $227 million. "Football, per usual, carried the load. The sports books won $113.73 million on college and pro football in 2014, a giant 40.73 percent increase from 2013. Overall, $1.74 billion was bet on football in 2014 [believe it or not, the International Centre for Sports Security estimated that *$152 billion* was wagered on the NFL in 2014 in legal markets *outside* the US], $12 million more than in 2013. Nevada Gaming Control does not track pro and college football separately, but sports book managers estimate the NFL accounts for around 55-60 percent of their annual football handle."[5] If true, that would mean the sports book won approximately $70 million from NFL bettors alone in 2014.

While every casino offers a sports book these days, some gamblers told me if I wanted to see real "sharps" in action, if I wanted to see a "whale" laying big money, then I needed to visit the M Resort. It's another off-the-Strip place. *Waaay* off the Strip. Like a $30 cab ride—one way—south of the famous "Welcome to Fabulous Las Vegas" sign off the Strip. The sports book there is operated by CG Technologies (formerly Cantor Gaming). They like to boast that they'll take any size bet on any game at any time. It's bullshit, but makes for great PR.

When I visited the M's sports book, I have to say, I wasn't impressed. I've been in basements that are bigger. Maybe not prettier, but definitely larger. Of course, one of the M's draws is its electronic, "In-Line" wagering. Here, you don't have to go to a window to place your bet; you can do it from an app on your smartphone. That's just the beginning. "In-Line" wagering, which got its start in Europe, lets you bet throughout a sporting event. It's no longer just about the opening point spread or the under/over line, it's about each individual event within a game. If you're so inclined, you can wager from the opening kick-off until the final gun sounds. It's not for the faint of heart.

My time at the M's sports book was short. Real short. I arrived on a quiet afternoon, took a look around, and then the journalist in me started asking questions. I was politely asked to stop. I pressed. These weren't deep, probing questions, just informational queries. I was asked to leave. Apparently lacking any witty repartee that day, I was instructed that any and all questions regarding the M Resort, its sports book, or CG Technologies needed to be directed to "corporate." Then I was told to leave. Firmly. Yeah, those five minutes weren't exactly worth the cab fare.

Jay Kornegay, the Vice President of Race and Sports Book Operations at the Westgate, offered a much warmer welcome. I was even treated to a behind-the-scenes tour of its sports book. It's not sexy. A couple of large copy machines, an audio/video control room about the size of a walk-in closet, a file room with a couple of boxes of promotional T-shirts scattered on the floor, and Kornegay's office made up much of it. But it's from here that one of the NFL's most influential betting lines originates.

Creating those lines are Kornegay's favorite part of the job. It is also the most secretive aspect of what occurs at the Westgate, and though many have asked, Kornegay has been hesitant to allow any outsiders in the room when he and his staff set their lines. He and four or five of his crew determine the numbers, often through conversation. Interestingly, that's how Scott Schettler told me the Stardust used to create its lines, only he had characters with colorful nicknames like "Roxy," "the Owl," and "the Hat" assisting him.

Though it may seem unusual to develop the point spread in such a casual manner, it's not. Pete Korner is the owner of Esportclub LLC (a.k.a. the Sports Club) which supplies betting odds and lines to a variety of customers. These numbers, which often are available four to six hours before most other outlets, can only be accessed by clients through a private website. Korner cut his teeth at a similar well-known operation, Las Vegas Sports Consultants. Now he employs three full-time and three part-time oddsmakers who operate much like their counterparts at the Westgate. "Although I have streamlined the process," Korner explained to me, "in effect, we do the same at The Sports Club today. Although everyone works independently, there is a 'round table' discussion for every game. Working independently and from a variety and unique sources, we can cover a lot more angles to a game. Upon discussion, we can hash out the best line possible with everyone's input."

So what's the big mystery with the line? There really isn't one. It seems as though most everyone, bookmaker and gambler alike, believes they have a pretty good bead on the NFL. Bookmakers can rattle off new lines for upcoming games rather quickly, as if off the top of their heads. They don't necessarily need computer programs or statistical algorithms to determine the proper numbers because the line is phantom. It's real, but it's not. The secret to an NFL betting line is knowing what it really is. Why it exists. It's not that the bookmaker thinks the Lions will beat the Bears by exactly seven when he sets the line at Detroit -7; it's that the bookmaker believes this is what the betting public *assumes* will happen in that game. It's the public's perception on which a point spread is truly based. It's a mind game which may explain why the betting public is often wrong when they plunk down their money. But that's why the line is there: to split the opinion on a game, hopefully getting 50 percent of all bettors' money on each side of the proposition so that the bookmaker can profit from the vig (that is, the fee for booking the bet).

While that's all the line is, in actuality, it's been a complete game changer. The NFL, the NBA, and their NCAA counterparts are no longer viewed or discussed in the same way since the development of the point spread. It wasn't an overnight sensation, and in fact, what was originally known as the split line was almost counterproductive for bookmakers. The split line might be set at 6/8 on a football game, meaning that if the game ended with the favored team winning by 7, it wasn't a push as it would be today at -7. Instead, the bookies kept both sides' money, and they were rather adept at hitting their own middle. However, by the 1950s the point spread became an established gambling element, and not so coincidentally its popularity mirrored the growth of the NFL.

Television and the point spread continue to be joined at the hip. At the Westgate "we're writing more college than pro these days," Kornegay reported, "but that is mainly due to the diversity of the college schedule." For example, when I met with him, one of the games Kornegay followed on the 14 televisions in his office was a Tuesday night Mid-American Conference football game. "This game would be widely ignored if it was played on the Saturday schedule. But tonight it's getting probably 30 percent more action than it would have because it's on TV. The television coverage makes a difference."

If a Tuesday night MAC match-up can draw out more bets and increase viewership, what do you think it says about the NFL's commitment to *Thursday Night Football*? The league can continue to fill those games with blatant schedule fodder because a primetime, regular season NFL game will garner two to ten times the betting action of a typical Sunday afternoon game. And betting fans are watching fans.

For Vegas, these primetime games can be a headache. Kornegay's "biggest decisions of the week" is often the Sunday night game. *Monday Night Football* is still an attraction, no doubt. In fact, MNF has always been a gambler's delight since its debut in 1970. It was either one last chance to win more, or more likely, a last gasp to recoup Sunday's losses. But due to its "flex" scheduling, *Sunday Night Football* often features a premiere match-up which creates an abundance of betting action. "Hopefully we had a good day so we don't have all of this liability going into the Sunday night game, but most of the time we do, so it's always a stressful game," said Kornegay. "Usually everything is on the line with the Sunday night game because of all the residual parlays that can carry over, especially if it's looking like a one-sided game."

One can understand Kornegay's Sunday night stress when you comprehend what he deals with during a Sunday of NFL football. He'll arrive at the SuperBook when it opens at 7 am—three hours prior to kickoff—sometimes passing a line of waiting, eager customers. Once inside, he will check to see who's there guest-wise in case anyone requires special attention. His job involves a lot of glad-handing, including awarding (and sometimes denying) "comps" to his best customers. This is the true nature of his job: customer service with a bit of public relations thrown in for good measure. Kornegay spoke that way as well. Bettors were referred to as guests or customers, not gamblers. His job is to make sure all have an enjoyable experience at the SuperBook.

"Sports books are no longer just amenities for a casino," Kornegay explained. "It's a revenue producing machine. As the public becomes more educated about gambling, they know and are discovering the true value, the entertainment value, of sports betting. For $20, you can sweat it out for three hours. How about that?" he added with a smile.

Kornegay is a jack-of-all-trades on NFL Sunday. Usually two local Las Vegas sports radio stations conduct remote broadcasts from the SuperBook, and Kornegay will briefly guest on both. Occasionally he'll do other radio spots via his cellphone while at the same time checking to make sure everyone is where they are supposed to be for when Football Central's theater opens at 9 am. Then he'll check on the lines, seeing where the book stands in case he's not comfortable on a position. "If I feel like we need to change some lines, we'll do it," he added. "I'll say, 'let's move that because it's getting kind of high, and maybe we can get some of it back.' Sometimes we can, and sometimes we can't."

Why move the lines? To limit liability. Though the Westgate can book millions of dollars in bets on a given NFL Sunday, it's run much like your local illegal bookie's shop. No one wants to get killed (monetarily) on a single game. So the lines will move in an attempt to attract money on the less-wagered side. But as Kornegay pointed out, "It's almost like 19 out of 20 games aren't balanced. We always have a decision. We try to be in the best possible position to win." What does that mean? "Well, most likely you have a pretty good opinion of what the line should be and what they are betting," he explained. "If they are betting the Packers -10 all night long and you know the line should be at 7 or 8, you know they aren't getting a very good number. I don't need to move it. I'll let them bet it because I know that they are not getting away with anything. It's a little cat and mouse game we play every single day in here. It's doesn't matter if it's basketball, baseball, hockey, football; it's always a little battle to position ourselves where we want to be on *that* particular game. We're going to go ahead and let them play even through we're accumulating liability. I don't need to move the line because it's the type of money we're comfortable with."

Since small fortunes can be won and lost betting on the NFL, "People can get a little...*hot* at the end of the games," Kornegay admitted. Like the rest of the casino, security is never far from the scene. It's one of the pitfalls that come with working in the book. "Sometimes you have to make decisions that aren't too favorable for a particular customer," Kornegay lamented. "But that's part of the job. They don't want to hear 'no.' Sometimes they get the wrong ticket, but it says right on there that it's their responsibility to check the accuracy of the ticket. You know why it's spelled out that way? It's because you are the only one who knows what it was supposed to be. I've seen people come up and say, 'Give me 514 for $100.' 'Here's 514.' 'I said *515.*' And this happens *all the time*! That's the nature of the beast. 'Give me $100 on the Redskins.' 'Here's your $100 on the Redskins.' 'I said *Raiders!*' Sorry. Check your ticket, sir. We make mistakes, certainly. It's a keystroke difference. It happens, and I believe the customers. I believe they wanted the other side or they didn't want that game, but I can't change it now. Occasionally, someone gets the wrong ticket and it turns out right. But in twenty-something years, I've never had someone come up to the window, apologize, and hand me a winning ticket and *not* want the money attached to the winner."

Because of such mix-ups and misunderstandings, Kornegay can take some abuse. "The joke with some of my regulars is, 'What's part of your interview process, Jay? You ask them what two plus two is, and if they get close to four you hire them?'" But you might be wondering how does one land a job at a sports book? "I've hired some people that didn't know the Cowboys are from Dallas," Kornegay told me. "But I've got other guys who know every quarterback on every college team out there. What people don't understand about this industry is that we get an overload of applicants from all over the country from people who want to work in a sports book. But to do so, you have to pay your dues. It's such a unique industry. We, or at least, I like people to know what a teller goes through—the process of opening a window and closing it down, filling out the paperwork—what goes on in that control room, learning all the different types of equipment back there and understanding that you just don't change the channel to 34 to get the Lakers game, we have to take three or four steps to make that happen. So they might get a little disappointed at what goes into the job."

Because the Westgate employs 40-60 people in the book at any given time, not all are true "bookmakers." In fact, the majority are not. To get to a post like Kornegay's takes time. A lot of time, along with a few lucky breaks. He explained, "Due to the consolidation within the industry in the past 15 years, there are fewer higher ranking jobs available. There used to be 15 director positions available, now there's maybe five or six. Where their used to be seven directors running seven independent books, now there's one director running seven books because so many are interconnected due to the corporate ownership."

As for Kornegay's own employment, he said, "The biggest misconception is people think I know who'll win. I'm not a handicapper; I'm a bookmaker. I'm an administrator. I'm a director."

Many NFL fans and bettors alike would say that Kornegay left out one job in that list: co-conspirator. It's believed that the NFL and Vegas are joined at the hip, and the results of games are manipulated for the bookies' benefit. What else could explain Vegas winning $70 million in a single NFL season? A longtime casino veteran swore to me that there's no way a casino even would allow a sports book on its premises if the games weren't stacked against gamblers. He theorized that if slot machines, keno, roulette, craps, blackjack and all the other table games clearly favored the house, why would sports betting—essentially a 50-50 proposition—ever be offered? Something else has to be afoot in order for that one Sunday or

Monday night favorite not to cover and kill many a bettor's parlay.

What I discovered in asking around, however, is that the NFL has had zero contact with the Vegas sports books. This hands-off approach has existed since at least the 1980s. Schettler—who believes NFL games have been and continue to be fixed—was the most open person I spoke with on the subject. Yet he had little to report as he could not recall a single instance when the NFL was in contact with the Stardust during its time as the country's premiere sports book. If the NFL wasn't talking to them, who else would it contact? Kornegay echoed this, stating that he has had no direct contact with the NFL regarding the Westgate's operations. Only occasionally does he cross paths with an NFL representative, and that usually occurs at a once-a-year industry conference.

In truth, Vegas doesn't need the NFL. Its casinos make far more money from slot machines than they ever would through sports betting. But the sports books certainly enjoy the NFL's contribution to its coffers. "The NFL portion is the key to everyone's yearly success," Pete Korner told me. "The NFL totally understands what is going on around the betting world. They don't have to support anything related to our industry to feel the positive effects for their product. It's just bad PR to say they want anything to do with us. And who can blame them?"

BRIAN TUOHY

WEEK 4
vs. BOOKIES

I returned from Vegas a winner. Scratch that. I walked out of the sports book a winner. Overall, I came home with less money than I had left with and not simply due to cab rides, cocktails, or overpriced hamburgers. I gambled on other things besides the NFL, and as a result, well...have you ever noticed that plane rides leaving Las Vegas are much more muted than inbound flights? It's darn near impossible to leave with some of the casinos' money in your pocket.

If I was going to continue my personal gambling odyssey through the NFL, I couldn't fly to Vegas each and every weekend. Enticing though the possibility was, I doubted the IRS would believe each trip to Sin City would've really constituted as a "business expense." No, like the rest of America, if I was going to bet on the NFL every week, I was going to use a good ol' fashioned bookie.

But how do you locate one?

I'll make a little wager with you right now, dear reader. I bet you know a bookie. And if you don't know one personally, I can almost guarantee that at least one person in your smartphone's contact list could put you in touch with a bookie lickety split. Myself, I know a handful of guys who bet with bookies on a regular basis. One phone call and I'd be in.

Yet that didn't seem very challenging to me. I wanted to approach this as a total newbie. How hard would I have to search to find a bookie? How long would it take? What would I have to do to get "in?" As it turned out, it didn't take much at all.

Bring up the subject of sports gambling to nearly anyone and it was almost certain at some point in the conversation I'd be told, "Yeah, I gotta guy." It wasn't like I was talking with scumbag street hoods, either. These were everyday, salt-of-the-earth people. The more I asked around, the more I felt like *everybody* was betting on sports. Even sports writers and sports radio show hosts confessed to me they bet on the games they cover. It was no secret. One even outright offered, "Do you need my guy's phone number?" Heck, without asking, my financial planner revealed that his father used to be a bookie.

Finding one was not a problem. Bookies seemed more prevalent than Starbucks. Getting a bookie to talk about his operation—*that* became my true quest.

I wasn't alone. It seemed the more New Jersey squawked about trying the legalize sports gambling, the more journalists sought out information with which to craft gambling-related stories. I received several offers to exchange information with writers and filmmakers along these lines. The most interesting came just prior to the start of the NFL season.

I was contacted by Vanessa, a British film producer associated with National Geographic. She was working on a new TV project titled *Misfit Economy* (later changed to *Underground Inc.*) which was being created by the same outfit behind the series *Drugs Inc.* The show intended to investigate black market economies in the US. Vanessa was in charge of an episode relating to illegal gambling, covering everything from sports gambling to cockfighting and beyond. She contacted me seeking help in accessing this "underground community." When we talked, I learned what Vanessa was mainly after was a bookie who would talk.

Despite living in Wisconsin, I do know a few people who know people. Some of these people know (or at least claim to know) some heavy hitting bookies. But none would talk. Introductions would lead to refusals. There wasn't even an "I'll think about it" offered. Even friends of mine who deal with low level bookies couldn't get their guy(s) to open their mouths. Vanessa was a passenger in the same boat I was. She, too, found bookies, but none wanted any sort of spotlight put on their operation (though *Underground Inc.* eventually did feature a bookie).

The reason why this search was so difficult is actually quite obvious: bookies are criminals. Oh, I know that statement gets sports gamblers up in arms, but it's a fact. *Bookies are criminals.* By booking bets, they are breaking the law. And the truth of it is the bookies realize this. They know what they are. They know what they are doing. It's just that the public doesn't necessarily see them as lawless.

If I said my brother was a drug dealer, most people would become upset simply because of the connotations associated with the illicit drug world. It wouldn't matter if he was Walter White or not; he'd be seen as a "drug pusher." Many would call for his incarceration. But if I said my brother was a bookie, those same people would probably just shrug their shoulders. A bookie? Oh, he's not hurting anyone. He's not a "gambling pusher." He's just performing a "service."

But take a step back. Remember that perhaps as much as $80 billion or more is wagered illegally on sports each year. And remember that this "service" might just be organized crime's most profitable endeavor. Bookies are the foot soldiers of this illegal empire. They make the wheels turn, grinding those profits into the mob's coffers each and every week. And while it's true the bookie himself may not actually be physically harming anyone, that doesn't mean his operation is guilt-free.

Greg Lauer, an attorney for an alleged Florida-based bookmaker, told the court in attempting to lower the bond set for his client, "They were not selling drugs, there were no guns involved. Guys betting on sports is what's being alleged here. If we were in a different jurisdiction, this would be 100 percent legal."[1] This is the typical mindset. Sports betting—though illegal—is no big deal. It's only a crime because some law says it's a crime. True. The same argument, however, could be made of a lot of laws on the books. I'm only ticketed for going 95 mph on the highway because some stupid sign claims the speed limit is 65. Why should I have to obey that law when I don't want to? I wasn't hurting anyone going 95. What's the big deal?

In above quote, Lauer conveniently didn't address the charges of racketeering and money laundering that authorities believed accompanied the illegal bookmaking in that Florida case. Bookmaking in and of itself might not be a "big deal," but in bigger operations, it's rarely the only crime being committed. For example, in "Operation Shore Bet" Monmonth NJ authorities arrested 25 individuals ranging in age from 27 up to 80 on a variety of gambling and bookmaking charges. According to news reports, "Members of the gambling ring used Monmouth County banks to launder money, while other members sold drugs to an undercover detective from the Monmouth County Prosecutor's Office."[2]

Much hoopla was made of a federal case brought against "Gentleman Gambler" Joe Vito Mastronardo Jr. and his bookmaking operation. Mastronardo was a well-known Philadelphia bookie for two reasons: (1) he was so good at setting point spreads that the "Vito Line" was nationally recognized and (2) he is the son-in-law of the late Frank Rizzo, former mayor of Philadelphia. Even wilder, an uncle of Mastronardo's was credited with developing the formula for Pepsi Cola, making the family extremely wealthy. Despite a previous arrest in 2006 on bookmaking charges in which he forfeited well over $2 million, Mastronardo went right back into business. When arrested again in 2012, authorities seized over $6 million from his operation. Though he wasn't connected with organized crime—and actively avoided associating with the mob—it didn't mean Mastronardo's operation wasn't organized. He had over 1,000 bettors placing individual wagers of $50,000 or more through a Costa Rican-based website, and used his wife and other family members to hide the millions in profits he was earning.[3]

Despite the notoriety, Mastronardo might have been small potatoes. An anonymous tip to police in Plano TX launched a 10-year investigation into a sports betting ring that allegedly handled more than *$5 billion* in wagers.[4] Though ringleader Albert Reed Jr. lived in a $2 million penthouse in Dallas, his bookmaking operation took bets from nearly all of the 50 states, including individual wagers of over $1 million (try to get that kind of money down on a game in Las Vegas). The government confiscated nearly $10 million from those involved including cash, gold, Las Vegas real estate and sports memorabilia.

Eighteen men in total were arrested, all of which pleaded guilty to charges ranging from money laundering to illegal gambling and tax violations. Remarkably only Reed Jr. served jail time. His sentence for running a $5 billion sports gambling ring? One year and one day. The other 17 defendants were given probation. As John Bales, US Attorney for the Eastern District of Texas, told reporters, "They are receiving what I would consider lenient sentences. But sentencing guidelines for a gambling case are quite low and actually provide for first time offenders to get probation."[5]

Notice that only the bookies are the ones getting arrested, not the gamblers. In fact, illegal sports gambling is incredibly safe, legally speaking, for those making the wagers.

Sure, a bookie might shaft you out of some money, but it's highly unlikely a bettor will be arrested for engaging in this illegal activity. Which makes you, Mr. and Ms. Weekend Bettor, part of the problem.

Though I'm sure some recreational bettors may consider their bookie a bit "shady," few realize that when you call your guy to plunk down $50 on the Browns this weekend, you're likely funding organized crime. Here's why: Most bettors are "homers," wagering on the teams they closely follow or the games they typically watch. For a local, small-time bookie, this can create a highly unbalanced book. Like his corporate casino bookmaking counterpart, an illegal bookie desires an even, 50-50 split of the money coming in on a game, hoping to profit mainly from the vig taken from each winning bet. Such a lopsided game can create havoc for the bookie, so he's often forced to "lay off" some of this one-sided action by betting with another bookie.

In the ocean of sports gambling, the small fish feed the medium fish, who in turn feed the larger fish, who are swallowed whole by the sharks. Lurking at the top of this food chain is organized crime. The mob set up a national lay-off system in the 1950s, connecting bookies in Cincinnati with those in Los Angeles to others in Miami, and so on. It smoothed out the process while maximizing the financial return. Today, that system continues to operate by encompassing not just local bookies, but many online and offshore sports books as well.

So while your $50 may have been bet with Donny in the backroom of the neighborhood bar, it's quite possible that your cash circulated throughout the country. And even Donny doesn't realize it. Because Donny might not really be "your guy." Donny might be an agent for the real bookie.

Much like the lay-off system, bigger bookmakers today incorporate an agent system in which smaller fish again feed the bigger fish. Where possible, bookmakers employ "agents" to do most of the heavy lifting. These are the guys that find the new clients. They are the ones that collect the bookie's winning, or occasionally, pay off the gamblers. They're middlemen, and do all of this running for a cut of the profits—usually based off of the income generated from the losing gamblers they handle.

"Yeah, I gotta couple of goons like that who work for me," said Neal (not his real name) the one bookie I managed to get to kinda, sorta talk to me on the record about what it is he does. "I call 'em goons because that's what they look like. It's not like they're leg-breakers. But sometimes it don't hurt that they have that look about them."

Neal is an old-timer. He's been a bookie since the 1970's, but swears he's not mob-connected. "Back in the day, yeah, I'd pay what I'd guess you'd call 'protection money' so I wouldn't get my door knocked down, but I tried to keep my business clean." His goal has always been to maintain a steady income based off a manageable number of clients. But the older he gets, the more the pressure of the job affects him. "It may sound cliché," he told me, "but this life gave me ulcers. Doing this for 40 plus years, I still have problems controlling the highs and lows. And today, there's just more, more, more."

Though he may not be tech-savvy—he has a "kid" that helps him with that—Neal is continually wired to both his smartphone and laptop. Long since divorced, his mind is always playing with numbers: the point spread, the outcomes, and the money going in and out of his operation. He keeps extremely detailed records, using spreadsheets to track his clients' bets and even their betting patterns. He learned the necessity of this the hard way. "Used to be that some of my bigger bettors would outright lie to me, saying 'I didn't take that team' or 'I didn't bet that game,' even though they called it in yesterday. What could I do? This isn't a 'go to the cops' operation. And since most of them liars would already be into me, I couldn't afford to cut them loose because of a single bet. So I'd eat it. But I quickly learned to avoid such troubles. Now there's no denying what was bet and what wasn't."

As for the lines Neal uses, most of the time they are the straight Vegas numbers. "I've been at this long enough, I have a feel for which numbers are right and which might be off." He added, "But that don't mean I don't shade."

What Neal is referring to is the time-honored tradition of bookies shifting a line a half-point or more against the hometown team. Bookies know full well that recreational gamblers tend to bet the popular area teams. So he will take advantage of his bettors' ignorance and alter certain point spreads to make them more favorable for himself, since the bookie knows those games will likely be the most one-sided action-wise. "Some guys," he told me, "they'll bet [the local team] no matter what. *No matter what*. But especially when they're winning. So I move the line so they have to give up a point or two. Most don't care because they don't know better. But I'll get a few who bitch and moan about it, and for them I can make an exception. But if I don't have to, I won't."

Though Neal wouldn't go into too much detail about his business, but he did say it's "pretty much what you think it'd be." It's not glamorous, that's for sure. "I'm not a suit-and-tie guy, and I've never had to be." He doesn't even have to leave his home to go to work. But being a bookie is, Neal claimed, "a constant headache." "Not only do I have to be on top of everything and try to be one step ahead of my clients," he lamented, "I think I think about money more than most bankers." One thing he doesn't seem worried about is the law. "I'm probably lucky, but I've never been pinched. I know a couple of fellas that were way back when, but I doubt I would be now. I used to worry about every new bettor who came in, you know, wondering if he was undercover or something. But now, at my age...?"

I could be wrong, but my guess was that Neal handled most of his clients' bets online which would explain his constant companions the smartphone and the laptop. When pressed, he was silent on this subject. But the trend today for bookies is to use what are called pay-per-head websites, often based outside the United States in countries like Costa Rica and Antigua where sports gambling is legal. Perhaps you've stumbled across one of these. They look like the typical gambling website, but there's no admission beyond the homepage. What's required is a key or password. Where do you find this? It's supplied to each new client by the bookie or his agent.

Once inside, a bettor has access to all the games and lines that bookie offers. It's a bookie's personal sports book. No phone calls are needed. The gambler bets right through the website while the bookie can monitor everything that's happening in real time. For such a service, the bookie pays whoever runs the website a fee (usually monthly) based on the number of bettors signed up; hence the title "pay-per-head." As for the actual money, it never leaves the country. The bookie and the gambler either meet face to face to settle up or the agent handles all of the monetary transactions.

Though a bookie may not be seen in the way a casino sports book is, they are known to have a few tricks up their sleeves. Shading lines is a time-honored one. Another is to offer odds worse than the typical -110 (that is when a bettor has to wager $110 in order to win $100). On certain games, a bookie may bump that up to -115 or worse. What's a bettor going to do? Go somewhere else? Not every gambler has more than one bookie with which to work. When the bettor accepts that -115, the bookie may turn around and make the same bet through a rival book at -110 or better, hedging the play and making a bit of profit in the process. Bookies of course can also limit bets. A gambler may want to bet $1,000 or more on a game, but there's nothing that says a bookie has to take that much action. Maybe he just wants a piece of that bet—or none at all.

The lament of many winning gamblers is when their

bookie flat out refuses to accept their bets. It happens. Win a few too many, look a little too sharp, and a gambler can easily find himself blackballed. Bookies prevent mounting losses by eliminating sharp bettors. It might not seem fair, but it's the bookie's house. It's his rules. There isn't any oversight because, well, this is a criminal enterprise.

That's what makes what I uncovered in an old FBI file a bit shocking. In 1979, rumors abounded that two (maybe three) NFL referees were fixing games. Both the FBI and the IRS investigated this case which I wrote about in my book *Larceny Games*. The NFL caught wind of it and offered a bit of help to the FBI in its investigation. What the league provided to the Bureau were seven weeks worth of betting lines on NFL games. These weren't the Vegas point spreads because, remember, the NFL didn't seem to associate with the legal sports books. These were the lines *bookies* were offering.

The NFL had access to at least one bookie in each of the 28 cities in which a franchise resided at that time. These hand-drawn spreadsheets listed each of the bookies' closing lines on every NFL game (and there were variations in the point spreads offered). Also included was whether the favorite covered or not. The FBI file contained no information as to why the league was doing this on such a regular basis, but one thing was for certain: the NFL wasn't turning in these bookies. It wasn't attempting to stop crime nor was it attempting to prevent wagering on its games—despite the NFL's supposed hatred of the practice. No, the league was apparently in cahoots with illegal gambling operations in order to monitor the betting activity on its games.

There's no way of telling when the NFL began such a practice or if it ever stopped. The league isn't very forthcoming with this sort of information. But finding the most widely accepted lines on today's games is a mere mouse-click away. When the NFL was doing this in 1979, however, it had to make several phone calls to several difference sources around the country. If the league wanted to seriously clamp down on illegal betting, it had the connections—both to the illegal bookies and the federal agents mandated with arresting them—to do so. Yet there doesn't appear to be any record of the NFL assisting in closing an illegal sports betting operation.

It's not really a surprise. The biggest bookies operating right now are in New York City, the same town in which the NFL's headquarters are located. If the league cannot stop—or won't assist in stopping—the illegal gambling occurring right under its nose, why should it do anything about the betting going on in Atlanta, St. Louis, Denver or elsewhere?

WEEK 5
vs. OFFSHORE

I don't know about you, but I enjoy checking my email. Unlike some writers, I keep a public email available to anyone seeking to contact me. I never know what I'm going to find in my inbox. Sometimes it's a lead on a story, sometimes it's an interview request, and sometimes it's just a kind word that helps keep me motivated.

In early 2014, I received something unusual. It was an inquiry asking if I would be interested in ghostwriting a book. Though I had no experience in the field, when I saw the potential pay and travel opportunities I couldn't type "yes" fast enough. Before a single word would be written; however, I had to interview with the fellows who would be credited as the future book's authors: brothers Gary and Neil Kaplan.

Who are the Kaplans? Gary was the founder of one of the first major offshore sports gambling websites, BetonSports. Neil was his partner in crime. I write that not as a cliché, but as reality. Both pleaded guilty to federal offenses for their roles in BetonSports.

I was warned ahead of time that these guys were...let's say quirky. They had already interviewed a dozen other writers and rejected them all. I was being brought in by the company the Kaplans hired to find a ghostwriter because the company had literally run out of writers to pitch. They were desperate for a match. To them, I appeared to be a good option. My background in writing books about sports, gambling and corruption seemed to be a solid fit for the Kaplans' project.

Or so the company and I thought. The Kaplans, mainly Gary as Neil didn't say much, had different ideas.

After I rattled off my writing background—the books, the articles, etc.—Gary sounded underwhelmed. "What we need," he told me, "is someone who can tell our *story*. Someone good with characters that can bring our personalities to life on the page." I countered by highlighting my screenwriting past. Prior to wading into sports writing and well before I earned the title of "America's leading expert on game fixing," I went to film school at Columbia College in Chicago. My focus was screenwriting. That education landed me a manager, a couple of Top Ten placements in nationally recognized screenwriting competitions, and zero purchased/produced scripts. But I assured them I knew how to develop characters and write dialogue.

Though I sent them a pair of "award winning" screenplays to review, I didn't get the job. In fact, no one ever got the job. No book "written" by the Kaplans has yet to surface to my knowledge. What it may boil down to is the impression I took away from talking with the brothers. They're delusional. And not just in believing that their personal story is equivalent to *The Godfather* or *Goodfellas*. After detailing my knowledge about sports gambling, Gary said to me, "As far as I'm concerned, the fact that we ran a sports betting website doesn't matter. Our story would read the same if we had made tables and chairs." Though I verbally agreed with Gary in a feeble attempt to win him over, my bullshit meter had maxed out.

Gary Kaplan was a high school dropout turned New York bookie. After enduring felony charges of bookmaking and forgery, his moment of genius came when he founded BetonSports in 1995. Kaplan set up businesses in Aruba, Antigua, and later Costa Rica to offer sports wagering services to a largely American clientele through toll-free phone numbers and the then-emerging internet. Though based offshore, the FBI pointed out, "Technologically, Kaplan's toll-free telephone lines terminated in Houston, Texas or Miami, Florida and then were forwarded to Costa Rica by satellite transmitter or fiber-optic cable. Some of Kaplan's web servers were located in Miami and were remotely controlled from Costa Rica."[1]

In the time just prior to the passage of the Unlawful Internet Gambling Enforcement Act, US-based customers had no problem depositing or withdrawing money from BetonSports accounts. The ease of these transactions coupled with their prominent advertising caused the site to explode in popularity. By 2004, BetonSports had "1 million registered customers and accepted more than 10 million sports bets worth more than $1 billion."[2] The Kaplans' enterprise by then required over 1,700 employees, most of which were based in Costa Rica.

But they didn't stop there. Though he admitted that by 2000 he thought that BetonSports was operating in violation of US law—and legally confirmed that fact in 2002[3]—Kaplan took BetonSports public on the London Stock Exchange's Alternative Investment Market in July 2004. Despite its criminality, early investors included the likes of Goldman Sachs, Merrill Lynch, and Morgan Stanley.[4] The stock offering raised over $100 million in capital which Kaplan funneled into Swiss bank accounts. Then the wheels fell off.

In 2006, while BetonSports was handling just under $2 billion annually in wagers, the United States District Court for the Eastern District of Missouri issued a sealed indictment against the company and many of its employees as part of a larger federal crackdown against internet gambling. The first to fall was BetonSports CEO David Carruthers. He was arrested in

July of that year while changing planes at Dallas-Fort Worth Airport during a United Kingdom to Costa Rica flight. Though the company dismissed Carruthers and continued to operate, a federal judge issued a restraining order preventing BetonSports from taking any further wagers from American bettors. It effectively shut down the site.

A little over six months later, Gary Kaplan was arrested in the Dominican Republic and extradited to the United States. His brother Neil and sister Lori Beth Kaplan-Multz were also arrested. "Prosecutors said the company falsely advertised that its Web-based and phone-based gambling operations were legal, and misled gamblers into believing that money transferred to BetOnSports was safe and available to withdraw at any time. In fact, they said, the money was used to expand operations, including purchase of a rival betting firm."[5]

In this instance, no one got away with anything. Gary Kaplan, "pursuant to a complex plea agreement," pleaded guilty in 2009 to charges including violating RICO statues and the Wire Wager Act. Sentenced to 51 months in prison, Kaplan was required to forfeit over $50 million and ordered to get his high school diploma. His brother and sister pleaded guilty to racketeering charges. Neither served jail time, but both also forfeited millions of dollars to federal authorities. Carruthers, who lived under house arrest in St. Louis for nearly three and a half years, reached a plea agreement which allowed him to return home to the UK, yet he wasn't fully released from custody until July 2011.

Gary Kaplan ultimately served just over a year in prison. He was released in late 2009, yet four short years later he might have decided to go back into the BetonSports business. Gambling news website CalvinAyre.com reported that, "The once mighty domain name [BetonSports.com] was sold this week via registrar GoDaddy for a mere $4,900 to a Costa Rica resident named Deana Morley. Morley was once the president of

Bulma International SA, a Costa Rica-based firm that listed BetOnSports founder Gary Kaplan as its secretary, which suggests that Kaplan may have just got his baby back."[6] In fact, as of this writing, BetonSports.com is up and running, offering wagering information, sports news and more—but it's not booking bets. Yet.

At the time of Kaplan's plea deal, acting United States Attorney Michael W. Reap stated, "Kaplan was unique in the scope and scale of his illegal operation. Despite his immense profits, he is living in federal custody. This case should serve as a warning to others who might choose to defy the laws of the United States on such a grand scale."[7] Reap also noted that, "Kaplan's business model itself was built on a wager that the U.S. could not and would not enforce its anti-sports book laws to reach Kaplan. Today, Kaplan lost that wager."[8]

When it was shut down, the Kaplans (and others involved in the company) held millions of dollars in a variety of bank accounts. Yet those who invested in BetonSports on the London Stock Exchange were left holding fistfuls of worthless stock certificates while bettors were out an estimated $16 million locked in inaccessible accounts. It took three years for BetonSports' account holders to begin to see any sort of reimbursement, and even then the court-mandated settlement was only going to repay three to five percent of the amount truly owed.

This should have served as a lesson well learned, yet major online sports books continue to thrive. Some are even active on Twitter. They also continue to run headlong into legal trouble because they refuse to turn away zealous American bettors.

In 2012, an investigation into illegal sports betting tied to the Curaçao-based website PinnacleSports.com led to the arrest of 25 individuals spread out across five states. They were charged with 225 counts of conspiracy, promoting gambling, and money laundering as the operation reportedly handled over $50 million in payouts. Surprisingly, eight of the suspects were from Las Vegas, including Mike Colbert who happened to be the sports book manager for my favorite place, The M Resort. At the time the charges against Colbert were being dismissed (it is not known if he struck some sort of deal with prosecutors as this case was ongoing at the time of this writing) yet another online sports book was besieged by US authorities.

Legendz Sports incurred the wrath of the US Department of Justice in early 2013 as it unsealed indictments against 34 individuals and 23 companies connected to the website's operation. Those charged were accused of racketeering, money laundering, and operating an illegal gambling business which netted over $1 billion in profits since 2003. Three Florida men—Paul Francis Tucker, Luis Robles, and Christopher Lee Tanner—were convicted in March 2015 for their roles in Legendz Sports. According to the Department of Justice, "The evidence demonstrated that Tanner and Tucker worked as bookies in Florida, and illegally solicited and accepted sports wagers and settled gambling debts. Tucker also used [his business] Zapt Electrical Sales and its bank account to launder gambling proceeds collected from losing bettors. The evidence showed that Robles worked as a runner for the enterprise, delivering cash to Legendz Sports bookies to make payouts and picking up cash profits from the bookies. According to the evidence at trial, bookies and runners for Legendz Sports transported millions of dollars of gambling proceeds in cash and checks from the United States to Panama. The checks were made out to various shell companies created by Legendz Sports all over Central America to launder gambling proceeds."[9]

Assistant Attorney General Leslie R. Caldwell echoed the Kaplan case when he said of these convictions, "In the age of the internet, what used to be a crime conducted by bookies on street corners is now an international criminal enterprise.

Operating on-line but off-shore, the individuals convicted in this case raked in more than a billion dollars in illegal gambling proceeds. But as these convictions demonstrate, no matter where or how organized criminals operate, the Criminal Division will bring them to justice."[10]

That's the thing with these offshore sports books. Many, if not all, are owned and/or operated by expatriated Americans who choose to take up residency in these Caribbean nations because they believe they are outside the reach of US law. The fact is, much like their bookie brethren back in the states, these guys are *criminals*.

This notion was best described by Marisa Lankester in her book *Dangerous Odds: My Secret Life Inside an Illegal Billion Dollar Sports Betting Operation*. Lankester fell in love with, married, and later divorced Tony Ballestrasse, one of sports gambling legend Ron "The Cigar" Sacco's bookmakers. Her book details the trials and tribulations of living the life of an offshore bookmaker. Ultimately, what it boiled down to for her was described during a dinner party, "The photographer's bright flash had revealed the true nature of my companions. Tony, Ron ["The Cigar"], Carmine, and Vinnie were nothing more than career criminals. They would spend their entire lives rootless, hunted, always trying to stay one step ahead of the law. It was a defining moment for me. Working in the [Dominican Republic] only gave them a veneer of legitimacy."[11]

Even so, it's actually rather safe, legally-speaking, to bet with these offshore sports books. No gambler has ever been arrested for betting with any of these sites. The biggest legal threat would lie in not reporting any big wins on one's tax return. Otherwise, you really don't have to worry about John Q. Law kicking down your door after you electronically bet the 49ers-Rams game.

Finding a sports gambling site isn't a problem, either. Finding a *reputable* one is a different story. What you have to concern yourself with is three-fold: getting through security and opening an account, getting money into that account, and then getting paid (should you win).

For example, the UK-based gambling behemoth William Hill operates approximately 20 full service sports books in Las Vegas and many more worldwide. They also have an online presence where customers can wager from the comfort of their couch. Yet when I attempted to access their site, what I was met with was this message: "WE HAVE DETECTED THAT YOU ARE CURRENTLY LOCATED IN THE USA." The barrier prevented me from going any further, even just to view the available odds on any game. Now I could (and did) mask my IP address and gain access to their site. Doing so isn't much of a hacker trick. For those interested, a quick internet search provides all the details on how to accomplish this, the NSA be damned. But what's the point for those interested in betting? Even if you could get money into an account there, the chances of getting it back out would be slim to none.

I could access all the games and odds at the Curacao-based Pinnacle Sports website; however, since 2007 the site has not allowed any US-based customers to register an account. Yet it still handled about $40 billion in sports wagers in 2014. When I accessed Pinnacle's registration page, there was no United States "country" option to choose. But if I resided in Canada, Iran, Vatican City or a multitude of other little known countries, they would've welcomed me—and my US currency—with open arms.

Then there's Bovada. This site—with the odd .lv suffix—is perhaps the American sports gambler's number one choice. It's owned by Mohawk Morris Gaming Group which is headquartered in the Kahnawake Mohawk Territory in Quebec, just across the Saint Lawrence River from Montreal. In 2014, it handled about $8 billion in sports wagers. Though Bovada accepts clients from every US state with the exception of

Maryland, Washington, and New York, the US Justice Department considers it an illegal gambling operation. Yet I created an account at Bovada in seconds. Interestingly, the email I received to confirm my new account for Bovada featured a picture of the famous Las Vegas Strip. Why would Bovada use such an image? They're not based in Las Vegas, much less Nevada. Why not a photo of a Canadian casino or a moose? Either would be slightly more apropos. Could this Vegas image be used to make them look a bit more legitimate to new, US-based subscribers?

When it came time to deposit funds into that newly created Bovada account, I stopped short of proceeding. Why? The Unlawful Internet Gambling Enforcement Act. Though Bovada stated it accepted a credit card for a deposit and offered me a payment window not unlike one at Amazon's checkout, the UIGEA made it illegal for banks and credit card companies to process payments to gambling websites. Which leads to a little known fact: make a deposit with your credit card at a site like Bovada and it's quite possible your credit card company will close your account. Immediately. To the credit card companies, this one payment will make you "undesirable" as a customer.

I may have been perfectly fine in giving Bovada my credit card information, but I wasn't about to risk my credit score to find out. Besides, there's many other ways to deposit money.

Ever hear of cryptocurrency? Virtual money? Bitcoin? Not only does Bitcoin and its ilk have actual monetary value (at least for the moment), but it has the added component of anonymity. This is why black markets like the defunct Silk Road was quick to adopt it as its preferred payment option. And what's a bigger black market than the $1 trillion worldwide illegal sports gambling business? If you search around on the internet, you're certain to find a sports gambling site which accepts Bitcoin as payment. One such entity is NitrogenSports.eu. Another is the Ireland-based Predictious.com. Though

Predictious is not a traditional sports book (you can bet on government elections, box office returns for movies, and more) it certainly behaves like one. The site will even accept "bets" for as little as 1 Millibitcoin (0.001 Bitcoin).

If you want to deal in good ol' US dollars and cents (how Byzantine), then you'll have to get off the couch. Some sports gambling sites allow its clients to send them a money order by courier with which to open an account. It's rather safe since nearly all courier services include a tracking number, but it can be rather slow. If you want to gamble *right now*—and who doesn't?—the more preferable way to get money to these sports gambling websites is via what's known as a person-to-person transfer.

In the on-demand age of Paypal and Apple Pay, wiring money to other person sounds like something that went out of fashion with the porkpie hat. Yet companies like Western Union transfer money all over the world and can be easily accessed from stores like Wal-Mart. Now, these money transfer companies don't advertise that they are an excellent conduit between sports gamblers and offshore sports books, but they don't refuse this business, either. You just need to talk to the gambling site's customer service department to ensure your money is headed to the proper location. This method of funding an account is often recommended because it's also the preferred way to get your money out. And that's sometimes the stickiest problem when it comes to offshore sports books: getting paid when you win.

Every site acts as if getting your winnings back from Antigua or wherever the hell they are located is a breeze. But many a gambler has been screwed out of his or her winnings never to be paid a dime of what's owed. Some of these sites are flat out scams. You can pay in easy enough, but they have no intention of ever paying out. Others just flat out shut down. Some will swear your money is "on its way," and they may in fact pay you...sometime next year. Then there's the always lingering threat of US law enforcement closing down the site and arresting those involved a la BetonSports. These sorts of stories go on and on as it is truly a "bettor beware" situation no matter with which site one chooses to deal.

Places like Bovada, 5dimes and others do have good reputations in paying off winning bettors. But because they still exist outside US law, when a dispute between gambler and website occurs, who do you think holds the upper hand? Bettors have zero recourse in these matters. Their only option is merely to plead with whoever is on the other end of the line and hope they are in a good mood that day. Otherwise, your account—and the money in it—may be closed. Sorry. You are at their mercy, of which they often have very little.

In the end, these websites are nothing but glorified illegal bookies and often act like it, limiting winning bettors, offering inflated lines (especially on high profile match-ups), adding extra vig to bets, etc. They have even been known to offer different point spreads depending on whether or not the customer is perceived to be a sharp bettor. Login with one account; get a certain set of numbers to bet. Do it through a different account and those numbers magically change. These sites may seem like gambling at a legitimate Nevada sports book, but it's not. Nor will it be until they are fully legalized and regulated. Some of these sites and the people who operate them are all for that because chances are they will make even more money with a lot less risk attached to it. They want to be legit. But others prefer things as is. Organized crime has an aversion to oversight.

BRIAN TUOHY

WEEK 6
vs. TOUTS

Sometimes even the best of us can use a little advice. The proper guidance. A push in the right direction. A trick, a tip, anything to correct the present course and lead one down a more desirable path. Because the truth is there's a huge difference between knowing a sport and knowing how to wager upon it. From the outside, it appears as if those two should go hand-in-hand. Knowledge of a sport—its intricacies, coaching tendencies, etc.—seems like it should lend itself to financial prosperity when betting on that sport's outcomes. But it doesn't. The point spread is a wily beast, and the vig, personal money management, and other associated pitfalls can easily make the smartest football fan appear to be an absolute idiot while robbing him of a small fortune in the process.

Luckily, there are all sorts of people out there ready to assist the willing gambler, to be that beacon of light in the dark forest of NFL wagering. But I wouldn't trust a single one of them. Seriously. I'm not sure I can write this next sentence emphatically enough. Do NOT pay for anyone's—and I mean *anyone's*—picks, moves, locks, or wagering advice, especially when offered for sale on the internet.

Free advice is fine. It's not necessarily trustworthy either, but all it can cost you is some time and perhaps a bit of sanity. Plenty of books exist to teach you how to "beat the bookies." I'm sure many offer sage advice and will in fact help the novice gambler improve on his plays. But who's willing to pick up a book these days (current company not included)? Reading takes time, and the game is about to kick off. Why did the line move? Where's the advantage? Who should you take? What the recreational gambler needs is clarity—and he needs it *now*. So the first place many turn is to boob tube.

The legendary Jimmy "The Greek" Snyder was perhaps the first sports gambler to be given network television air-time to discuss NFL betting. The Greek was legit. He had a pedigree that made his "dees and dose guys" talk palatable to Middle America. Of course, The Greek wasn't allowed to actually mention the point spread on a game, but many armchair bettors hung on his every word prior to phoning a bet to his bookie.

Alas, The Greek's time on TV was cut short by a few very un-PC words. His ill-advised statement gave CBS the out it sought, and ever since discussion of gambling on network NFL pre-game shows was verboten. But cable TV was not so shy. Though limited for a long time to public-access cable programming (remember that?), wagering and point spread discussions have today found a home on many national cable sports networks, including the granddaddy of them all, ESPN.

The NFL mandates that none of its broadcast partners mentions the betting lines or any sort of wagering information during its telecasts. Occasionally Al Michaels will allude to such things during *Sunday Night Football*, but otherwise the major networks abide by the league's wishes. Even NFL pregame shows like when Jimmy, Howie, Terry, and the rest on FOX make their "picks" for a given week, they won't make those selections against any sort of point spread. Yet tune into a pre-pregame show, such as ESPN's *Colin's Football Show*, and the attitude changes.

On November 9, just prior to the Sunday kickoff of Week 10 of the 2014 NFL season, I tuned into *Colin's Football Show* to see what (former) ESPN radio host Colin Cowherd and ESPN the Magazine's Editor-in-Chief and host of the "Behind the Bets" podcast Chad Millman—the experts—had to say about wagering on this week's games in a segment called "Three Big Bets." It began with the following exchange:

Cowherd: "This isn't a week of good games, but it could be a week of good bets."

Millman: "*Very* good numbers available if you like to invest."

Cowherd: "I never thought of it as investing, but…"

Let's stop right here. Though there are similarities between playing the stock market and gambling on sports, the word "invest" should never cross the lips of someone discussing betting on an NFL game. "Investing" sounds intelligent. "Betting" sounds risky. And these two talking-heads were basically telling their viewers which three NFL games were the best "investments" of the day. This is wrong. And honestly, it got worse as the conversation progressed.

The first game brought up was Kansas City -1 versus Buffalo. Cowherd raved why he liked the Chiefs. Millman countered by calling him a "silly, silly, silly man." "The wiseguys are all over Buffalo in this one," Millman informed him, and by extension, the audience. At the same moment he spoke these words, a graphic with the word "Sharps" covered the displayed Buffalo logo (which, by the way, wasn't actually the Bills logo, but rather a cartoon variation of it—probably as a concession to the NFL). Millman explained how the line in the game moved from KC -3 down to KC -1, throwing in a few NFL-related stats like QBR to explain everything.

Game two was the New York Giants +8.5 versus Seattle. Cowherd decided he'd take the points and New York. Smiling,

Millman nodded because "The wiseguys are on the Giants as well." Once again, the "Sharps" logo covered the fake Giants emblem. Millman explained, "The bookmakers can't make the number high enough because they know they are going to get a ton of Seattle money. So the wiseguys have been coming in and taking it," moving the line from -10.5 to -8.5. Then Millman questioned how Seattle could possibly run up the score with such a weak offense. Clearly, the Giants were the smart bet, sorry, investment.

The final game discussed was St. Louis +6.5 versus Arizona. Cowherd took the Rams which Millman again informed him was the wiseguys' play and was again accompanied by that stupid "Sharps" graphic. Cowherd actually cheered for himself for picking two of the three games the sharps liked. Millman did caution that the Rams were a "tricky, tricky" team because they beat the Seahawks, but were "killed" by the Chiefs. Millman also added that the game's line was "inflated" because everyone "loves" Arizona at the moment.

Now, granted, this was just a TV show. It's meant to be taken with a grain of salt, or in this case, maybe an entire salt lick. But it sounded like the informed conversation of two experts. Two experts—and a slew of unnamed "wiseguys"—who wound up being incredibly wrong. The Chiefs covered the one-point spread and beat Buffalo 17-13; Seattle's "weak offense" whooped the Giants 38-17; and the "inflated" Arizona line wasn't blown up enough as they crushed the Rams 31-14. How's that for some free gambling advice?

It may seem as if I cherry-picked this particular episode of *Colin's Football Show*, but honestly it was the only one I bothered to watch. Maybe he and Millman nailed the other 48 games they discussed during the "Three Big Bets" segment over the course of the season. I don't know. But the fact that "Three Big Bets" even exists is bothersome. Not only because it gives the illusion of an informed discussion on the subject of NFL gambling, but because it's also indirectly encouraging it.

Colin's Football Show, *The Linemakers*, and every other program like it are meant "for entertainment purposes only," much like *The Anarchist's Cookbook* described bomb-making methods "for informational purposes only." The argument follows that none of those talking heads can know if someone watching the show will actually go out and bet using the information they just saw. Yet then why are any of these shows on TV? Whether intended or not, these programs are promoting what's (at this time) a largely illegal activity. What might be worse is that these "experts" are providing their viewers with junk information on which to make those illegal wagers.

No matter how you dress up this behavior, those involved are acting like touts. And to a recreational gambler, nothing short of a gambling addiction is as dangerous as a tout.

What is a "tout?" It's a sports gambler/handicapper who claims to be so good at picking winners that he sells his information to weaker gamblers seeking help. There is good money to be made in being a tout. One tout I spoke with flat out told me, "I can make more money selling my moves than betting them myself."

Take a look at one extreme (and likely exaggerated) example. Adam Meyer, a tout who went by the title "sports consultant to the stars," told CNBC the following in 2011: "Meyer says he has more than 11,000 people who pay $199 a month, which buys them 15 to 20 picks a week. There's also a group of bettors who pay him $10,000 for even more games. And finally, he says there are 67 gamblers in the Platinum Club, which costs $250,000. Those gamblers can work with him until they net $1 million. If they don't within a year, they probably don't use Meyer again. If they do, they can choose to pay him another $250,000 for their next million."[1] Do a little math, and that added up to Meyer allegedly clearing over $40 million a year. Yet in late 2014, Meyer was arrested for attempting to extort $25 million from a client. As of this writing, he was facing a six-count indictment for wire fraud, extortion, and racketeering. Meyer was planning to plead "insanity" to these charges.

Many touts and tout-related websites sell a season-long subscription package for upwards of $200. Land 500 subscribers as a tout and you've just earned $100,000. That's without laying down a single bet or even giving out a single correct pick. It's a zero risk move. This is why many publicly known sports gamblers have turned themselves into touts of varying degrees. Once one builds up any sort of reputation (even a fake one), it's easy to monetize that persona by becoming a tout. Set up a website, send out a few tweets, and boom! You're in business.

"I can tell you with 100 percent certainty that all sporting touts are smoke and mirrors and marketing," former tout Brad (not his real name) told me. "They have a million tricks that temporarily make them look good to new customers, but sooner than later the customer loses his or her bankroll and then they are out of tout [subscription] money as well. Then the tout markets himself to the next 19- to 29-year old gambler that doesn't know better. I'm quite surprised that none of these guys have been assaulted in a dark alley by a disgruntled customer. I know I almost was!"

Brad transformed himself from a gambler to a bookie to a tout in a relatively short period of time. Part of this goes to show you the irony of touts. Many do have a solid understanding of sports gambling. They built their bankable reputation somehow, and though luck and/or lies may have played a role, many touts have a proven track record—no matter how distant—to promote. Of course, past performance is not indicative of future results. This is why most touts are as effective as a coin toss in picking winners.

For Brad, the path to becoming a tout started with the purchase of Wayne Allyn Root's book *Betting to Win on Sports*.

Root is a trip in and of himself. A biography of Root can be found on Al McMordie's "Big Al's Sportsline" website (which is a tout site, and interestingly, is linked to Root's WinningEdge.com tout site featuring a biography of McMordie). It begins, "Wayne Allyn Root is quite simply one of the most honored professional sports handicappers and Vegas oddsmakers in the world. He is the brand name of sports gaming—dubbed by the national media as 'the King of Vegas Sports Gambling,' 'The Face of Las Vegas Gambling,' 'America's Oddsmaker,' and 'The Prince of Prognosticators.' His rags-to-riches story is truly remarkable. Born a S.O.B. (son of a butcher), Wayne has morphed into high profile CEO, entrepreneur, best-selling author, TV celebrity and nationally recognized politician. Wayne is living proof that the American Dream is alive and well."[2]

Brad was drawn to Root's book because it was a contrarian guide to sports betting. "It's a good book," he recalled, "it really is. And it tempted me enough to call his company sometime in the early 2000's. They sold me on a $1,200 college basketball package which I can't believe I fell for, but I whipped out my credit card and signed up. All up front without seeing anything. I was hypnotized."

Root's service assigned Brad a handler who would consult with him on his bankroll, picks, etc. This wasn't any sort of tape recorded message as touts were once famous for. It was an honest-to-goodness human being. "So I told the guy," Brad remembered, "look, I got $2,000 to work with, and really, that's a lot of money to me [at the time]. That's what I have to utilize. And right off the bat, the guy has me play four $500 games. I'm like, 'Really?' and he's like, 'Yeah, yeah. Don't worry about it.' So I ask, 'What if we lose all four games?' and he says, 'We won't. I guarantee it.' He lost all four of his picks. He bankrupted me in a night."

Luckily for Brad, he was crafty enough to record the conversation complete with the guarantee. He decided to take

Root's service to task. "I raised enough hell with them that I got Root himself on the phone. They gave me my money back. Not the full $2,000, but $1,000 in order for me to keep playing. I was impressed with that. Root said, 'I'm pretty impressed that you had the due diligence to record a guarantee on picks from someone at my company.'"

But Brad was not impressed with the touts at Root's service. "They sucked worse than a dog picking biscuits with team names on them. They never won. They never did anything contrarian, nothing like Root's book. They never followed that line of thinking."

While he was locked into Root's service, Brad started getting phone calls from other touts attempting to sell him their services as well. He couldn't figure it out at first, but then Brad realized Root had given (or sold) his phone number to other touts! "These guys [which included the aforementioned Big Al McMordie and Adam Meyer] would call and tell me they were going to change my life. So, I tested them because I knew they were desperate for commissions. Some would give me just a free pick or two, others an entire week's worth. I did this for two years, when I was really deep into this, testing these guys. And in all that time, I only found two out of maybe 30 or 40 who were the real deal. The rest were like the lowest of the lowlifes."

Then came Brad's brainstorm. "I thought, especially after the Root incident, that if they're doing this for big bucks, then I could do the same thing for pennies on the dollar, but still make a good buck doing it as well as having a bit of fun along the way." Having booked bets while in college, Brad enlisted his computer-savvy brother and launched his own tout website in 2005. "My hope was that I'd get decent info from those other guys and re-sell it. It's slimy, I know, but it was fun. I went at this venture very hard, going as far as putting up a full-print logo on my truck and driving to popular Midwest sporting events such as Wisconsin Badgers football games and the Big Ten basketball tournament. I even recruited and paid college kids to sell my services. I had professional tri-fold advertisements, a radio ad, and more."

Like many others, Brad's service offered daily, weekly, and monthly packages. Once set up, he handled everything himself, despite acting like "I had people in the boiler room looking over the numbers and crap like that." He wrote each day's rundowns, recalling "I never typed so much in my life." And though he lied about a lot of things, he claimed the one thing he couldn't fake was his betting record. "You couldn't do it. Instead, I would focus on the good things. I'd use a fresh streak or go back a ways to make the long-term record look good. You know, use the 'big pick,' the 10-dimer that won as a selling point."

Not all touts are so honest. Rick Reilly once wrote a piece on touts for *Sports Illustrated*. In it, he informed readers, "SI took a two-month test drive through the world of sports-advisory services and found misleading ads, bait-and-switches, repeated claims of fixes coming down, misrepresentation of records, unforgivably high-pressured sales techniques, phone harassment, phone threats, phony guarantees, mail fraud, wire fraud and some perfectly dreadful manners."[3]

That was 1991. Twenty-five years later, nothing within this so-called industry has changed. Many touts fake or alter their betting records to look more desirable to prospective clients. One of the most absurd attempts at this was by "John Morrison" on SportsBettingChamp.com who was alleged to be a "celebrated Ivy League graduate from Cornell University with a PhD degree in statistics." He claimed a win rate of 97 percent, adding that his system went 79-0 during the 2008-09 NBA season and 63-0 the following year. Unbelievable to all but the highly gullible.

If touts don't resort to outright bullshitting, then they might post picks against phantom lines, use point spreads that were only available momentarily, or pick against numbers at sports books that are closed for the night, leaving them with lines that have yet to be updated. It's equally as shifty, but more difficult to prove given the wide variety of sports books in the world. Yet touts have to constantly look over their shoulder when erasing such "mistakes" because sports betting message boards are filled with chatter on this subject. Some sports gamblers are more than happy to play the role of watchdogs, revealing which touts are the most egregious fakers.

For Brad, it didn't take long to reach his breaking point. "It fell apart because the amount of work became laughable," he said. "I wanted something on the side, something fun because I've always been really interested in this, and it just became a monster. And I started to realize that people were actually relying on me. So I'm up at all hours of the night, deciding what game is what."

At this point in our conversation, Brad invoked the name of Brandon Lang. Perhaps Lang's biggest claim to fame—one he makes sure to point out time and again on his website—is that the film "Two for the Money" starring Matthew McConaughey and Al Pacino was based on his life. Lang leverages this fact to his advantage, writing on his website, "Let's just say Hollywood would not have made a movie based on my life in the sports gambling business if I weren't a winner!"[4] Sure, Brandon, sure.

Brad recalled a different Lang in the past. "In videos Lang posted, you could see he was drunk, stressed out, and reaching. Then he'd post apologies on which games were picked and why. You could tell the life was killing the guy, yet he was running other people through the grinder. But for anyone in this business, there's always a new group of up-and-coming gamblers to take advantage of."

And Lang continues to make his sales pitch today. At least he includes one extremely truthful statement on his website, "Understand something right now: **I am not going to win every**

game, every week or every month. [emphasis in original]"[5] From the point of that safety net onward, however, Lang goes full tout, writing, "But, I can put you on the right side of more games that you've ever been on in your gambling life, and by doing that, you will make money. By the way, if you're curious about whether my record is legitimate, let me assure you it is, and let me explain why: You see I offer long-term packages of 7, 30, 60 and 100 days. Anyone who buys a package gets EVERY play I release, day in, day out. Now, if I lied, even once, how many customers do you think I'd have remaining? See, that's the beauty of the Internet. I don't need some phony monitoring service to document my wins and losses. Instead, you—my customers—do that for me. **You validate my opinion and assure my credibility. And that's why we're a team.** [emphasis in original]."[6]

I hate to brake it to Lang, but there's no "team" in the tout business. Especially not one made up of the tout and the clients...unless you want to discuss affiliate programs. You see, most touts exist only in cyberspace. Oddly enough, many sports books operate only in the virtual world as well. Wouldn't these two entities make for a profitable team? In fact, they often do. Visit enough touts, and you'll find that their sites will often direct perspective clients to online sports books ready and willing to accept their bets. This is just a convenience; an example of the gambling "expert" informing the novice where there's a safe place to make a wager, right? Wrong. Most likely, the tout is an affiliate of the sports book and will get paid for every player that creates a new account with that book. But the tout doesn't get paid a flat fee for each sign-up. Instead, he'll earn a percentage on *every losing wager that client places*. Depending on the deal, this might amount to as much as a 30 percent kickback. In other words, the tout has a monetary incentive to give his customers bad information.

This might lead you to wonder, "Is this legal?" I'm

afraid to inform you that being a tout and selling such information is 100 percent legal. Though the Wager Wire Act reads in part, "Whoever being engaged in the business of betting or wagering knowingly uses a wire communication facility for the transmission in interstate or foreign commerce of bets or wagers or **information assisting in the placing of bets or wagers on any sporting event or contest, or for the transmission of a wire communication which entitles the recipient to receive money or credit as a result of bets or wagers**...shall be fined under this title or imprisoned not more than two years...[emphasis added]," touts are free to operate in the United States.

Just imagine what happens if sports gambling is legalized. The tout world with absolutely explode with new "experts" and "pros" who know who to bet, when to bet, and perhaps most importantly, where to bet. This is a budding industry in need of oversight if not outright regulation. Right now, it's the Wild West; a "buyer beware" situation which easily suckers in newbies, then chews them up and spits them out without fear of retribution.

The only hope, and it's a distant one, is if the evil little voice inside each tout's head has an epiphany. Brad had one. It may have taken two-and-a-half years for him to have it, but ultimately he gave up the business. "My wife said I got was I deserved," he said, "I was full of shit, and that's why it didn't work out."

Believe it or not, Brad now leads a "way calmer lifestyle." He's a school teacher. And the reality of touts is a lesson every bettor needs to learn.

WEEK 7
@ GAMBLERS

When you think of a gambler, what sort of mental image do you conjure up? My guess is it would fall into one of two stereotypes.

The first would be the stylized, Hollywood version. A dashing, well dressed, James Bond-esque figure who's ready to bet his entire bankroll when he perceives the deck to be stacked in his favor. He *never* sweats. Can't with ice in his veins. This gambler won't ever lose his final bet because to do may be true to life, but would be completely out of character.

The other variation is the degenerate gambler (does the word "degenerate" ever precede anything but "gambler?"). This guy lost 50 cents in a playground bet and has been chasing it ever since. *Mad* magazine published "The Anatomy of a Gambler" back in the 1960s. The cartoon cross-section of a man labeled various body parts with descriptions such as "itchy fingers for dipping into petty cash drawers and wife's pocketbook," "drooped shoulders from carrying burden of heavy losses," "sensitive nose for smelling a sure thing," "sharp eyes for finding bookies, and spotting cops," "deaf ear to starving family's pleading," and in the brain a "desire to get something for nothing" as well as a "desire to avoid working." This gambler cannot win, and if by some miracle he does, he'll blow it all by doubling down the next chance he gets.

The reality, of course, falls somewhere into the vast gray area between these archetypes. With sports gambling, most bettors tend to resemble what I saw milling about the Westgate's SuperBook while the Germans shot their quasi-legal documentary footage. The place was jammed elbow-to-elbow with men. Just regular, nondescript guys. They covered a variety of ages, races, and body types, though their collective BMI skewed toward the unhealthy. Most did share one commonality—they were decked out in their best Sunday outfit, an NFL jersey. Hats were optional.

What were sorely lacking were women. It was a complete sausage-fest in there. Though a couple of females clung to their man's side, lazily checking their smartphone while he scanned the updated lines, none were approaching the windows to bet. Except one woman. A middle-aged blond clad in a bedazzled pink and white Tony Romo jersey. She carried a fistful of betting tickets. I wanted to ask her a few questions, but after stalking her for some 20 minutes during which time she never stopped talking on her cellphone, I gave up. I didn't need security ushering me out like at the M.

This got me wondering, where are the female sports bettors? As the NFL actively attempts to expand its product awareness, it has set its sights directly on women. Half of the NFL's online retail shop is devoted to women's apparel. More female broadcasters are filling the sidelines as well as the talking-head shows. And did you really think the NFL's month-long breast cancer awareness program (which adds pink accents to every team's uniform causing you to assume something is wrong with your TV) is being conducted because the league actually *cares*? This is all part of a greater marketing strategy.

And it's working. The best proof may lie in the fact that

more and more women are signing up for fantasy football leagues with each passing year. Of course, fantasy football isn't gambling (yeah, sure). Yet women do frequent casinos. You can find plenty of women at the blackjack tables, shooting craps, and playing the slots. The poker room is no stranger to the female form either, as a handful of women have become respected poker professionals. So why hasn't any of this translated into women betting on sports?

Certainly some woman somewhere must be dropping a nickel or a dime on the Dolphins and the over. It can't be 100 percent men. It just can't. Yet to prove this required finding that girl. It wasn't as easy of a quest as I expected. I asked many sources if they could point me towards a professional woman sports bettor. Every time I asked the question, it was answered with the same "I dunno" shrug. Oddsmakers, bookies, gamblers…no one could seemingly name a female pro until finally—*finally*—I received a response from the Westgate's Jay Kornegay. He suggested a woman by the name of Kelly Stewart.

"I'm just a nice girl from Kansas," Stewart told me, quickly adding with a laugh, "but we know that's kind of bullshit." Stewart was interesting to speak with. She was open and honest, admitting that though she gambled on sports, it couldn't be a full-time gig for her just yet. She had to maintain another job to make ends meet—something a lot of male "pros" won't publicly confess to needing.

She also acknowledged that she was still learning the trade, wisely taking advice from those who know more than her. "I like to see where the sharp guys are," Stewart said. "I'm not saying that I am one of the sharpest players by any means, but it's always that old adage, 'You're as smart as the people you hang around.' So if I'm with them and hear there's steam coming in on a team which matches my thoughts, I listen. Don't get me wrong, I've been known to make a square play or two, but at this point in time I've learned from those mistakes. I learned how to create power rankings and match those against the line which I think really helped push me over the edge from a good sports bettor to a great one."

Even having waded waist-deep into the sports gambling world, Stewart herself couldn't name another female sports gambler. "For the longest time, I thought I was the only woman doing this," she said, "but then I talked to some of the old school guys, and they were like, 'Oh, no. There's been other women.' But I wonder where are they now?" She guessed why this is, saying, "I think it's because women don't understand sports. I've been playing sports all my life, going to games forever, and I'm a question asker. Even as a kid, when something would happen in a game, I'd ask my dad, 'Why did that happen?' But most women just have a team they root for. They don't bother to really learn the game."

If there was a woman who wanted to learn, Stewart claimed she'd be all for it. "I really want to see a woman who knows what she is talking about, who has the ambition to learn. But I think that's the problem with most women...and why I don't get along with them. They are more concerned with hair, makeup, and nails. That might sound sexist of me, but I hope they really are willing to do this. If any would reach out to me and ask, 'Kelly can you teach me?' I'd be more than happy to take on an intern."

Stewart might soon need one. Besides spending hours working on her plays, she can be heard on Las Vegas radio picking games, seen on local TV discussing point spreads, and writing about all things sports gambling for the *Las Vegas Review-Journal*. "I wouldn't say I use my looks to an advantage," she explained, "but obviously it helps. There are thousands of men trying to break into this industry that I'm sure are great handicappers, but because they are men they will never succeed."

Though the uniqueness of Stewart's presence has helped

her go as far as she has, I wondered if she had encountered any discrimination. "From the Las Vegas sports betting community, everyone I've physically met has been absolutely amazing," she claimed. "I think when people met me, they come away thinking I'm cool, legit; a real person." But on Twitter, it's been a completely different story. "I get eaten alive by men," Kelly lamented. "I thought, 'No one cares that I'm a girl.' But, of course, men are always threatened by a powerful woman. I can understand that."

I learned this for myself when I wrote a profile of Stewart for Vice Sports. What's known as "Gambling Twitter"—a collection of anonymous "pro gamblers" who act as watchdogs (and sometimes trolls)—tore me apart for writing that feature. The problem for them was Kelly Stewart is also known as KellyinVegas, the face (and body) of a tout website with the same name. Though I mentioned this fact in the article, I was instantly seen as touting the tout, helping the KellyinVegas website sucker even more noobs out of their money. This was never my intention. The point of my article wasn't to promote Stewart per se, but to be about Stewart's experience of being a woman in a truly man's domain. Yet once my editors at Vice decided to title the piece "The New Face of Sports Gambling is 'Kelly in Vegas,'" I knew trouble would be afoot.

I understood why these Twitter-based attacks were slung at me (and at Stewart as well). The anonymous gamblers bashing me were "protecting the industry." Now I could debate how much of an "industry" sports gambling actually is (exactly what does this industry produce besides wealth for those who control it?), but what I took umbrage at was when I countered these viciously personal attacks by asking the "pro gamblers" for interviews to learn more about the reality of "the industry," they all cowered in the safety of their Twitter spider holes. Not one accepted my offer.

This is the second biggest irony surrounding touts. They

are the ones willing to have public personas. They are willing to be known, to be interviewed, and to become the public faces of sports gambling. Obviously many have an agenda tied to this—they want to lure in more lambs for the slaughter. More press means more exposure which eventually will lead to more subscription packages sold on their website. Why wouldn't a novice gambler trust that voice on the radio or that talking-head on TV? Would these guys really be getting air-time if they weren't "experts?" Hell, that's what the host just introduced that guy as, a "betting expert."

Of course, this just leads to more vitriol from the "real" pros. They point the finger of blame at us "lazy journalists" for our willingness to give touts a soapbox from which to preach. This criticism might have been best summed up by authors Strine and Isaacs in their 1978 book *Covering the Spread* when they wrote, "The gullibility and ignorance of the press, radio and television in matters pertaining to betting on professional football (and other sports) is astonishing. Excellent reporters, columnists and broadcasters, who in other instances check and double-check their facts and sources, are easily led into a blind-switch when confronted with the hustling handicapper's false glamour. Thanks to the media we see Monday-morning quarterbacks who have never lost and one-year-wonders who get lucky once with their public picks, go underground, and then live off the streak for six or sixty seasons."[1]

What Strine and Isaacs (and many others) overlooked was that some of us in the media do try to dig deeper and find more honest and intelligent voices, but most of those guys refuse to talk. It doesn't matter if it's on the record or off. If they can be found, these pros maintain their silence. So, as I wrote in the previous chapter, because touts do know a thing or two about sports gambling—perhaps just enough to be dangerous—they wind up being the best sources available. With gambling information gaining more and more traction within the national sports media, it's not like this industry won't be covered. ESPN now has an entire subsection of its website—ESPN Chalk—devoted to sports gambling. Others are certain to follow suit. This will likely lead other writers and broadcasters to run headlong into issues similar to the one I encountered with my Kelly in Vegas piece.

The solution to this problem lies in one of two paths. Either some sports writers have to themselves become professional sports gamblers, or else the real pros have to step into the limelight. If a sports writer does take a whack at sports gambling, he's only setting himself up for ridicule. Even though a sports gambler needs to be correct only 52.38 percent of the time to be profitable against the typical vig, can he really survive writing a column in which he is correct only half the time? The public—and the sports betting pros—likely wouldn't allow it. So, it leads us back to the real pros. If these guys truly want to protect sports gambling as they claim, then they have to speak up. Snarky Twitter comments won't do the trick, not when hated touts are getting national coverage.

Yet the silence from the pros is understandable. The number of sports bettors that are profitable over the long haul, those that can make a true living doing this, is extremely slim. I'm talking about maybe one percent of all of those betting regularly. If you happen to be one of those select few, why would you give away your secrets? What, besides stroking your vanity, is there to gain? Becoming a talking-head will do nothing except limit your profitability. So it's better to just keep your head down, your mouth shut, and stick to the winning game plan. Even Stewart acknowledged this, telling me, ""Many of these guys are very, very intelligent, statistical guys. I'm talking, really, really smart guys. Most are fairly introverted. A few guys have more of a personality and you might hear them on the radio. Most of these guys, though, you'll never know who they are."

The best example of this is Billy Walters. He is perhaps the most named-dropped American sports gambler, having been featured on *60 Minutes*. One of the earliest members of the legendary "Computer Group" which was the first to utilize computer algorithms for sports betting, Walters has stretched out to become an all-around entrepreneur. He is also an alleged criminal, having been acquitted in past of conspiracy, illegal transmission of wagering information, and money laundering. As recently as 2014, Walters was under investigation for insider trading along with his friend, PGA golfer Phil Mickelson.

Despite having always worked within a betting syndicate, few know how Walters really operates. But that's the point. Walters isn't about to reveal his tricks because then he wouldn't be nearly as successful as a sports bettor. People just know he wins. He *always* seems to win. Walters claims to have had only one losing season in the past 39 years. And no one's arguing against that boast.

Walters' plays move the lines. That's the kind of reputation he has. He's well aware of this fact, too, so he's been known to exploit it. "He would use us," Scott Schettler, former head of the Stardust Race and Sports Book in the 1980's, explained. "Walters' people would come in the morning and bet with us at the Stardust on the games they wanted to lose. So say USC is playing UCLA and they wanted UCLA. Well, they would come in and bet on USC. We would change the line, and the whole country would wait for us before they put their line up, even the illegals around the country. Billy and his crew had successfully altered the line, and then they'd just go to all different places around the country and bet the other side. It was pretty neat."

Schettler was impressed not just with Walters' savvy, but also with his respect for the bookmakers. "Billy and his crew also put out false games because they knew people followed them. They didn't want to put all the bookmakers out of business, so they'd put out false games, false moves, and all the dumbbells, no matter what those guys bet, they would just blindly bet [what Walters did]. It was really funny. You'd listen to these bettors, 'Billy Walters has USC.' 'No, he's got UCLA!' They don't know who the hell he's got. It was just a riot." The same of Walters' 1980's-era shenanigans could be said today.

Walters employs an unknown number of "runners" who place bets for him since he can no longer walk into a book and bet for himself. The anonymity of the runners allows Walters to bet much more than he possibly could, permitting him to exceed normal limits while keeping his plays a secret. Though what's known as messenger betting is illegal and Las Vegas is supposed to be cracking down on the practice, Walters has been smart enough to ensure his operation is fully compliant with the law. How much betting he even does in Las Vegas is a question mark. It is likely Walters' crew also bets with legal and illegal bookies offshore and throughout the world. According to an ESPN article, "the headquarters of Walters' international operation is located outside the United States. The last known location was in Panama, according to sources, after earlier offices were based in London, the Bahamas and Tijuana, Mexico."[2] But again, who knows for sure? The secrecy has equated with his success.

What if you have it in your mind to be the *next* Billy Walters? Someone will have to take his crown when he retires. Walters is 68. He can't go on forever. So how can you gain nationwide recognition without having the "tout" label attached to your name? How do you prove yourself as a great sports handicapper to others in the industry?

The answer, if betting on the NFL is your thing, might just be the Westgate's SuperContest. Begun in the late 1980s, the SuperContest pits some of the best football handicappers in the country against each other in a season-long NFL pool. The entry fee is $1,500 with the top 30 finishers collecting prize money. Thanks to a good deal of promotion and a push from social media, the SuperContest has taken on an air similar to that enjoyed by the World Series of Poker. In 2014, 1,403 people/teams entered with a $736,575 prize awarded to the first-place finisher.

What's great about the SuperContest is the fact that anyone can enter. There's no prerequisite. All a player needs is confidence, $1,500, and the ability to be in Las Vegas to sign-up. (You do not need to reside in Nevada to participate. You can have a local proxy submit your weekly picks). It's also an extremely level playing field. Each participant must submit five picks every week of the regular season against a set point spread. Whoever gets the most picks right over the course of the season is the champion. Simple, right? The catch is you have to be really good (or really lucky) to win.

Historically, first place was won by a player/team hitting between 61-69 percent of his picks. That is an extremely profitable win percentage over the course of a season. Recall that to be a winner against the vig, a bettor needs to hit on just over 52 percent of his bets. Winning 54 percent or more and you're making bank. Going over 60 percent is unheard of, at least when talking about more than a single season. Records seized in some of the raids on Billy Walters' operation showed his crew winning 58 and 60 percent of their bets in a certain seasons, and by all accounts, Walters is a multi-millionaire. *That's* how big of a difference a few percentage points can be when it comes to picking winners—51 percent over the long haul and you're a loser, 58 percent over the same time frame and you're on a private beach sipping margaritas with super models.

To see how difficult this would be in practice, I entered the SuperContest to test my handicapping prowess. Okay, I didn't have the $1,500 to blow by entering the contest, but I did the next best thing. On my semi-popular website thefixisin.net, I played the home-version of the SuperContest, picking five games a week against their numbers and posting my picks prior to the start of Sunday's games. This verified my picks (in my mind at least), and kept me honest because the intention was to see what I would've done had I entered, using those results for this very section of the book you now hold.

I am by no means a sports gambler. Have I bet on sports before? Certainly. I'm quite familiar with the machinations of betting, but I've never attempted to wager on every week of an NFL season, especially by picking five games a week. The last time I did something similar to this was when a group of my friends ran a season-long pool some 10 years ago in which each week we'd have to pick 15 NCAA football games along with every NFL game against the point spread. Just one small problem: I knew next-to-nothing about NCAA football. Each week I'd look at the NCAA rankings, and then guess who'd win and/or cover. Well, at the end of the first week I was in first place. I never looked back, winning the pool wire-to-wire.

This was shaping up to be something different. Here, I'd have the control. Gone would be the days of merely guessing. In its place would be *educated* guessing. My top five NFL picks determined each and every week by hours of research and deep statistical analysis.

Actually, anything close to resembling that notion fell apart by Week 4. Instead, such deep thinking was replaced by a more holistic, experimental way of picking NFL games. As I posted on my website alongside my picks, the reasoning behind each week's picks would change. Sometimes I'd be contrarian and bet against the public. Sometimes I'd take all favorites (or all underdogs). A couple weeks I found "free picks" on tout websites and used those. Otherwise I'd take which teams I felt the NFL wanted to win, the point spread be damned. Whatever was my whim that week, whatever my gut told me, that's what I went with. I was all over the place. A terrible strategy, and yet I was remarkably successful.

Believe it or not, I finished the 2014 season with a

record of 49-34-2. That's 59 percent (if you throw out those two pushes). Had I actually entered and played those exact picks in the SuperContest, I would've finished tied for 18th place and won about $20,000. By the way, this did not convince my wife to allow me to enter the 2015 SuperContest.

One of the 23 people I would've tied for 18th was Kelly Stewart (aka KellyinVegas) who posted a record of 50-35. Another person who I would've tied, and who posted the exact same record as I did, was a guy by the name of David Frohardt-Lane. Let it be known that Frohardt-Lane was the 2013 SuperContest champion with a record of 55-26-4 (68 percent). His victory made the 37-year old a rather hot commodity and talking-point because he used analytics as the basis for his picks.

This is the growing trend in sports betting as well as in sports in general thanks in large part to the success of Oakland A's GM Billy Beane and the best-selling book about him, *Moneyball*. Now analytics is the rage. ESPN has its own off-shoot website, Nate Silver's FiveThirtyEight, dedicated to all things number, statistic, and analytic related. The "Worldwide Leader in Sports" also sponsors the MIT Sloan Sports Analytics Conference which will enter its ninth year in 2015. The event's conferences are heavily covered, sometimes presented as Gospel truth, and seem to be able to explain just about every behavior and trend in sports these days. But can they decipher how an author haphazardly picking games equaled the results of the 2013 SuperContest champion who utilized analytics to make his selections? I mean, Frohardt-Lane has a master's degree in statistics from the University of Chicago, works in finance as an algorithmic trader, and was hired as a consultant after his 2013 victory by an unnamed professional sports franchise to evaluate potential draft picks.[3] I graduated from Columbia College in Chicago, teach guitar on the side, and have been called "America's foremost sports conspiracy theorist." Analytically-speaking, we were equals last year. So, where's my major league consulting job?

The actual 2014 SuperContest champs were a collective of four guys all about 30-years old who went by the name "CH Ballers." They posted a ridiculous record of 64-20-1 (76 percent), setting a SuperContest record in the process. How'd they do it? Was it analytics that pushed them over the top? Not according to them. In an ESPN interview, the "CH Ballers said it was a total collaborative effort, with no single person making most of the picks and no math model or system in place....They would all handicap the games individually and then do a conference call every Thursday night to go over all the games on the weekend card (never using a Thursday game). They would usually have seven to nine plays and just narrow down to their five strongest."[4] As for their backgrounds, two were economic majors, one is a commercial real estate broker, and the other is a private equity investor. And though they admitted to being "all long-term sports bettors," this was their first attempt at anything like this.

Interestingly, one of CH Ballers' rallying cries was "What is Fezzik doing right now?"[5] This was in reference to the only two-time SuperContest winner (back to back at that), Steve Fezzik. I can tell you what Fezzik is currently up to: he's a tout, selling picks on the website Pregame.com. This is not an uncommon result for SuperContest victors. In fact, it's really the perfect gateway to such a career. Because even though Fezzik won in 2008 and 2009, Frohardt-Lane won in 2013, and the CH Ballers walked away champs in 2014, it doesn't mean any of them will ever win at such a clip again. History would dictate a regression was certainly forthcoming. Yet when it comes, and no matter how hard it hits, no one can ever take away those SuperContest victories. So I'm sure it would be easy to think, "Why not profit off that reputation?" Because who knows what the future will hold? A gambler is only as profitable as his last bet.

But all of these gamblers—the pros and the recreational—are profitable for the NFL. It doesn't matter if they are betting in Vegas, with bookies, through offshore websites, or playing in weekly pick'em pools with friends; betting on NFL games creates viewers. It drives ratings. It makes the most unwatchable Thursday night game a "must see" event. This is what the NFL craves more than anything. A person with a financial stake in the outcome of a game is much more likely to tune in and watch until the bitter end than the casual football fan. The money is a motivator.

As we've seen, the NFL fears legalization of sports gambling will twist every fan into nothing more than a "gambler," someone worried about the outcome of a game against the point spread or the under/over line more than what it may mean in the league's official standings. So the league publicly fights against these undesirables. But deep down the league knows it needs them because in reality, most of these gamblers are just normal, everyday guys. The league can only fight off this hypocrisy for so long.

"Does anyone believe that the NFL is naïve enough not to know that if it weren't for people betting on sports and playing fantasy football that they wouldn't have 20 percent of the people that are watching now?" Billy Walters stated in a recent (and rare) interview. "If you're running the NFL and admit what you already know, then why wouldn't you want to legalize it? That way, people involved in it are licensed and have to undergo background checks, and it's regulated, taxed and up front. That's the most positive outcome for everyone involved."

WEEK 8
vs. ADDICTION

"I'm addicted. One hundred and ten percent. I'm not going to lie to you," Kelly Stewart confided to me. If true, it was an unusual admission from someone within the professional gambling world. Addiction is a dark truth to all the fun that this industry sells. An evil little mentioned, much less publicly discussed. And Stewart was quick to throw others under the addiction-riddled bus, adding, "And don't let anybody else that does what I do say that they're not either. You just can't give it up."

The reason for this is simple. "I like winning money," she said. "A friend of mine likes to use a quote, and I'll probably screw it up, but it's, 'Money won is sweeter than money earned.' It's so true."

Such an attitude coupled with the pressing need to have action on a game is one that many gamblers can never overcome. Stewart herself seemed to teeter on compulsive behavior as she said to me, "Since football's started, I've probably not bet on maybe two days. I'm talking like a Tuesday and a Wednesday. Sometimes that attitude costs me money. A lot of the older guys get on me about it and tell me, 'Kelly, you've got to work on your discipline.'" It's something she was trying to conquer. "I went 2-3 on Saturday which was awful, and considered betting a few of the late games I liked, but I thought, 'I've had enough.' That was good otherwise I would've lost a couple more games. It's about maintaining discipline within that addiction."

Those two words—"discipline" and "addiction"—don't mix. To have the former while being crushed under the weight of the latter is nearly impossible. Addictions blur the lines of discipline, and most never recognize when they've crossed over.

Like downing that first shot of whiskey or inhaling that initial toke of marijuana, a gambling addiction is able to dig its hooks into a person in a heartbeat. "There's a weird thing that happens in gambling," Brad the tout said to me. "It seems like no matter who starts gambling—young, old, bingo players, sports gamblers, whatever—they have that initial luck. I don't know if it's an evil entity, but whoever starts just *wins*…but just enough to give you a taste. It's like an illusion. Few start out losing and say, 'Damn, I'm never doing that again.'"

The National Council on Problem Gambling (NCPG) states that two to three percent of adults meet the criteria for a gambling problem. According to a 2008 ESPN survey, about 118 million Americans gambled on sports in the past year. If the NCPG's number held true for sports gambling, it would mean 3.5 million sports gamblers would fall under the "problem" banner. Many might be younger than expected. Wagering by 18- to 24-year olds has increased 30 percent in the past 20 years. The NCPG states that about 67 percent of all college students bet on sports, making it second in popularity only to poker within that age group. But sports gambling even grabs a hold of younger kids with 44 percent of male high school seniors reporting to have bet on sports. In fact, sports betting is the number one form of gambling among children aged 14-22.[1]

Keith Whyte, Executive Director of the NCPG, told ESPN's *E:60*, "One of the reasons college campuses are such a hot bed of gambling is that you almost have a perfect storm of factors that have come together. The average college student has access to four credit cards. We've got the fact that college students tend to be high risk takers. They tend to be intensely competitive. And they think they're bulletproof."[2] These are just some of the risk factors the NCPG cites. Others include family history of addiction, substance use/abuse, ethnicity, and sex, with males more likely to succumb than females.

What else might be a contributing factor for America's youth? It would be easy to trot out the clichéd response accusing television, but...well...is it to blame? Without seeking an expert, I feel safe in exonerating TV. But like low-fat ice cream, it may not be completely guilt-free. With every game from all of the major leagues available to anyone willing to pay a subscription fee, each bar, restaurant, and basement "man cave" has the ability to transform itself into a Las Vegas-style sports book. All that is missing is direct betting access. As chronicled, that issue can be solved with a few clicks of the mouse or swipes on a smartphone. Why go to Vegas when the at-home experience is virtually the same? This reality feeds into sports gambling's circular effect: people bet on what they watch and watch what they bet.

While not outwardly promoting gambling (yet), sports television networks aren't shying away from such talk, either. For young adults, this could result in a de facto acceptance. ESPN's Lisa Slaters raised such a point during a 2013 *E:60* report, stating, "I think that we're [ESPN] are talking out of both sides of our mouths. You know, we have poker on every night of the week it seems like. You know, quite frankly, we kind of promote gambling on our air all the time. Betting on sports. Every Sunday you can see the analysts giving the lines on the games. You know, what kind of society do we live in when we tell kids, 'This is bad, this is bad, this is bad,' and then yet we turn around and give them all the access in the world, and kind of glamorize and promote the very things we tell them not to do?"[3]

Beer commercials avoid depicting binge drinking. They never show people vomiting after over-indulging. Their actors don't portray the morning-after hangovers that can result from consuming their product. It's easy to understand why. The same can be said of casino commercials, sports book websites, and gambling-related talking-head programs. It's all about the action and excitement of wagering; never the potential for addiction. Should they be required to provide it lip-service? With only a small percentage of people "at risk," it's easy to argue against doing so. Yet to their credit, most gambling outlets do add a written or quickly spoken disclaimer to any promotional material. For the most part though, addiction is treated as a non-entity.

A similar feeling appears to permeate most of society. Gambling addiction was reclassified in The Diagnostic and Statistical Manual of Mental Disorders from being a problem with impulse control to an actual addiction only recently. This mirrors the biggest issue with gambling addiction: recognition. Of course, it doesn't help when most people tend to think of gambling the way Charles Barkley does. (Thinking like Barkley might be a mental disorder in and of itself.) Back in 2006, Barkley admitted to losing $10 million gambling. About this he said, "Do I have a gambling problem? Yeah, I do have a gambling problem but I don't consider it a problem because I can afford to gamble. It's just a stupid habit that I've got to get under control, because it's just not a good thing to be broke after all of these years."[4]

By writing it off as just a "stupid habit" he needed to "control" regardless of the amount of cash he lost, Barkley was falling into the trap. The money is meaningless. The behavior is what's at issue. The NCPG defines problem gambling as "Gambling behavior which causes disruptions in any major area of life: psychological, physical, social or vocational."

The internet is littered with stories about gambling addiction. You're just not going to find these unless you actively search for them. Any music fan that has seen an episode of VH1's *Behind the Music* is well aware of how many bands have endured members going through an alcohol or drug addiction. Most, but not all, have lived to tell their tale of desperation and woe. Other celebrities and even a few athletes have come forward to talk about their battles with these demons, but finding a spokesperson for gambling addiction is difficult. Yet in reading stories of gambling addicts, their tales sound remarkably like those who fought against substance abuse. Compulsive gambling even feeds off of the same areas of the brain that affects those with drug and alcohol problems.

Yet a gambling addiction is perhaps the easiest compulsion to conceal. Alcoholics and drug addicts often have outward features that are difficult to hide. Their breath may reek of booze or their clothes may stink of weed; they may be physically or cognitively impaired; and the effects might physically punish the body, outwardly changing one's appearance. But gambling has none of those visible warning signs. No one broadcasts their bank account balance on their foreheads. You cannot readily see the urge, the stress, or the depression that accompanies a gambling addiction. It's locked away in the addict's brain.

Debt may be the only limiting factor for a compulsive gambler. This aids in avoiding detection. Even if a drug addict craves more, the body will control the amount of heroin or cocaine one can imbibe. Certainly overdoses occur, but in many cases the body shuts down prior to reaching that deadly limit. But you can't overdose on money (or the lack thereof). One can gamble all day, every day as long as there's cash with which to play. How can family and friends know that the loan they just gave to the problem gambler is going to the rent or to the Bills-

Broncos over if they can't recognize their loved one might have an addiction?

More frighteningly, the problem gambler doesn't necessarily get their "high" from winning. The rush doesn't come from being up $100 or $100,000. Studies have shown that over time, problem gamblers actually lose their sensitively to winning.[5] Winning merely allows them to keep pushing their boundaries. The thrill is found on the edge of losing control; in either betting money they don't have, or as some have claimed, outright *losing*.

Hiding such an addiction can take a mental toll on anyone. It can be difficult, if not seemingly impossible, to admit to a loved one that the rent money or one's retirement fund has been gambled away. And believe it or not, gambling might be the deadliest addiction of them all. According to the NCPG, as many as one in five problem gamblers attempt suicide. It is the highest rate amongst all the addictions and second only to schizophrenia among mental disorders. This is why recognizing a gambling problem and seeking help for it is so important.

Thankfully, there are treatments which can help compulsive gamblers regain control of their lives, coming in the form of medications, therapy, and support groups like Gamblers Anonymous. Yet it's known that only a fraction of those with gambling problems ever seek this sort of help. Most remain untreated. As gambling proliferates throughout America and as it loses its negative stigma, it's undeniable that more and more people will fall prey to this addiction. By limiting gambling's availability, it can repress the amount of problem gamblers created. This might be the one place where the NFL's anti-gambling argument actually works.

However, compulsive sports gamblers don't necessarily function like a problem lottery player or a slot machine addict. One study has shown that effective treatments for most gamblers might not work with sports bettors. Why? Because sports gamblers believe they know more than they actually do.

"Professor Pinhas Dannon of the Sackler Faculty of Medicine at Tel Aviv University and the Beer Yaakov Mental Health Center explains that sports gamblers appear to see themselves as more attuned to their game than other types of gamblers. They believe that their knowledge and experience of the game, including a team manager's habits or stadium style, can help them accurately predict the outcome of the match."

"The researchers used soccer betting, an area growing in popularity for sports gambling, in their study. The participants included 53 sports gamblers who gambled professionally, 34 soccer fans with no gambling experience and 78 individuals who had no knowledge of soccer and no gambling experience. The participants were tasked with betting on final scores of second-round matches of the Champion's League. The task required that the participants choose the exact scores of the games."

"In their study, Professor Dannon and Dr. Ronen Huberfeld found that successful outcomes had no ties to the knowledge or experience of the gamblers. In fact, the two greatest winning gamblers in the study did not have experience in gambling and had no prior knowledge of gambling. The findings of the study provide evidence that suggests that gamblers who participate in sports gambling games are acting under a belief that they can control the outcome, based on their knowledge."[6]

The "knowledge" that many sports gamblers rely upon often comes from hours and hours of work crunching numbers. Many professional sports gamblers will say they spend upwards of 40 hours, if not 60 hours a week, working on their bets. And after all of that time and energy, the best gamblers might not see an advantage anywhere and refuse to place a wager. Or they might bet every game on the slate. Might this behavior lead to obsession? Might it not create "disruptions" in their life, including those of the "psychological, physical, social or vocational" type, the very definition of problem gambling according to the NCPG?

Remarkably, one writer saw such a problem develop in his own life. Not in sports gambling, but in the (supposedly) non-gambling endeavor of fantasy football. C.D. Carter, a writer for the fantasy football website The Fake Football, published an article at the *New York Times* Fifth Down blog titled "When Fantasy Football Becomes an Addiction." Though you might assume his piece was written in jest, reading it fails to give that impression.

Carter wrote, "I cannot watch football the way it was meant to be watched. I watch for stats. I fret about fantasy points, not game outcomes. The game, in short, is meaningless. I don't watch playoff games. I don't care who wins the Super Bowl. I have loyalty to no one but myself and my pretend roster of random players from across the league. I can't recall the agony of emotional investment in a real team—the ability to feel that joy and pain has long left me, crowded out by fantasy obsession. There is no joy, only anxiety, only pain, only disappointment. When I win a fantasy game, I'm only happy not to lose. When I lose, I'm crushed. Of all the daily constructive exchanges, petty spats and frenetic 140-character volleys among Twitter's fantasy freaks, the issue of obsession—addiction—is rarely broached. It goes unacknowledged, I think, because in a dank flophouse, junkies don't ponder the ill effects of their addictions. They just do their drugs. They get high."[7]

Carter found he wasn't alone with these feelings and the actions that accompanied them. Another lost soul appeared to be that of Austin Lee who writes "in-depth fantasy analyses for Pro Football Focus, a daily resource to any hardcore fantasy footballer." Lee told Carter, "I was losing a lot of sleep over waiver wire moves and trades and other decisions. It had a lot of weight to it, a lot of meaning. You just lie there awake and you think, I know I can find the right fit, I can come up with the right combination. I just need to try harder. If you're a real addict, you have lots of people who can make your obsession seem completely normal. If you need that kind of confirmation, lots of people are there to tell you it's O.K., because they're addicted, too." Lee concluded by saying, "You can see the terrible impact of being an alcoholic right away. But this consumes your thoughts. It really eats away at you."[8]

Though Carter didn't differentiate between regular and daily fantasy football in his piece, it doesn't matter. Neither has been deemed gambling, despite both having certain gambling components. These are more easily recognized in daily fantasy sports, and it is likely addiction factors such as those Carter described will be more prevalent there. While many will brush aside these comparisons (including the NFL), the NCPG's Keith Whyte related a story to me in which one habitual daily fantasy player lost upwards of $50,000 "in a matter of months." Clearly, this poor fellow was addicted...to something that wasn't considered gambling.

WEEK 9
vs. GAMBLING ATHLETES

"Some days I thank the good Lord I'm still breathing; other days, I pray to the good Lord that I'll stop breathing. That's what kind of misery I've been through."

Former Baltimore Colts quarterback Art Schlichter said that quote in an interview for the FBI and NBA co-produced film titled "Gambling with Your Life" (which you can't see. The FBI released a redacted version of it to me by mistake and warned not to make it public). The Bureau used it as part of a larger presentation they would provide to both pro and college teams in the preseason, educating players of the dangers of gambling and drugs. Schlichter was the poster child for such problems.

He is also supposedly just an aberration.

In 1977, Schlichter signed with Ohio State as perhaps the most highly touted quarterback prospect in school history. He didn't disappoint. A *Sports Illustrated* cover boy, Schlichter finished fourth in Heisman Trophy voting in 1979, sixth in 1980, and fifth in 1981. He was chosen fourth overall in the 1982 NFL Draft by the Colts, one pick prior to Jim McMahon and six picks ahead of Marcus Allen. The Colts quickly locked Schlichter up with a three year deal worth $530,000 plus a $350,000 signing bonus and a $125,000 low-interest loan from Colts' owner Robert Irsay.

Schlichter was expected to compete with—and beat out—Mike Pagel and David Humm for the starting quarterback job. Instead, he finished the 1982 season as the team's third-string QB. He wouldn't even play in 1983. Why? Schlichter was a pathological gambler.

"I thought maybe I could control it," Schlichter lamented in the FBI video. "I never really thought about it being an addiction for a long, long time."

Schlichter was known to gamble in high school, visiting local race tracks with friends despite being underage. This habit continued at Ohio State where he frequented the nearby Scioto Downs. "By his senior season at Ohio State, at least three agencies—the Columbus Police Department's organized crime bureau, the Ohio Bureau of Criminal Identification and Investigation and the Ohio State University police department—had been aware of Schlichter's fondness for the race tracks, according to officials with the agencies. Steve Hall, a former OSU police officer, said that Schlichter's fondness for the track 'was common knowledge around the campus.'"[1]

This behavior apparently slipped past both the Colts and the NFL. Armed with his signing bonus, Schlichter spun out of control. His race track wagers increased from $50 into the hundreds then expanded into the thousands as he bet on baseball and college basketball, and then into the tens of thousands as he began betting on the sport he knew best, football.

Schlichter would call his bookies from the pay phones in Baltimore's Memorial Stadium. When on the sidelines, Schlichter wouldn't be charting plays on his clipboard like he was supposed to be; he'd be tracking his bets on other games. It's been said that when he did get in the huddle, which didn't happen often his rookie season, he'd call a play and then forget it by the time he got under center because of his preoccupation with his wagers.

It turned ugly when Schlichter got down over $600,000. Bookies began threatening both his life and that of his family's. Cornered, Schlichter sought help from the FBI. "I didn't go there willingly," he recalled in the video. "I went there because I had no choice."

His cooperation with the FBI led to the arrest of four Baltimore-area bookies. Meanwhile, he began receiving treatment for his gambling addiction. That was in the real world. In the realm of the NFL, things were a little different.

The league launched an investigation which found, according to one NFL source, "I don't think there were too many days of the week that Art didn't bet on something."[2] The investigation determined Schlichter bet on "about 12" NFL games which were "mostly Monday night games and playoff games."[3] In a meeting with Commissioner Pete Rozelle and NFL Security Director Warren Welsh, Schlichter was forced to reveal on which games he wagered as well as specific details about the Colts' 1982 season.

According to the *New York Times*, "'What bothered us most,' said one league official, who spoke on the condition that he not be identified, 'is that if he won, he collected his money. But if he lost, the bookies would carry him. If they were carrying him, they were carrying him for a reason. At some point they were going to want the money or a favor. And what's the favor?' However, there has been no indication that Schlichter had been asked to do any favors for the bookmakers."[4]

Regardless, Rozelle suspended Schlichter, proclaiming that Schlichter's reinstatement would hinge on his rehabilitation. He sat out the entire 1983 season. Schlichter returned to the NFL in 1984, even starting five of the Colts' games. But he was far from cured.

Five games into the 1985 season, the Colts cut Schlichter. By the start of the 1986 season, he was out of the

NFL entirely. Though he reemerged in the Arena Football League and won the MVP with the Detroit Drive in 1990, he never stopped gambling. When he filed for bankruptcy in 1998 citing $1 million in debts, Schlichter had already been arrested four times on charges of bank fraud, unlawful gambling and writing bad checks. He would serve time in 17 different jails and prisons, ultimately bottoming out in 2012 when "a federal judge sentenced him to nearly 11 years in prison for scamming participants in what authorities called a million-dollar sports ticket scheme."[5]

"Gambling has eaten me alive. Okay?" Schlichter said in the FBI video. "It has ruined my family, it has killed my self-esteem, it's taken every dollar I've had. It will eat you until you haven't gotten anything left. And I'm the living proof of that."

Despite numerous players receiving suspensions for drugs, domestic violence, child abuse, manslaughter, and other "conduct unbecoming of the league," no player has missed a down in the NFL due to gambling since Schlichter's 1983 season-long suspension. In 1947, New York Giants RB Merle Hapes and QB Frank Filchock were handed lifetime suspensions for their involvement in an attempt to fix the 1946 NFL Championship Game (the NFL denies this game was, in fact, fixed). Both were reinstated in the 1950's. Sixteen years later, a well-documented NFL gambling scandal resulted in two players, Detroit Lions DT Alex Karras and Green Bay Packers RB Paul Hornung, sitting out the entire 1963 season under suspension. Both players returned in 1964, and the black mark didn't prevent Hornung from being elected into the Hall of Fame in 1986.

How is it that in 95 years of NFL football only five players have fallen under gambling's spell? Something just doesn't add up here.

Other sports have had their fair share of betting athletes. Basketball endured gambling-related stories related to Wilt Chamberlain, Michael Jordan, Charles Barkley, and Allen

Iverson (among others). Baseball's two biggest scars resulted from the gambling of Pete Rose and the fixing of the 1919 World Series. The NHL cringed when all-star player turned head coach Rick Tocchet plead guilty to charges of conspiracy and promoting gambling related to his participation in a bookmaking ring. Yet Tocchet was quickly reinstated by the NHL and currently serves as an assistant coach for the Pittsburgh Penguins.

Perhaps the NHL's biggest gambling story related to another (former) Penguin, future Hall of Famer Jaromir Jagr. In the late 1990's, Jagr racked up nearly $850,000 in gambling debts owed to two offshore sports books.[6] One Jagr bet through was owned by Steve Budin who today operates the tout website SportsInfo.com which is connected to Brandon Lang's eerily similar website. In fact, Lang wrote the foreword to Budin's book *Bets, Drugs, and Rock & Roll: The Rise and Fall of the World's First Offshore Sports Gambling Empire.*

In that book, Budin discussed Jagr's betting. "Jagr loved to bet football, and he loved calling in his bets right from the locker room."[7] One night, Budin related, Jagr's Penguins were in New York to play the Rangers. Jagr phoned Budin with bets from Madison Square Garden (using his "special code name: 975 JJ"). But there was a problem. "Jagr's credit card was maxed out, and he couldn't get action because we did not, under any circumstances, extend a credit line."[8] Undeterred, Jagr made a 3-way call between himself, his bank, and Budin to get his credit extended in order to place his bets. While still on the phone with his banker—and with his teammates on the ice warming up—Jagr confirmed his wagers.

"Jagr was a great customer, mostly because he couldn't pick his ass from his elbow," a trait Budin claimed all athletes possessed. "I don't remember him ever receiving a payment from us in all the time he played. He may have won a bet or two, but I am 100 percent certain he never had a winning week, ever.

He might have been the biggest sucker I have ever dealt to in my entire career. He never met a favorite that he didn't just adore. It just goes to show you that nobody can win at betting sports, not even star athletes."[9]

When Budin wrote "athletes," he meant to use the plural. If he is to be believed, several professional players bet with Budin's company though he never named names beyond that of Jagr and teammate Len Barrie. "One thing I want to make clear," Budin wrote, "We didn't let athletes bet on their own games or on their own sport. That would be wrong, not to mention illegal [he's actually incorrect on that point]....Now, don't get me wrong. Athletes wanted to bet on their own sport, even on their own teams at times, but we never let that happen."[10] Budin admitted the fear of taking those bets was more from the worry of being connected to a potential scandal and not from some sort of moral high ground.

When Scott Schettler ran the Stardust sports book in Las Vegas during the 1980's, he occasionally witnessed athletes bet, including Art Schlichter. "He was just sick," Schettler recalled of Schlichter. "Sick, sick sick. If he won, he wouldn't take the cash; he'd take it in tickets."

Other sports figures came through the Stardust sports book as well. "There had been athletes in there and some of them would just sit quietly and hope no one would recognize them," Schettler told me. "Others would stand outside it like there was a fence, looking in. Like one time I got a message that Johnny Bench was outside and he'd like to talk to me. I said, 'Well, tell him to come on in the office.' And the guys say, 'Oh, no. He won't come in the book.' 'Well, then screw him. I don't want to talk to him.' Big deal, Johnny Bench. But he wouldn't come into the office. But other guys...I do remember a player, an NBA player, come right up to the window and bet. Nothing sinister. You know, just a bet. But that was rare. I even thought to myself, 'Is this guy nuts or what?'"

Another Vegas insider, who chose to remain anonymous for this book, told of a woman who frequented the Dunes sports book in the late 1970's. She would usually arrive Sunday mornings and bet big money on NFL games, winning far more often than she lost. It became a regular sight, and one that many of the guys in the Dunes looked forward to because this woman wasn't just attractive, she was downright gorgeous. But she never said much, nor did she seem overly familiar with gambling when she did talk. Yet almost without fail, she was there on Sunday betting the NFL. Finally, one casino employee recognized her. She was a professional model. She was also married to an active NFL quarterback. It didn't take long to realize she was placing the bets at the direction of her husband. The story goes that the marriage didn't last, and neither did her visits to the sports book.

While these tales are revealing, they are also anecdotal. Unfortunately, no serious studies exist discussing the gambling habits of American professional athletes. You can probably guess why. The closest we've come was an anonymous poll of 73 NFL, NBA, NHL and MLB players published by ESPN in 2015. It revealed that 58 percent of respondents gambled on things other than sports, 42 percent were aware of point spreads, 37 percent suspected a teammate of having a gambling problem, and 34 percent gambled money on sports other than their own.[11]

A more formal examination of professional athletes and gambling was conducted in 2014 by NatCen, Britain's largest independent social research agency. Authored by Heather Wardle and Andrew Gibbons, "Gambling among sports people" was conducted in part "to examine how many professional sports people gamble and experience problems."

NatCen obtained responses from 44 percent the professional cricket players (176 athletes) and six percent of pro soccer players (170 athletes) in the UK. Their two main findings were a bit shocking. When compared to the general public,

"Sports people [were] more likely to gamble," and "Sports people [were] more likely to experience problems." By extrapolating their data, the authors estimated that "at least" 192 cricket and/or soccer players had a gambling problem and another 440 were "at risk." They found that responding athletes admitted to (in descending order) "chasing losses," "needing to gamble with larger amounts of money," "betting more than [he] could afford to lose," "gambling caused stress, anxiety or health problems," "borrowed or sold things to get money to gamble," and "gambling caused financial problems." Despite these admissions, less than three percent of players claimed to have sought help for their gambling problems.[12]

Though NatCen's study focused on professional athletes and though it found clear evidence of problem gambling within those ranks, its findings cannot be compared directly to the activities of America's pro athletes. That doesn't mean their study should be viewed as meaningless. Though there are cultural and legal differences between the British and American views on gambling, all professional athletes tend to possess similar traits that lend themselves toward such a lifestyle: a lot of free time coupled with a lot of excess money.

An ESPN insider once told me of an NBA star who had a monthly allowance for strippers and gambling. The writer had no apparent issue with it because the player was under control. The fear regarding a gambling player—especially one gambling illegally with a bookie—is that somewhere down the line that behavior turns. The player loses control, becomes compromised by the bookie (or the mobsters controlling the bookie), and bad things happen. That was the concern the NFL had with Art Schlichter, and it should be a worry with any player treading that path.

Yet how can we know if any pro athlete has a gambling addiction or is even teetering on one? The leagues don't make pronouncements about such things. In fact, if we're to believe the leagues, no one within their ranks has fallen prey to a gambling addiction since Pete Rose's banishment from MLB in 1989. Can that be the reality of the situation?

If probing questions about gambling behavior cannot (or will not) be asked of pro athletes, then the next best thing might be to pose similar questions to those poised to become major leaguers: college players.

The NCAA has one hard, fast rule relating to sports betting: don't do it. The NCAA's yearly manual features Bylaw 10.3 which states that no NCAA athletic department staff member, non-athletics staff member with athletics responsibilities, conference staff member, or student-athlete may knowingly participate in sports gambling, solicit (or accept) a bet on any intercollegiate competition for any item that has a tangible value (including food and clothing), or even provide information that would assist an individual in gambling. Players are even barred from participating in March Madness or Super Bowl pools as well as fantasy sports *if* an entry fee is required. If caught gambling, a first time offense for a student-athlete is supposed to carry a punishment of loss of eligibility for one year. But student-athletes have little to worry about. The NCAA has one—count 'em, *one*—full-time employee whose focus is investigating athletes gambling.

This has propelled some to conduct studies into the actual gambling habits of NCAA players. In 1996, a University of Cincinnati study found that 25 percent of athletes gambled on sporting events, 4 percent gambled on games that they played in, and 1 percent took money in exchange for a change in athletic performance. Not to be outdone, the University of Michigan Athletic Department did their own study in 1999. Of the 3,000 NCAA Division I football and men's and women's basketball players asked, 758 responded to the UM survey. The results showed that approximately 35 percent of respondents had broken NCAA rules and engaged in some form of sports betting. What's worse, 21 student-athletes admitted to providing a bettor within inside information, four student-athletes bet on games in which they played (and all did so more than once), and three admitted to "accepting money to play poorly."

If these two studies were the only examples of college players engaging in sports gambling, they might be disturbing enough. Yet the NCAA has run its own anonymous survey of its student-athlete population over the course of the past twelve years, and the results are equally as troubling. Conducted in 2004, 2008, and 2012, the NCAA study received results from approximately 20,000 student-athletes on each occasion. For male respondents, anywhere from 23.5 to 29.5 percent admitted to breaking NCAA rules by gambling on sports (between 5.2 and 6.7 percent of females stated the same). The most popular way to make those wagers was via the internet and/or texting (33.7 percent) while 17 percent claimed to have used either a student bookie (8.4 percent) or an off-campus bookie (8.6 percent). By far the most popular sport for either sex to wager upon was the NFL with 60 percent of males and 58 percent of females saying they've done so. The NBA was a distant second.

Focusing on just Division I football and men's basketball, some of the most disturbing questions/answers from players included:

Percentage Reporting Having Been Contacted by Outside Sources to Share Inside Information:

Basketball:
2004 – 1.2 percent
2008 – 3.8 percent
2012 – 4.6 percent

Football:
2004 – 2 percent
2008 – 3.5 percent
2012 – 2.2 percent

Percentage Claiming to Have Provided Inside

Information to Outside Sources:
    Basketball
        2004 – 1.2 percent
        2008 – 0.9 percent
        2012 – 0.8 percent
    Football:
        2004 – 2.5 percent
        2008 – 1.1 percent
        2012 – 0.3 percent
    Percentage Reporting Having Bet on Their Own Team:
    Basketball:
        2004 – 2.7 percent
        2008 – 2 percent
        2012 – 0.8 percent
    Football:
        2004 – 2.9 percent
        2008 – 2.2 percent
        2012 – 1.3 percent
    Percentage Reporting Having Bet on Another Team at Their School:
    Basketball:
        2004 – 1.8 percent
        2008 – 1.4 percent
        2012 – 1.5 percent
    Football:
        2004 – 4.9 percent
        2008 – 3.4 percent
        2012 – 2.6 percent
    Percentage Reporting Having Been Asked to Influence the Outcome of a Game:
    Basketball:
        2004 – 2.4 percent
        2008 – 1.6 percent
        2012 – 2.1 percent

Football:
  2004 – 2.3 percent
  2008 – 1.2 percent
  2012 – 1.2 percent

While some solace might be taken in recognizing that the percentages in most of these categories has diminished every four years, the fact that none of these—including the question related to *point shaving*—is zero should stop every sports fan in his or her tracks. Apparently corruption, if not outright criminality, is prevalent in major college football and basketball programs across the nation. And it's not simply the NCAA or some sports writer saying this; it's an admission coming straight from the players themselves.

"The decrease in the rate of gambling among male student-athletes is encouraging," Rachel Newman Baker, the NCAA managing director of enforcement, told the Associated Press. "However, the explosive growth of sports wagering has caused a noticeable increase in the number and severity of sports wagering cases investigated by the NCAA."[13] Though the number of investigations may be on the rise, one would be hard pressed to find any instance of the NCAA taking away a player's eligibility for his gambling—despite a quarter of the student-athlete population admittedly breaking NCAA rules. More needs to be done on the enforcement end as well as on the educational side to slow gambling's hold within the collegiate ranks.

The NCAA has attempted to be proactive in these regards. It launched a program called "Don't Bet On It" which provides educational material to campuses nationwide. Its effectiveness remains to be seen. The NCAA has also attempted legal maneuvers to stem the growing tide. In 2000, the NCAA supported a bill meant to supplement PASPA which would have made it illegal (even in Nevada) to wager on all amateur sports, college and the Olympics included. Alas, the High School and College Gambling Protection Act was defeated thanks to an assist by Las Vegas lobbyists. A similar measure, the Ted Stevens Olympic and Amateur Sports Act, was introduced in 2003, yet it, too, failed to pass.

Imagine if either of these Congressional Acts had become law. Might it not have altered the collegiate sports landscape in its entirety? Approximately $1 billion is wagered in Nevada on NCAA basketball and football each year with even more wagered quasi-legally offshore and still more bet illegally in the US. If gambling on college sports was actually prohibited (and that prohibition strictly enforced), the ongoing debate of what constitutes a "student-athlete" and whether these players should be paid and/or unionized might vanish. As this book argues, people are watching the NFL in the record-setting numbers because "fans" often have a monetary stake in each game's outcome. The same can clearly be said of NCAA football and basketball. Remove that monetary incentive by eliminating betting and perhaps the tap pouring billions of dollars into college sports can be squeezed shut. By no means would it be a cure-all, but it's a good place to start—especially if people are supposed to believe the myth that these games are being played by true amateurs.

Preventing players from gambling is another trick entirely. What's needed is a strong voice from which athletes can learn, preferably a player who was an addicted gambler and then reformed. Finding a player courageous enough to come forward may be difficult. No one wants to be known as "that guy." The speculation that would follow—the questions regarding credibility and on-the-field performance—would be difficult to withstand.

Yet the Georgia Council on Problem Gambling apparently had access to such a player. Though anonymous, the testimony provided for its website is powerful: "I am one of many professional athletes gambling to excess. I spent most of my time at casinos in Las Vegas. I would often lose $40,000 within a few hours. I used to think that since I had a lot of money that I could afford to gamble. During a conversation with one of the Gamblers Anonymous meetings members I realized I was no different from them. They had little money and were broke from gambling. I made a lot of money but was broke just like they were. The Georgia Gamblers Anonymous meetings have been very helpful. If you are a one of so many professional athletes gambling out of control, please seek help."[14]

It's an important message not just for players, but all people with a gambling problem. One person who desperately needed such guidance was Denver Broncos wide receiver Kenny McKinley. Drafted in the fifth round of the 2009 NFL Draft, McKinley played sparingly in his rookie season prior to a knee injury cutting it short. In the ensuing offseason, McKinley found himself tens of thousands of dollars in debt due to a gambling addiction. Shortly thereafter, he committed suicide.[15] He was 23 years old.

WEEK 10
@ LOTTERIES

"Did you know I can bet on football at church?"

"What?!" I said, turning to look at my mother as if she had just informed me she was the shooter on the grassy knoll.

"Yes," she assured. "It's $20 for the season. What me to put you in?"

Without hesitation, I handed her a crisp $20 bill. Of course I wanted a piece of that sacred action. A week later she presented me with my entry, a ticket labeled "Football Mania."

Created by the company Charity Mania, Football Mania (and its brethren Baseball Mania, Basketball Mania, etc.) wasn't gambling per se, rather a donation to the church. However, couched within my contribution was an added bonus. With the Football Mania card, I, the donator, possessed an opportunity to not just get back my $20, but win one of "189 prizes totaling more than $17,000!" Charity never paid so well.

The game was simple enough. Each week, the card assigned me three random NFL teams. If my teams scored the highest (or lowest) total combined points for that week, I'd win. I could conveniently check the Charity Mania website (or the church bulletin!) for the weekly results. There was also a grand prize awarded at season's end for both highest and lowest total cumulative scoring card. Being average didn't pay. I was average; despite the card informing me that I had a 1 in 26.7 chance of winning.

The genius of this promotion/charity/fundraiser lies in the fact that Charity Mania paid no licensing fees to any of the major leagues on which it based its cards. In Week One, I didn't have the Colts, Raiders, and Steelers. I had Indianapolis, Oakland, and Pittsburgh. Oh, we all know what that meant, and we all know in which games I needed which teams to score (or not score) a ton of points, but without those names and logos on the card, not a dime went to the NFL.

In fact, Charity Mania's website states, "You sell CharityMania Tickets to raise money and keep 70 percent as profit." Any sort of licensing agreement would certainly cut into those charitable proceeds. I have a sneaking suspicion that as Charity Mania continues to grow; teams of lawyers from each of the major leagues are going to be paying its founders a visit.

Maybe I'm wrong. Many major league teams offer in-stadium 50/50 raffles to raise money for charity. If you're new to these, they're rather straightforward. Raffle ticket sellers scour the stadium, hawking $2-3 entries like beers. Late in the game, a winning ticket number is announced. Half the money raised goes to the designated charity, the other half to the lucky ticket holder in attendance. A winner can walk away with upwards of $20,000.

In a sense, it's fundraising via gambling. And it's effective. People like to get something for their contribution, even if it's insignificant. It makes them feel as if their money didn't just get thrown into a hole. And perhaps the best gift to receive is in return is a heap of cold hard cash. Not that anyone is donating just to win big money (at least I hope not), but that element exists nonetheless. And in the case of the 50/50 raffle, it's team sponsored.

Teams sponsor another sort of ticket...in a way. Take, for instance, the following:

"SEAHAWKS FANS AREN'T AVERAGE SPORTS FANS. They set Guinness Book world records. They cause earthquakes. They make a game in New York feel like a home game. All season long, they earn the right to wear the number 12."

"For this zealous fan base, there's the 'Seahawks 12' Scratch ticket from Washington's Lottery. While this ticket gives our 12s an opportunity to win money and get in the game, it's also a tribute to everyone who lives and dies with the team. Thanks for the many ways you inspire the team on the field."

"DIEHARD HAWKS FANS, THE 'SEAHAWKS 12' SCRATCH TICKET IS FOR YOU."

Though the NFL abhors the idea of its fans gambling on its games, starting in 2009 a league-wide policy was implemented that enabled teams to license their names and logos to state lotteries. They weren't the first league to traverse this path. The NBA began it in 2002, the NHL followed in 2003, and MLB joined in 2006. "We examined how other sports had been working in this area," NFL spokesman Brian McCarthy told me via email, "and we concluded that it [lottery licensing] did not conflict with our policies against gambling on the outcome of games."

That was key. "Our concern has always been with gambling on the outcome of NFL games," McCarthy informed me. "Use of a team logo in a scratch-off game is not an issue."

That idea may be true, but isn't it a bit disingenuous?

Lotteries have a long history in the United States. They helped fund Colonial America's fight for independence and played a significant role in financing early American roads, bridges, libraries, railroads, and more. Over time, lotteries took a turn for the worse and became associated with "policy making"—great for organized crime, but bad for most customers who were often from lower income neighborhoods.

The lottery went legit a second time thanks to New Hampshire which reinstituted it on a state level in 1964. Fifty years later, 44 state governments rely on the lottery for revenue. It's a huge business. The lottery system makes approximately $70 billion a year—three times what the NFL, MLB, NBA, and NHL earn combined.

The problem with lotteries—and scratch-off tickets in particular—is that states now profit in the same fashion the mob used to when "running numbers." "While approximately half of Americans buy at least one lottery ticket at some point, the vast majority of tickets are purchased by about 20 percent of the population. These high-frequency players tend to be poor and uneducated, which is why critics refer to lotteries as a regressive tax. (In a 2006 survey, 30 percent of people without a high school degree said that playing the lottery was a wealth-building strategy.) On average, households that make less than $12,400 a year spend 5 percent of their income on lotteries—a source of hope for just a few bucks a throw."[1]

The NFL willingly stepped into this morass. It didn't have to. No one person, no one team compelled the league to become a partner of any state lottery. But the league saw an opportunity to pluck a few more dollars out of the lottery's $70 billion revenue stream and waded right in.

The odd part of this deal is that though the league opened the door for every team to sell itself to a state lottery, the Chicago Bears and Buffalo Bills never did. Other teams that started later stopped. However, the revenue generated from these local deals is one of the few manners of income that are not shared league-wide. Whatever money a team makes whoring itself out to the lottery, it keeps.

Not all deals are created equal. In 2009-10, the Wisconsin State Lottery paid the Green Bay Packers $260,000 for its rights—10 times the cost for the rights to Tetris.[2] At the same time, the California State Lottery paid the Oakland Raiders, San Francisco 49ers and San Diego Chargers a combined total of $1.73 million in licensing fees.[3] Three years later, the Kansas City Chiefs earned a paltry $45,000 for its rights while the Atlanta Falcons received $250,000.[4] Meanwhile the winner in all of this just might be the New England Patriots who Sports Business Daily estimated earned $5.7 million since 2009 by licensing their name and logo to the Massachusetts State Lottery.[5]

Even when teams are located within the same state, the fees they earn from selling their brand can be different. According to Katelind Powers, the Open Records Coordinator for the Texas Lottery Commission, in 2014 the Dallas Cowboys were paid $558,981.96 in licensing fees. In the same fiscal year, Powers informed me the Texas Lottery gave the Houston Texans less than half of that—$195,842.11 to be exact—for the same rights.

This money isn't just for the rights to use the team's name and logo on scratch-off tickets. Oh, no, there's more to it. As Erica L. Palmisano, Assistant Director of Communications for the Maryland Lottery and Gaming Control Agency, informed me, "In 2014, the Maryland Lottery paid the Ravens a total of $1,165,000 for a sponsorship agreement that included advertising assets and opportunities such as onsite activations, merchandising, prizes and the ability to use the Ravens' marks."

See, despite the NFL getting all sanctimonious about gambling on its sport, it has no issue with its teams working in conjunction with a pure gambling entity such as a state lottery. Many of these NFL-themed scratch-off tickets have "second chance drawings" in which losing tickets can be sent in to potentially win everything from team apparel to season tickets. For example, the Wisconsin Lottery's 2014 Packers' tickets offered fans a chance to win two "Champions Club" season tickets and home playoff game tickets for the 2015 season. "The grand prize also includes a parking pass to each home game for the 2015 season and two pregame sideline passes for Packers-Bears and Packers-Vikings home games during the 2015 season....First place winners will receive one of 95 officially licensed NFL helmets autographed by a current Packers player and Packers Pro Shop gift cards. Second place winners will receive one of 100 Packers Pro Shop gift cards valued at $500."[6]

There was so little separation between the Packers and the Wisconsin Lottery that when the new Packers-themed lottery game was announced in 2014, the news conference took place at Lambeau Field. In attendance was both Wisconsin Lottery director Mike Edmonds and Packers President and CEO Mark Murphy. "We're happy to be working with the Wisconsin Lottery for a fifth season of games," Murphy said. "It's great to see our fans win season tickets and we're excited that in 2015 our grand prize winner will be able to experience game-day in the Champions Club and have the opportunity to spend time on the sidelines as we prepare to face two of our biggest rivals."[7]

State lotteries print sport-themed tickets because they believe it attracts a different type of lottery player, one that it typically cannot reach. "Wisconsin Lottery officials assert that the sale of licensed games results in ticket sales among individuals who would not otherwise purchase lottery tickets and that the sale of licensed games may actually increase overall ticket sales. For example, they believe that offering tickets involving a professional sports team encourages ticket purchases among sports fans who would not otherwise purchase lottery tickets. However, they were unable to provide data to support this assertion."[8]

Wisconsin's lack of statistics is interesting because "the state's [Wisconsin's] audit bureau says games requiring a licensing fee are not a good gamble for the state....The report recommends the Wisconsin Lottery stop offering games which involve license fees. That's because according to the report, non-licensed games outperform them."[9] Instead of giving the Packers $260,000 every year, "the report recommends diverting those funds back to taxpayers through property tax relief."[10] As a Wisconsin resident, I'm completely in favor of that.

The evidence related to the overall success of NFL-themed scratch-off tickets is scattershot. Palmisano of the Maryland Lottery and Gaming Control Agency started that regarding their Ravens-themed $5 scratcher, "One important note: this ticket generally sells out in half the time it takes to sell an average unadvertised $5 ticket." In the case of the Massachusetts and its sports-themed scratch-off tickets, its lottery noted a "direct correlation" between a team's performance and the success of its logo-bearing tickets.[11] Yet in California where the goal was to "connect with the younger demographic," sports-themed tickets did not attract the key 18-to-34-year old consumers.[12] It's one state which initially sought out team licenses, then abandoned the practice.

The ironic part in all of this is that there is one state lottery the NFL despises. In 1976, the state of Delaware began an NFL "lottery" which operated more like pari-mutuel wagering in horse racing. In essence, the state offered NFL betting by way of parlay cards which featured computer-generated point spreads. It was a complete disaster. The state's posted lines were often out of whack (by up to 7 points!) with the numbers offered in both Las Vegas and the illegal books. Smart bettors in and around Delaware quickly exploited the system. And while the amount of money wagered each week increased, the system fell apart in less than a month—with Delaware being the loser.

Being one of the four states grandfathered by PASPA, Delaware took another stab at offering NFL parlay cards through its lottery in 2009. This time Delaware brought in UK bookmakers William Hill to act as the state's "risk manager" (read: bookie), and everything went according to plan. When it debuted with the 2009-10 NFL season, Delaware sold over 750,000 tickets and handled nearly $11 million. By 2013-14, those numbers tripled with over 2.2 million tickets sold and a $31.5 million handle.

Delaware still had to fight its share of legal battles with the NFL over this maneuver, winning some and losing some. "We have pushed the PASPA envelope," Delaware Lottery Director Vernon Kirk told me via email. Though it failed to obtain the right to offer single game wagering like Nevada enjoys, the Delaware lottery has plenty of NFL action available for fans at its three "racinos" (a combination horse track and casino) and at 83 licensed "sports retailers." As Kirk explained, "This would include plays like our futures wagers for picking the championship winner (at odds), our teasers, super teasers and reverse teaser cards, point totals, etc. We also have half-time wagers and a play-off special card whereby you pick 2 games against the spread and one game straight-up."

The soft spot in Delaware's current system still lies within its point spreads. To avoid any ties, the state only offers half-point lines (i.e. -3.5 or +7.5). The lines are then locked on Wednesdays which means Vegas action doesn't alter Delaware's numbers. Player injuries, too, have no affect on the lines although occasionally the state will take a game off its cards. All of this adds up to a decided edge for sharp players, and it's no coincidence that Delaware's busiest racino on NFL Sunday is Delaware Park which is a mere 45 minute drive from the heart of Philadelphia and an hour from Baltimore.

Delaware isn't dumb. They recognize these weaknesses and have seen an influx of more sophisticated bettors. Although many gamblers avoid parlay cards in general because they don't like being forced to make at least three picks per wager, what the state offers is enticing. Unlike betting through a bookie, there's a guarantee here every winning gambler will get paid on the spot.

This is how sports betting could be operating in every

state which desires it. Licensed, regulated and monitored to keep both the state and the bettors safe, Delaware has proven how effectively this system can operate. Yet PASPA and leagues like the NFL continue to stand in the way of any other state enacting such a program.

The biggest hurdle to jump in this path towards legalization is the league's continuing mantra of "integrity." As we'll see, what sounds so noble and strong in sound bites is actually only a concept catered to when the NFL feels like trotting it out.

BRIAN TUOHY

WEEK 11
BYE

WEEK 12
@ OWNERS

The sentence "Roger Goodell is a tool" can be taken in a couple of ways. Many people, football fans and pundits alike, might agree that such a statement pertains directly to the NFL Commissioner's personality. Having never had the chance to sit down and talk to the guy, I'll abstain from piling on.

For me, the most important take away is the recognition that Goodell is an instrument of the owners. An actual tool. And nothing more.

When most fans sense an injustice within the NFL or feel the league is not listening to them, they point an accusatory finger at the commissioner. "Goodell did that wrong," "Goodell screwed this up," and on and on it goes. While those sorts of statements may be correct, they aren't entirely accurate. True, Goodell has done himself no favors since obtaining his office by wielding the NFL's hammer of justice with an inconsistent power which has made him look incompetent at times. Yet despite this, he is still seen as sitting atop the NFL pyramid, ruling over the league like a demented child king. But in fact, his is a paper throne.

Goodell was placed into his position by the cabal of true power within the league, the NFL owners. He never ran anything before in his life. He landed a job as a league intern in 1982 through a letter writing campaign and worked his way up the proverbial ladder from there. Twenty-four years later, he succeeded Paul Tagliabue when he retired as commissioner in 2006.

It makes little sense that the businessmen who own the NFL would want someone with an economics degree from Washington & Jefferson College presiding over their multi-billion dollar baby. (And, in fact, it was not a unanimous vote which put Goodell into the position). Yet what they have in Goodell is a true puppet. He knows of no other professional job other than working for the league. He's willing to live and die for "the shield" because it's his lifeblood. Hey, you pay me $40+ million dollars a year and I'd fall on a lot of grenades for the NFL owners, too.

But that's the key difference. Goodell gets paid a (ridiculously high) salary. The NFL owners, they earn profits from the league. No one pays them. They receive the earnings and dole them out to guys like Goodell. As with everything else, that's the telltale sign of who's truly atop the power structure—follow the money.

While only a few pages here will be set aside to discuss the men who really run this league, an entire book could (and should) be devoted to NFL ownership. I was tempted to write such a tome myself and still may someday, but the undertaking involved is enormous. That is, if someone truly wanted to delve into the subject and not cover it in the typical kiss-ass sportswriting nature. To look into the business dealings of the men who built and continue to run this league is akin to untangling multiple deals with the devil. The further one goes the more complex and dark it becomes. So when one or more of the NFL owners talks of maintaining the league's "integrity," such comments should be taken with tongue firmly planted in cheek. This is most evident when the subject of gambling on the NFL arises.

History, as they say, is written by the victors. This is true of the NFL as well. The league loves to celebrate (certain) milestone dates and moments, but the history of the league is often discussed in regards to the pre- and post-Super Bowl era. What occurred prior to the advent of the Super Bowl—the league's battles with the AFL and the AAFC, and even the founding of the NFL itself—is often written in vague, sometimes mythical terms.

The stark reality isn't often laid out as bare as Hugh Culverhouse Jr., son of former Tampa Bay Buccaneers owner Hugh Culverhouse Sr., once did. He told author Denis Crawford, "Most of your owners were financially unsophisticated. You got to understand that the league was started by gamblers. There is this façade that these guys are from high society, and no more bullshit could be found. It is a collection of gamblers and rejects."[1]

Much like calling Goodell a "tool," Culverhouse's "gamblers" may not mean what you think. He might have been referring to the gamble of entering the fledgling NFL as an owner. It was no sure thing money-making-wise in the 1920s. It was more of a boondoggle. Teams came and faded from existence in a matter of days. The Green Bay Packers, the only small-town franchise which survived that era, did so because the town bought the team. It has no true owner; a practice the NFL outlawed.

But if you take Culverhouse's "gamblers" to mean just that—one who bets for a living—it's not too farfetched a statement either. The best case in point is Timothy Mara. Mara bought New York's first NFL franchise, the Giants, in 1925 for the tidy sum of $500. He told his young son Wellington, "In New York, an empty store with two chairs in it is worth that much."[2] Mara made the investment despite having never witnessed an NFL game. This is interesting given his job description: bookmaker.

At the time, bookmaking was a legal profession. Mara started out as a runner then advanced to taking bets on his own at the age of 18. Nearly all of this gambling related to horse racing. Mara could be found "upon his high stool in the clubhouses of the five New York tracks" handling "between $20,000 and $30,000 on weekdays. On Saturdays and holidays he handles $50,000 or more."[3] Needless to say, having control over that much action in the days prior to pari-mutuel wagering made Mara a small fortune. Through different business dealings, he would come to own three NFL franchises at the same time—the Giants, the New York Yankees, and the Detroit Wolverines—never once quitting his bookmaking endeavors. What would now be seen as a major conflict of interest (on two levels) was inconsequential to the NFL then.

Of course, Tim Mara owned the Giants for a mere blink of the eye. "In 1928, Tim Mara obtained a bank loan to help finance Al Smith in his campaign for the Presidency. Tim thought that after the campaign the loan would be repaid out of the coffers of the Democratic National Committee. But when Smith lost the election, the Democrats denied ever having made such an agreement. The bank took Mara to court and won its case, but it failed to collect a penny. In the interim, Tim had transferred everything he owned, including the Giants, to a corporation composed of his blood relatives, with son Jack the president, and son Wellington the secretary of the Giants."[4] Instead of paying his debt, Mara declared bankruptcy. That financial decision failed to damper his bookmaking activities or his well-to-do lifestyle. Yet the Giants remain in the Mara family's control to this day.

Tim Mara's contributions to the sport and the league led to his enshrinement in Pro Football Hall of Fame's inaugural class of 1963. His biography on the Hall's website fails to mention his bookmaking career. It also ignores his friendship with another Hall of Famer (Class of '64) who was a well-known gambler, Pittsburgh Steelers founder and owner Art Rooney Sr.

Legend has it that Rooney first met Mara in a NYC restaurant when there to bet $50,000 on a horse. It won. Rooney was so elated he told Mara he'd name his soon-to-be-born son Timothy in his honor. Decades later, Timothy Rooney's daughter would marry Tim Mara's grandson, intertwining these two NFL franchises while producing a pair of Hollywood actresses in Kate and Rooney Mara.

Rooney Sr. bought into the NFL in 1933 for $2,500. His Pirates, later renamed the Steelers, were kept afloat in the lean Depression era by Rooney's race track winnings. Never one to shy away from gambling—he held nightly poker games in the Steelers' office in the Fort Pitt Hotel[5]—Rooney once won $300,000 in an amazing two-day span at the track in 1936. Such activities may have kept Rooney preoccupied. Despite being hailed an NFL "legend," Rooney's Steelers only posted eight winning seasons between their 1933 founding and 1971, and they didn't win a division title until 1972.

Even into the team's 1970s dynasty years, Rooney and his family were entrenched in horse racing. As author Don Kowet wrote in 1977, "Now Art Rooney's five sons have assumed the day-to-day management of the family's sporting enterprises. Together, under the company named Ruanaidh (pronounced 'Rooney' in Gaelic), father and sons comprise a total of ten different corporations. Art's second son, Art Jr. ('Artie') is president of the Penn Racing Association; Pat is president of Green Mountain Park in Vermont and, along with his brother John, runs Liberty Bell Park in Philadelphia; Tim operates Yonkers Raceway in New York and is general manager of the Palm Beach (Florida) Kennel Club, another of the family properties; Dan, the oldest, runs the Steelers."[6]

Apparently the betting activities that happily surrounded Rooney's horse racing holdings were the same ones that would lead to the destruction of the NFL's beloved integrity. But gambling cannot be fine for one sport and horrific for another. So which is it? Is sports gambling okay? Or does it mean horse racing is corrupt? (I mean it *is* corrupt, and if you love horses you'd be horrified to know how those animals are often treated in order to win a bet). To have the Rooney family stand shoulder-to-shoulder with the other NFL owners to prevent sports gambling's legalization is hypocrisy at its finest.

Want another hypocrite? How about one-time Cleveland Browns/Baltimore Ravens owner Art Modell? Sure, a loyal Browns fan could attack Modell for firing the team's namesake in founder/head coach Paul Brown while at the same time turning a one-time league powerhouse into a joke. Or there's Modell tearing the heart out of the city by moving the team to Baltimore (a city he claimed had "no business" hosting an NFL team) because Cleveland refused to give him the new stadium he demanded.

But keeping on this theme of owners being "anti-gambling," there's this statement Modell made during the Art Schlichter scandal as quoted from the *Miami News*, "Cleveland Browns' owner Art Modell says gambling is the biggest threat facing the National Football League. Modell, speaking in Columbus, Ohio, described gambling players as 'the one thing we fear more than anything else. I hope it isn't prevalent.'"

Notice Modell wasn't concerned with gambling *owners* because, well, he was one. In fact, the Browns have a history of problematic ownership. The team was formed by Arthur "Mickey" McBride and the aforementioned Paul Brown in 1946 as part of the rival All-American Football Conference. McBride was a bookie and the sole owner of the Continental wire service.

Once labeled by the federal government as "public enemy number one," the Continental was mainly used for the mafia's nationwide bookmaking operations throughout the 1940s. When McBride sold his stake in the franchise after it joined the NFL, it went to Saul Silberman who owned two horse tracks and was known to wager upwards of $2 million a year. Silberman in turn sold it to another well-known gambler, Art Modell.

Modell had some shaky connections. He partnered in a horse racing stable with Morris "Mushy" Wexler who was connected with McBride's wire service as well as other Mafioso. Modell's 1969 Las Vegas wedding to TV actress Patricia Breslin was an allegedly "mobbed up" affair hosted by Caesars Palace president William Weinberger (whose silent partners included mobsters Sam Giancana and Tony Accardo). Yet the NFL could forgive/forget/ignore his background and connections because Modell was instrumental in garnering millions of the dollars for the league as lead negotiator in its television contract talks.

No one within the NFL could (publicly at least) attack Modell for his background because doing so might have opened up the floodgates. Other owners had similar character flaws. Chicago Bears owner George "Papa Bear" Halas once sought financial help from Charles Bidwell, an associate of Al Capone and a noted bootlegger. Bidwell later bought the rival Chicago Cardinals (who Halas would push out of the city to St. Louis and later Arizona) which his heirs own to this day. Meanwhile, Detroit Lions owner and Mafioso friend George Richards was caught gambling on his own team's games, a heinous NFL crime which Halas helped cover up for decades.

While NFL apologists may point out that all of this happened in the league's formative years, the next generation of owners wasn't much cleaner. "The Chargers were founded by longtime gambler Barron Hilton, who had both a business and personal relationship with Los Angeles attorney Sidney Korshak, who was described by law enforcement officials as 'the link between the legitimate business world and organized crime.' A later owner was Eugene Klein, another Korshak friend with mob and gambling associations."[7]

"Sonny" Werblin, owner of the New York Jets, used his entertainment industry connections to singlehandedly save the AFL from extinction. Yet his dealings within the sports world weren't limited to his football team. Werblin also owned race horses. He once famously said of his horse Silent Screen, "I'd much rather own the horse than [Joe] Namath. Silent Screen has four good legs."[8] Sonny's partners in buying the Jets were also horsemen: three were fellow officers at New Jersey's Monmouth Park Racetrack, and another was president of Bowie Race Course in Maryland. Immediately after selling his stake in the Jets in 1968, Werblin helped build the original Meadowlands complex which many outside of New York don't realize is not just home to the Jets and Giants, but next door to a thoroughbred race track. They share a parking lot.

Shopping mall developer Edward DeBartolo Sr. had such a questionable past that Major League Baseball prevented him from buying the Chicago White Sox at one time. But a history of racetrack ownership was nothing new for the NFL, so the league welcomed him as the new owner of the San Francisco 49ers in 1977 (the NHL also allowed him buy the Pittsburgh Penguins the same year). DeBartolo transferred ownership of the team to his son Ed Jr.

The 49ers were a dynasty under Ed Jr.'s control, but in the late 1990's DeBartolo Jr. found himself in the middle of former Louisiana governor Edwin Edwards' corruption investigation. DeBartolo paid the governor a $400,000 bribe for a riverboat casino license (apparently partnering in a casino was no issue for the NFL either). He would later plead guilty to a charge of failing to report a felony, and received a $1 million fine plus two years of probation in return for his testimony against Edwards. The NFL also fined DeBartolo $250,000 and suspended him from the team for one year. DeBartolo later relinquished control of the team to his sister, Marie Denise DeBartolo York, whose son owns the 49ers today. Despite the conviction, fine, and suspension, DeBartolo was elected to Pro Football's Hall of Fame in 2009.

While we're in the Bay area, ever wonder how Al Davis became owner of the Raiders? The team was originally owned by F. Wayne Valley who foolishly hired a young Al Davis because, "Everywhere I went, people told me what a son of a bitch Al Davis was—hell, that's why I wanted him. Everybody hated his aggressiveness. The AFL people told me that he was too abrasive, too aggressive; they said he'd do anything to win."[9] Valley should've paid closer attention to those warnings.

Davis had been the AFL's commissioner prior to the league's merger with the NFL, almost becoming the NFL's commissioner had Pete Rozelle not won the vote. Davis then became a managing general partner with a 10 percent stake in the Raiders when he began to spread rumors that Valley wouldn't help out the team's troubled WR Warren Wells (who had thrice been arrested on separate charges of attempted rape, DUI, and battery during which a girlfriend stabbed him) because Wells was black. Fed up with Davis's antics, Valley decided to fire him when his contract expired. Behind Valley's back, Davis had team attorney Herman Cook draw up a new contract which would take effect the moment the old one expired. Davis and the team's third partner Ed McGah then signed it. This contract, finalized in July 1972, gave Davis a $100,000 a year salary for 20 years and absolute control of the team on and off the field, including the sole right to cast the team's vote at NFL meetings. Valley had no idea about any of this until it was publicized in the papers in 1973.[10] If that maneuver doesn't scream integrity, I don't know what does.

Carroll Rosenbloom may or may have not bet $1 million on his Baltimore Colts to win the 1958 NFL Championship

Game. He may or may not have also influenced the outcome of that game to win his bet. But during a 1958 investigation into Rosenbloom's ownership stake in a mafia-controlled Cuban casino, several people testified under oath that Rosenbloom often gambled on NFL games. The NFL and then-Commissioner Rozelle ignored all of this testimony. Instead, the league allowed Rosenbloom to trade his ownership in the Colts for the Los Angeles Rams franchise in 1972 so both parties could avoid any taxes associated with the deal. Rosenbloom died seven years later under mysterious circumstances (some believe he was murdered). His widow, Georgia Frontiere, moved the Rams to St. Louis only after getting a deal in which 96 percent of the new stadium was funded by taxpayers.

The man Rosenbloom cut that historic trade with was Robert Irsay. Today, the Colts are wholly owned by Irsay's son Jim who has been a recent embarrassment to the league. In 2013, Irsay skirted the league's anti-gambling policy by offering $8,500 on Twitter to the first person to correctly guess the final score of a Ravens-Patriots game. Amazingly, after a man's guess came within a point of being exact (27-13 against the actual final of 28-13) he received a FedEx package from Irsay with a personal note and the $8,500 in $100 bills. Irsay continued his strange foray into bookmaking on Twitter by offering money-laden contests for a 49ers-Falcons game as well as taking people's picks for the AFC championship.[11]

Though the NFL failed to punish Irsay for such behavior, just over a year later the league was forced to react to his latest headline-making blunder. On March 16, 2014, Irsay was arrested on charges of operating a vehicle while intoxicated and four counts of felony possession of a controlled substance. His arrest came about two weeks after a woman named Kimberly Wundrun was found dead of an apparent drug overdose in a $140,000 townhouse Irsay had given to her. During Irsay's traffic stop, police found $29,029 in cash ($12,000 of which was in a "laundry bag" found in the car) as well as numerous bottles of prescription medication. Toxicology reports showed he had both hydrocodone and oxycodone in his system. Though each of the four drug charges carried a potential six month to three year sentence, Irsay served no time. He pleaded guilty to driving while intoxicated and was sentenced to one year probation. His driver's license was revoked for a year, and Irsay was to be subjected to monthly drug tests.

Shortly after Irsay entered his plea, NFL Commissioner Goodell suspended him for six games and fined the Colts owner $500,000, the most allowable by rule. It was the first time an NFL owner had been suspended since Ed DeBartolo Jr.

There were two takeaways from Goodell's reaction. The first was that Goodell didn't act against Irsay until his case was fully adjudicated. Such a standard does not apply to players' suspensions and/or fines. Yet by Goodell's own words, that shouldn't be the case. In a letter Goodell sent to Irsay, the commissioner wrote, "I have stated on numerous occasions that owners, management personnel and coaches must be held to a higher standard than players. We discussed this during our meeting and you expressed your support for that view, volunteering that owners should be held to the highest standard."[12]

It's difficult to disagree with Goodell's statement, but again, this is the *owners'* league. Players, personnel, and management are the replaceable cogs in the machine which is fueled by the owners and their money. And no one, not even a figurehead like Roger Goodell, is going to dictate what the owners do. They are going to effectively punish themselves, if at all, when it might be called for. Irsay was a scapegoat, nothing more. Other current NFL owners have engaged in more egregious, (near) criminal behavior without any sort of punishment being handed down from league HQ.

Cleveland Browns owner Jimmy Haslam's family

company, the truck stop chain Pilot Flying J, was raided by the FBI in 2013. Haslam serves as CEO of Pilot Flying J, the nation's leading retailer of diesel fuel, which rakes in nearly $30 billion in annual revenue. The FBI alleged that a "conspiracy and scheme to defraud executed by various Pilot employees to deceptively withhold diesel fuel price rebates and discounts from Pilot customers ... for the dual purposes of increasing the profitability of Pilot and increasing the diesel sales commissions of the Pilot employees participating in the fraud."[13] One Pilot Flying J employee turned FBI informant provided a taped conversation featuring the Vice President of Sales for Pilot Flying J, John Freeman, admitting that Haslam not only knew this was going on, but "loved it."[14] It was also alleged that Haslam was included on emails discussing the scheme.

Despite FBI allegations that this conduct lasted for at least six years, Haslam claimed he was unaware of it. Yet a year after being raided, Pilot Flying J agreed to pay a $92 million penalty for its actions. "In an agreement with the U.S. Attorney's Office for the Eastern District of Tennessee, Pilot Flying J has accepted responsibility for the criminal conduct of its employees, ten of whom have pleaded guilty to participating in the scheme. For its part, the government has agreed not to prosecute the nation's largest diesel retailer as long as Pilot abides by the agreement."[15]

Evading any personal criminal charges, Haslam released a statement which said, "We, as a company, look forward to putting this whole unfortunate episode behind us, continuing our efforts to rectify the damage done, regaining our customers' trust, and getting on with our business."[16]

That was exactly what the NFL did with this case; they put it behind immediately them. Goodell had zero response. No fine, no suspension, not any form of punishment for an owner who sullied the league's reputation by making headlines for a variety of alleged criminal behavior. So much for owners being held to the "highest standard."

Players rarely get this benefit of the doubt thanks to the league's "personal conduct policy." The prime example of this was Ben Roethlisberger. The Pittsburgh Steelers quarterback was twice accused of sexual assault—once in 2008 and again in 2010—yet never had a single criminal charge brought against him. No matter, he was suspended in 2010 for six games (later reduced to four) for his behavior. Other players have run afoul of the league and were suspended and/or fined because they, too, made headlines for all the wrong reasons.

The "personal conduct policy" is somewhat ill-defined. Embedded in every player's contract, it reads: "Player therefore acknowledges his awareness that if he accepts a bribe or agrees to throw or fix an NFL game; fails to promptly report a bribe offer or an attempt to throw or fix an NFL game; bets on an NFL game; knowingly associates with gamblers or gambling activity; uses or provides other players with stimulants or other drugs for the purpose of attempting to enhance on-field performance; or is guilty of any other form of conduct reasonably judged by the League Commissioner to be detrimental to the League…The commissioner will have the right…to fine player…to suspend player…or to terminate this contract."[17]

As many would argue, Goodell and the NFL don't appear to truly be a "reasonable judge." They are biased. Heavily. Otherwise outside arbitrators wouldn't be required in many of these cases. Hell, at one point the league actually brought former commissioner Paul Tagliabue out of retirement to hear the appeals on Goodell's ruling in the New Orleans Saints' Bountygate scandal. But because the NFLPA can't collective bargain their way out of a paper bag, players are bound to these contracts and the whims of the league in determining their fate.

For the owners, however, such rules don't necessarily apply. Sure, each team owner and their staff are supposed to agree to and sign an "Integrity of the Game" certification which basically states that the team didn't/won't cheat, but it's a completely different set of regulations from what the players must agree. It's a loophole created by the owners, for the owners.

So it's no wonder why Minnesota Vikings owner Zygmunt "Zygi" Wilf's off-the-field tomfoolery slipped past Goodell's watch. In 2013, a 21-year long civil court case in which Wilf and his family's real estate development company had been accused of "organized-crime-type activities" finally reached a conclusion. The judge in the case ruled Wilf "had committed fraud, breach of contract, a breach of fiduciary duty and [violated] the state's civil racketeering statute."[18] The judge also stated, "I do not believe I have seen one single financial statement that is true and accurate. There was a consistent, pervasive method of removing funds so they would not reach the partners. The bad faith and evil motive were demonstrated in the testimony of Zygi Wilf himself."[19] The court ordered Wilf to pay $84.5 million in damages to the plaintiffs; the NFL stood pat. (And Minnesota taxpayers agreed to pay for half of the Vikings a new $1 billion stadium).

Last, but not least, let's not forget Dallas Cowboys owner Jerry Jones. Casting aside the unflattering photos of a long-married Jones and a pair of Texas strippers which surfaced in 2014 as part of a badly executed blackmail attempt, there were few questions raised when Jones discussed his team's point spread on Dallas radio. During his weekly radio show on 105.3 The Fan in 2013, Jones actually stated that though the Cowboys lost to the Chiefs 17-16 in the second week of the season, it was no big deal because Las Vegas had predicted that would happen. "We went in there as the underdog," said Jones. "The Cowboys were the underdog going in the game. The line actually expected us not to win that game. And so, let's keep that in mind."[20] Jones went on to add, "It never ceases to amaze me. Actually, they were right. I think, what were they a three-point favorite? End up losing by one. It never ceases to amaze me how close these things pan out."[21]

Now what if Cowboys quarterback Tony Romo had made such post-game comments? What if *any* NFL player referenced the point spread after a loss? What would the NFL and commissioner Goodell have done? Certainly a fine and/or a suspension would have followed which is why no player is dumb enough to make such statements. Yet here was an NFL owner, one of the men supposedly fighting to keep sports gambling illegal, talking about his team's point spread on the radio. How insane is that? Apparently not enough for the league because guess what sort of repercussions Jones faced? That's right: none.

NFL owners aren't completely naïve when it comes to their fans gambling on the sport. As Houston Texans owner Bob McNair explained to the *New York Times*, "It does show the depth of passion our fans have for our game. Ultimately, I think it falls under that old saying of 'Don't worry about the things you can't change.' We can't do anything about individuals. I play golf, and I like to play a $2 Nassau when I'm out there on the course. It doesn't mean I do not love the game, but sometimes it's nice to have a little something extra at stake."[22]

McNair seems to get it, even if he hasn't been very public about pushing the subject. Maybe it's because he's a touch hypocritical, too. Besides his apparently joy for gambling on golf, like many owners that have come before him McNair breeds and races thoroughbreds.

BRIAN TUOHY

WEEK 13
vs. PAIN

When a bettor decides to channel his inner NFL owner by stepping up to the window at the horse track, most assume the thoroughbreds are in peak physical condition. Injuries aren't an issue because if the horse couldn't race, it'd be scratched. Any use of drugs, including the often administered lasix, is prescribed and monitored by trained professionals. Odds favoring one horse over another are strictly based on variables such as race length, track conditions, previous times, and the betting public's perception of these factors; not the horses' health. Track insiders may have a "hot tip," but a savvy bettor can pick a winner with careful study of the program.

Or so the story goes.

Horse races can and are fixed because of one key element: the horses cannot talk. If they did, they would reveal a litany of abuses. Without exaggerating, I have reams of FBI files relating to fixed races, using methods of doping, shocking, and good ol' jockey manipulation to achieve the desired outcome.

Owners and trainers will do horrific things to cause a horse to underperform, all in the name of making some fast cash.

To combat decades of cheating and abuse, racing commissions are charged with monitoring the activities in every stable. Drug testing plays a big role in this anti-corruption battle. Even though blood samples are drawn after each race in an attempt to deter cheating, not every drug forced into a horse's body can be testing for and detected. Federal legislation has been proposed that would give the United States Anti-Doping Agency oversight of all equine medication and drug testing. Whether passing such a bill would remedy the situation remains to be seen.

Ironically, the non-gambling entity called the National Football League has similar protections in place. One of the most noted is the league's injury report. Released and updated during each week of the season, it lists players as either "Probable" (75 percent chance an athlete will play), "Questionable" (50 percent chance), "Doubtful" (25 percent chance), or "Out."

The NFL claims that the release of the injury report has absolutely nothing to do with gambling or gamblers' attempts to gain inside information. These exist simply to achieve competitive balance within the sport (and maybe help fantasy players better set their lineup). Yet the origination of the injury report dates back to the late 1950's and the antics of Hall of Fame quarterback Bobby Layne. "The Blonde Bomber" was known to fake (or at least exaggerate) an injury with a specific purpose in mind: altering next week's point spread. It's alleged that Layne not only bet on games but shaved points as well, using such tricks to better his gambling propositions. So, was it just a coincidence that during Layne's heyday the NFL's injury report first surfaced?

The injury report remains far from foolproof. Denver Broncos quarterback Peyton Manning was listed on the team's injury report as "Probable" for the last three games of the 2014 season as well as for their playoff matchup against the Colts. Questions swirled around his poor performance in those games. After the season ended, it was revealed that he had suffered from a torn quadriceps muscle in his right leg and played through the injury. As an outside observer, perhaps as a third party who had bet money on those Broncos games, a reasonable question to ask was did the term "Probable" really cover the extent of Manning's injury? There's a huge difference between saying, "Manning's leg is bothering him, but he'll play" versus telling fans, "Manning has a torn quad muscle." Granted, the first statement was accurate, but it undersold the situation a bit, don't you think?

The question not asked was, "Should Manning have played?" If a thoroughbred suffered a torn quadriceps (assuming they have quads, I'm not a vet), it wouldn't be shoved into the starting gate to race. Even if the horse could talk and was asked, "Do you think you can go?" it probably would respond by saying, "No."

Unless, of course, the horse understood the alternative. If the horse with the torn quad was asked that question knowing full well that by answering, "no," it might be "euthanized," the horse might just give it a whirl. A lifelong limp and a stable brimming with oats are better than a final bolt to the forehead.

Chicago Bears safety Chris Conte sided with the horse. Sort of. He told Chicago's Newsradio WBBM in December 2014, "I'd rather have the experience of playing and, who knows, die 10, 15 years earlier than not be able to play in the NFL and live a long life. It's something I've wanted to do with my life and I wanted to accomplish. And I pretty much set my whole life up to accomplish that goal."[1]

Conte was no stranger to pain. He sat out of four of the Bears' 16 games and left seven others due to injury in 2014. Of course, he was crucified on Chicago sports radio for a perceived lack of toughness.

"Football has been subverted into a made-for-television event," wrote former NFL player Nate Jackson in his book *Slow Getting Up*. "Everything is so clear. Except it's not. The third dimension is what makes it real, violent, and dangerous. Consuming the product through a television screen, at a safe distance, dehumanizes the athlete and makes his pain unreal. The more you watch it, the less real it becomes, until the players are nothing more than pixilated video game characters to be bartered and traded."[2]

It's difficult to explain a sensation like pain. Doctors and nurses will ask you on a scale of one to ten what your pain feels like at a given moment, yet that number can't do it justice. Running back Reggie Bush articulated football-caused pain this way, "Football games—I always try to relate them to for the average person—it's just like being in a car crash. Like literally every time you're getting hit is like being in a car crash. Imagine as a running back you're getting hit—I touch the ball at least 20 to 30 times a game, that's 20 to 30 car crashes you're in in two hours."[3]

I've been in a car crash. I remember the aftereffects. I don't want to be in another one.

I've never played in the NFL, or even organized football in college or high school, so even as a writer I cannot describe what it feels like to play with/through such pain and then continue to live with the debilitating effects afterwards. Some former NFL players have been brave enough to come forward and explain what they endured during their playing days. You might notice a reoccurring theme develop.

"The pain was so bad, my wife had to help me out of the car," former Pittsburgh Steelers and Dallas Cowboys wide receiver Buddy Dial told *The Pittsburgh Press*. "And that night, I sat in a tub of water, my wife had to call the neighbor to help pull me out of the tub. So I went to the hospital. Then, before the game, they gave me 10 or 12 shots of something—all these needles—and blocked the whole lower part of my back. And I played the whole game. After the game, when it wore off, I about died. It was brutal."[4]

One of Dial's fellow Cowboys flankers was Peter Gent whose semi-fictional account of his time in the NFL became the classic book *North Dallas Forty*. Gent wrote, "The trainers were responsible for the overall health of all player personnel. The problem was that their opinions carried little weight with management. The medical problems were constantly overruled by front-office tactical decisions, and there was no place for professional integrity. Each Sunday was its own problem that could only be solved satisfactorily by winning. If the trainers, highly qualified physical therapists, didn't finally bring their medical opinions into agreement with the current tactical needs of management, they would shortly find themselves administering enemas in the geriatrics ward at Parkland Hospital. As a result, a player who the trainers thought needed rest or even surgery often found himself shot full of Novocain facing a grinning Deacon Jones and the player was given the chance to exhibit the most desirable of traits—the ability to endure pain."[5]

Cardinals' linebacker Dave Meggyesy was a contemporary of Dial and Gent. In his book *Out of their League* he wrote, "When a player is injured, he is sent to the team physician, who is usually more concerned with getting the athlete back into action than anything else. This reversal of priorities leads to unbelievable abuses. One of the most common is to 'shoot' a player before a game to numb a painful injured area that would normally keep him out of action. He can play, but in so doing he can also get new injuries in that part of his body where he has no feeling."[6]

But that was just the high flyin' 1960's, right? Times have changed. As Bob Kravitz wrote in 1984, "Such treatment of a pro football injury is not likely today." Kravitz then quoted former Oakland Raiders offensive lineman turned National

Football League Players Association (NFLPA) director Gene Upshaw as saying, "Guys are aware now of the long-term consequences of playing hurt. It's still an individual choice, but players today won't just go out and play no matter what—the way we did years ago. Hey, let's not kid ourselves. When I played, lots of guys were using drugs. I'm not going to tell you that I didn't."[7]

Kravitz continued, "But now, painkillers—at least those legally obtained from NFL teams—are less abundant....Players are better educated about painkillers, too....The use of painkillers was curtailed in 1973 when the league developed its own drug monitoring program. At the beginning of each season, each team is required to provide the league office with an inventory of all drugs. Three times a year it must provide copies of all prescriptions for drugs. At the end of the year, each team must provide a final inventory. Further, each team is inspected once a year by regional security representatives—all former Drug Enforcement Agency agents."[8]

With all due respect to Kravitz, to the above paragraph I call bullshit.

In his book *Taking Flak*, former Houston Oilers quarterback Dan Pastorini wrote about "the Candy Store" in the training room. "There were glass jars the size of milk jugs, rows of them, across the entire wall on one side of the room. Valdoxan were the happy pills. Then there were Percocet, which we called red-and-yellows. Black Mollies were Amphetamines. There were pills of every color. I had no idea what some of them were. I just knew you could grab a handful whenever you wanted. The Quaaludes jar would be empty every day. Guys were just beat up and hurting and needed them to sleep. They'd take them out of the jars by the handful."[9]

Pastorini played throughout the 1970's and into the early 1980's when supposedly the NFL was monitoring these controlled substances. But Pastorini wrote, "It's like I was chemically controlled. I mean, when I was a rookie one of my linemen, Bob Young, talked about taking steroids. I was sure a lot of guys were taking steroids by '77, just like a lot of guys couldn't function without pain pills. But nobody asked and nobody cared, least of all me. Those guys were protecting my ass, you think I'm going to care? You think anyone cared? None of it was under doctor's supervision. Some guys were taking drugs to a level where no man should go. It's how you survived."[10]

Here was a player who knew pain firsthand. "From my rookie year until I walked off the field in Pittsburgh a few weeks earlier," Pastorini wrote, "I had suffered 12 concussions. I broke my nose 16 times. I broke my cheekbone. I cracked my sternum. I broke my collar bone twice. I separated my right shoulder four times and my left shoulder six times. I had two operations on my right shoulder and four on my left. I fractured four transverse processes in my back. I had some kind of fractures in my ribs 38 times. I couldn't count all the broken thumbs and fingers."[11] To play with broken ribs, Pastorini took 12 pre-game shots, then another dozen during halftime. At one point, he lost sensation in his throwing arm because one of the shots damaged a nerve near his shoulder blade.

He is by no means alone. And the methods of pain management in the NFL have not changed.

Three members of the Seattle Seahawks defensive unit known as the "Legion of Boom" played in the 2014 Super Bowl with serious injuries. Earl Thomas had a dislocated left shoulder. Kam Chancellor had a torn MCL and a bone bruise. Richard Sherman had ligament damage in his elbow. After the game, Seahawks head coach Pete Carroll said, "It was an extraordinary effort from guys who played through unbelievable issues. That was a heroic thing that those guys did to play. They wanted to play for their teammates and they did exactly that, and they did it in great fashion."[12]

How did they manage to play through such injury? No one mentioned drugs or injections. Chancellor claimed he made it through on "faith."[13] Sherman stated, "You just stop thinking about that and focus in on what you've got to do on the play. The pain is going to be what it is. If you've played this game long enough, you're usually playing in some kind of pain. That pain just happened to be more significant that day. But you just adapt, you just adjust and try to continue to do your job until you can't do it effectively anymore."[14]

And that's just it. NFL players often play through pain because the alternative is much like the fate of the injured horse—death. Perhaps not the physical cessation of life, but it can easily become a career-killer. If one player cannot go, another is there, eager to replace him. And who is to say the injured player will ever see the field again? The average NFL player's career is a mere three-and-a-half years long.

"You've got to realize, man, us NFL guys have a very small window to play this game," said 11-year NFL veteran defensive tackle Kevin Williams. "And you're always wired and talking about playing to the best of your ability and having success while you can. Because you won't have it long. You can't last forever."[15]

Because of that sentiment, Williams routinely took injections of Toradol to relieve his pain. Because so many other players do as well, stories of lines forming to get into the trainer's room for an injection are not uncommon. Former Bears linebacker Brian Urlacher told HBO Sports that he thought his regular Toradol injections were "like a flu shot."[16] Former St. Louis Rams wide receiver Torry Holt had a Toradol injection prior to playing in Super Bowl XXXIV, saying of it, "I felt like new money. You get that shot and you feel like you're 18, 19 years old. It's like a sheet of armor. I was a new man."[17]

"Toradol was originally developed as a postoperative drug, used primarily to treat moderately severe acute pain. When injected into the bloodstream, it can begin working almost immediately, quelling whatever pain may be present. That's been ideal for NFL players in need of a quick game-day fix. Equally important, the shot gives many players added confidence that they can perform worry-free, uninhibited by existing pain and able to more easily push through any new injuries that may occur."[18]

Though it's been used regularly in the NFL for nearly 20 years, there have been calls to limit, if not outright ban, Toradol's usage within the league. In referring to the NFL Physicians Society Task Force's updated guidelines for Toradol's usage, Dr. Thom Mayer, the NFLPA's medical director, said, "This task force recommendation is important as it, although indirectly, admits that the gratuitous use of Toradol to keep our players on the field is not, and was never, clinically sound."[19] Dr. Mayer believed Toradol should only be administered to players listed on the official injury report.

Thought FDA approved, "complications associated with Toradol misuse include potential kidney failure, liver damage and gastrointestinal bleeding. There's also increased risk of heart attack and stroke."[20] Toradol also increases the risk of brain bleeding should a player suffer head trauma while the drug is in his system. That is a huge red flag given the NFL's current anti-concussion crusade.

The legal battle between former players and the NFL over concussions, repetitive head trauma, and when (and how much) the league knew about its risks is a matter of public record. It's changed not only the way the game is coached, played and officiated, but how it's broadcast and covered by the media. There's good reason for this. According to the book *Is There Life After Football?*, "More than 4,500 living players maintain that they have symptoms of football-related brain damage. That's nearly a quarter of all living NFL alumni," the authors wrote, later adding that "former players are over five times more likely than other men their age to suffer from dementia."[21]

As bonkers as it may seem, these facts apparently mean little to many current NFL players. According to ESPN, "In an NFL Nation anonymous survey, 85 percent of the 320 players polled said they would play in the Super Bowl with a concussion."[22] When posed the survey question, Washington Redskins linebacker London Fletcher responded, "Did 100 percent say yes?"[23] Fletcher went on to comment about playing with a concussion, "If it's something where I'm having just a few symptoms and can hide it from the trainer, then yeah, I would do it. With some of them, you get in a game and you can't play."[24]

Saying a player "can't play" is a relative term in the NFL, much like referring to a concussion as "getting your bell rung" or being "dinged." As former NFL linebacker Dave Meggysey wrote, "Getting 'dinged' means getting hit in the head so hard that your memory is affected, although you can still walk around and sometimes even continue playing. You don't feel pain, and the only way other players or coaches know you've been 'dinged' is when they realize you can't remember the plays."[25]

Luckily, the sidelines are filled with trained personnel ready to assist the "dinged" player, such as the ball boy. Former NFL ball boy Eric Kesteroct wrote in the *New York Times*, "I lay awake at night wondering how many lives were irreparably damaged by my most handy ball boy tool: smelling salts. On game days my pockets were always full of these tiny ammonia stimulants that, when sniffed, can trick a brain into a state of alertness. After almost every crowd-pleasing hit, a player would stagger off the field, steady himself the best he could, sometimes vomit a little, and tilt his head to the sky. Then, with eyes squeezed shut in pain, he'd scream 'Eric!' and I'd dash over and say, 'It's O.K., I'm right here, got just what you need.' A sniff of my salts would revive the player in alertness only, and he would run back onto the field to once again collide with opponents with the force of a high-speed car crash."[26]

Though the NFL's latest concussion protocol is supposed to prevent this sort of behavior from occurring, there's leakage in the system. New England Patriots wide receiver Julian Edelman—who missed the final two games of the 2014 season due to a concussion—took a huge hit to the helmet in the fourth quarter of Super Bowl XLIX. Despite looking out-of-sorts, Edelman never missed an offensive play and eventually caught the game-winning touchdown pass. After the game, Edelman "inadvertently" referred to his opponents as St. Louis, not Seattle. The Patriots were elusive when asked if Edelman underwent the proper concussion protocol testing since he never went to the locker room as mandated by the league, though reports suggest the medical staff did question Edelman on the sidelines.

A player escaping such "mandatory" testing is not unheard of. During two separate 2013 Wildcard playoff games, the Green Bay Packers' David Bakhtiari and the New Orleans Saints' Keenan Lewis violated league rules by refusing to leave the sidelines to be checked. Bakhtiari actually took it one step further and re-entered the game. Yet in a league where donning the wrong type of socks is a fineable offense, neither player was docked pay for their actions. Why? According to NFL spokesman Greg Aiello, "This has never been an issue of a player defying doctors' orders and going out on the field. It's never come up before, so we wouldn't be able to fine a player in this instance, but obviously it's something we'll be looking at. This is the first time I've ever heard of it, where the player went back on the field against orders of the doctors."[27]

I would again call bullshit on the above statement.

But of all the impediments to a football player's safety, the most unlikely hindrance may just be the players' union itself. Regarding the situation of Bakhtiari and Lewis, NFLPA spokesman George Atallah said, "We have a disagreement as to whether or not the players were in violation of the protocols to begin with."[28] Atallah went on to state that he didn't believe player fines would be the correct punishment for such behavior because responsibility existed solely at the team level. As for either of Bakhtiari or Lewis's actual well-being, Atallah didn't appear to address it.

In the aforementioned ESPN NFL Nation poll, 60 percent of the players asked believed the NFL is committed to player safety. That's a majority, but not by much. It cannot help the players' perspective when the owners attempted to increase the number of games a season by two to 18. Nor did the decision to play weekly Thursday night games aid in keeping players healthy. As Houston Texans tackle Duane Brown said, "You talk about player safety, but you want to extend the season and add Thursday games? It's talking out of both sides of your mouth."[29] The NFLPA managed to curtail an 18-game season (for now), but those Thursday night games in which the players hate participating? They're much too valuable to quit.

The players union has failed in other aspects of player safety as well. One issue being that of concussions. Pro Football Talk's Mike Florio took the NFLPA to task on the subject, writing, "At a time when some are lamenting the fact that the settlement of the concussion lawsuits will prevent the public from knowing what the NFL knew and when the NFL knew it, those same questions will never be answered regarding the NFLPA. What did the NFLPA know, when did the NFLPA know it, and why didn't the NFLPA do a better job of protecting its men?" He continued, "The simple fact is that, under the late Gene Upshaw, the NFLPA was a major part of the problem. Consider this quote from NFLPA executive director DeMaurice Smith in his 2009 remarks to Congress: 'There is simply no justification for the NFL to have previously ignored or discredited Dr. [Bennet] Omalu and others with relevant, valid research. For far too long, our former players were left adrift; as I emphasized at the last hearing, *we were complicit in the lack of leadership and accountability*, but that ends now. I am here again to make it clear that our commitment is unwavering.'[emphasis added]"[30]

Another concern the NFLPA seems adrift on is drugs. Way back in 1969, San Diego Chargers defensive tackle Houston Ridge filed a lawsuit against his team, accusing them of conspiracy and malpractice in regards to drugs. Ridge "charged that steroids, amphetamines, barbiturates and the like were used 'not for purpose of treatment and cure, but for the purpose of stimulating mind and body so he (the player) would perform more violently as a professional...'"[31] The suit was eventually settled for $250,000.

Ridge's case should have been a warning shot, signaling the beginning of the end of the drug culture within the NFL. Instead, it seemed to become more pervasive.

If the NFL owners wanted a completely clean game—and judging from their behavior, it's difficult to believe that's the case—the only way they could achieve it is by convincing the NFLPA to allow such oversight. Yet to protect its rank and file, the NFLPA has fought hard at the collective bargaining table to prevent drug testing's spread more so than provoking its further usage as a deterrent and a safeguard. So drug testing within the NFL rolled out at a glacial pace. Many players still dislike having to subject themselves to the league's test. As one anonymous member of the Seahawks proclaimed, "We are being treated like criminals, tested like people on parole."[32]

Though the NFLPA has allowed testing for steroids and other performance-enhancing drugs for some time, the 2011 collective bargaining agreement between owners and players instituted a first. It allowed for the NFL to test players for human growth hormone (HGH). This was a major concession for the NFLPA. For one, it required players to submit to a blood draw and not just a urine sample. But more importantly, it opened up a lot of players to potential fines and suspensions. How so? A member of the Pro Football Writers of America told me on-air during an interview on his Florida-based radio show that his inside source informed him that 75 percent of NFL players used HGH.

Even though this was part of the CBA passed in 2011, HGH testing did not begin until October 2014. When it was about to be initiated, NFLPA president Eric Winston informed players through a letter which read in part, "As you know, the new Performance Enhancing Substances Policy includes HGH testing. Testing for HGH will begin on Monday, October 6th. Each week of the season, 5 players on 8 teams will be tested. No testing will occur on game days. We negotiated to ensure that the methodology of testing be conducted in the most professional and safest manner for players. Importantly, after three years of negotiating, players won the right to challenge any aspect of the science behind the HGH isoforms test in an appeal of a positive test."[33]

Amazingly, given a three-year heads up, not one single NFL player has yet to test positive for HGH.

Maybe it's not that shocking. As Nate Jackson wrote, "Oh, and there is a once-a-year drug test. If you can't pass it then you're either stupid or you have a drug problem. Either one, you need help."[34]

Jackson, who played in the NFL from 2003-2008, further elaborated on his experiences with the testing process. "The rules are strict. They want to catch people cheating. But I've never seen steroids around. I've never seen anyone get caught, either. I've never heard anyone talk about taking them, or heard from anyone that someone else was juicing. I've never seen HGH, either. I only learn about it through the media. They tell me it's undetectable, that it's a wonder drug, that its benefits are manifold, and that it can accelerate the healing process after an injury. Sounds great, if you want the truth, but even if I knew how to get them, I don't have the time or the peace of mind to arrange something so secret. Besides, I made it here without them. We all did. Steroids won't make you a good football player."[35]

Perhaps without realizing it, Jackson explained why he never saw another player using performance-enhancing drugs…while at the same time contradicting himself in his book. After a career full of injuries, he didn't want his football dreams to die. So he started using HGH. "I reach out to a connection I made a year earlier and acquire a supply of human growth hormone, HGH. The drugs come in the mail in a package stuffed with dry ice. I half expect to see the feds storm out of the bushes, guns blazing, as I pull the box off my front porch. But no feds. Just me and another needle."[36]

If, like Jackson, a player was inclined to give HGH or any number of other performance-enhancing drugs a try (and why wouldn't he? They work), obtaining many of these drugs is as easy as shopping at a third-world pharmacy. It's a quick hop, skip, and jump over the border to Mexico or some other Caribbean country where the drug laws are much more lax. On the shelves is every sort of PED a player could ask for. The only trick is circumventing America's crack TSA agents to get the stuff back into the country.

But a player may not even have to go that far. I have heard allegations from former players that team medical personnel not only provided players with PEDs, but they taught them how to use the drug so as not to get caught. This may oppose everything the NFL hypes about its anti-drug policy, yet given how easily teams provided players with painkillers, would it really come as a shock? Recent developments just may reveal how true all of these allegations are.

Under the direction of the U.S. Attorney's Office for the Southern District of New York, the federal Drug Enforcement

Agency (DEA) conducted "spot checks" of several NFL teams in 2014. The DEA was checking "whether visiting NFL clubs were generally in compliance with federal law. Agents requested documentation from visiting teams' medical staffs for any controlled substances in their possession, and for proof that doctors could practice medicine in the home team's state."[37] "The DEA likely will be especially interested in the record keeping of NFL medical staffs. Any facility where prescription drugs are dispensed must have a proper pharmacy registration and maintain effective security over controlled substances. The law also requires a complete and accurate record of each pill that is received, sold, delivered or otherwise disposed of."[38] Criminal penalties were not out of the question.

NFL spokesmen were quick to assure everyone that nothing sordid was taking place. Yet these mini-raids were conducted by the DEA because in May 2014 more than 1,500 former players filed a class-action lawsuit against the NFL over prescription medications. Their claim was that teams routinely and illegally distributed these drugs without the proper safeguards, leading players to addiction and other medical complications after their careers ended.

"Prominent plaintiffs such as former Chicago Bears quarterback Jim McMahon, former 49ers center Jeremy Newberry and former defensive end Marcellus Wiley, who is now an ESPN commentator, detailed physicians and trainers handing out addictive painkillers without prescriptions, in dangerous combinations, to mask injuries....McMahon, who played from 1982 to 1996, said in the lawsuit that he received 'hundreds, if not thousands' of injections and pills from NFL doctors and trainers, including Percocet, Toradol, Novocaine, amphetamines, sleeping pills and muscle relaxers. He said he became so hooked on pain meds that at one point he took 100 Percocets a month."[39]

Meanwhile, one painkilling drug that has become

increasing legal across the United States remains on the NFL banned substance list: marijuana. When the states of Washington and Colorado legalized marijuana in 2012, the NFL was quick to announce, "The use of medical marijuana is not permitted and the medical advisers to our joint substance abuse program with the Players Association do not believe it should be permitted."[40]

Despite such pronouncements, marijuana is perhaps the most widely used drug in the league. Lomas Brown, an 18-year veteran tackle who retired in 2002, countered the NFL's anti-drug statement with his own missive, saying, "I would just think that the use of marijuana for pain management, it would be a far better outcome to me than it would be for the abuse of heavy narcotics like pills of [Vicodin] or [Percocets] or whatever the pill of choice is for pain in the NFL....The NFL, they have to protect their logo, they have to protect their image, but I say at least 50 percent of the players smoke."[41] Yet despite testing players for marijuana usage, suspensions for the drug are few and far between. In fact, over the past few years many potential first round draft picks have admitted to using marijuana only to see the honest admission not affect their position on many teams' draft board.

The book *Is There Life After Football?* brought the following stats to light, "Nine out of 10 former players wake up each day to nagging aches and pains that they attribute to football. About eight in 10 report that the pain lasts most of the day. Among younger retirees aged 30 to 49, one third say their work lives are limited in some way by the after-effects of injury. Retired players are much less likely than their age peers in the general population to rate their health as excellent or good, and nearly 30 percent of NFL retirees rate their health as only 'fair' or 'poor.'" The league's younger alumni, age 30 to 49, are "five times as likely" as their non-NFL age counterparts to have problems with mobility and strength, from walking stairs to lifting objects, and 15 percent of this group are "unable to work as a result of football-related disabilities."[42]

Football has become to be seen as so dangerous that Chicago Bears Hall of Fame player and coach Mike Ditka of all people isn't so sure kids should continue to participate in the sport. He told HBO Sports that if he had a young son today, he wouldn't let him play football. "That's sad," Dikta said. "I wouldn't. And my whole life was football. I think the risk is worse than the reward. I really do."[43]

Yet people still bet on this game, even as it teeters on becoming a true blood sport. Some sickos will even cheer when an athlete is carted off the field because it'll help win a fantasy football game or possibly insure the point spread is covered. Former NFL player Don Reese laid it out bare in a 1982 *Sports Illustrated* article. "But even if you don't give a damn about the players," he wrote, "if you care about the game you have to be alarmed. What you see on the tube on Sunday afternoon is often a lie. When players are messed up, the game is messed up. The outcome of games is dishonest when playing ability is impaired. You can forget about point spreads or anything else in that kind of atmosphere. All else being equal, you line up 11 guys who don't use drugs against 11 who do—and the guys who don't will win every time."[44]

Reese wrote that in relation to his cocaine abuse during his playing days with the Dolphins, Saints, and Chargers. But the sentiment holds true, if only in reverse. Sadly, today 11 players using drugs might readily beat the team filled with 11 clean players because only the drug-fueled athletes might be able to take the field pain-free.

WEEK 14
@ NFL SECURITY

The biggest outrage in the NFL since perhaps the 1963 gambling scandal coincidentally took place inside an Atlantic City casino elevator. It's undeniable that Baltimore Ravens running back Ray Rice knocked his then-fiancée Janay Palmer unconscious with a single punch during a morning after Valentine's Day argument in 2014. What is questionable is everything the NFL did after that moment.

Much like the NFL's concussion lawsuit versus some of its former players, everything related to the Ray Rice incident revolved around how much the NFL knew and when the league knew it. This debate centered on one key piece of evidence: the security video of Rice's punch from inside the elevator. The NFL's version of how it came to see this graphic video—which wasn't obtained by ESPN or *Sports Illustrated* or FOX Sports or any other "sports news" organization, but rather the celebrity gossip outlet TMZ—goes something like this:

Four days after Rice was arrested for assaulting Palmer,

a member of NFL Security called the Atlantic City Police to request the incident report. The police told the NFL representative to file an official open records request, but the NFL failed to do so. Later that same day, the same NFL Security official attempted to contact the Atlantic County Solicitor's Office regarding the matter despite that office not being involved in the case whatsoever. Unsurprisingly, that phone call proved futile.

As fate would have it, the following day the NFL was scheduled to meet with New Jersey State Police to review security measures utilized for Super Bowl XLVIII which had just been held at the Meadowlands. During that meeting, a different NFL Security member inquired about the Rice incident. Since the state police were not investigating the case, they had no information available for the NFL.

Four months passed with the NFL apparently doing little more than reading news reports related to the case. Then in June a league representative asked the Atlantic County Superior Court pre-trial intervention director for "any and all" information related to the Rice case. The NFL only received back the previously available indictment.

Three months later, and a full seven months after the incident occurred, TMZ stunned the sports world by making the footage from inside the elevator public. And the NFL went into full-blown panic mode.

That was the league's story, and it was sticking to it in the face of an increasing amount of doubt. For example, ABC News spoke with the Atlantic City PD and learned that neither it nor their City Hall had any record of communication with the NFL in regards to this matter. Also, the two entities which did have a copy of the video—the Atlantic County Prosecutor's Office and the New Jersey Gaming Enforcement Division—told ABC News that the league never contacted either of them.[1] Even more damning was an Associated Press report which stated that the NFL *did* receive the inside-the-elevator video on April 9. The AP's source even played a brief voicemail message from a woman with an NFL office phone number acknowledging receipt of the video while proclaiming, "You're right. It's terrible."[2]

In an attempt to counter such reporting while saving its reputation, the NFL brought in no less an authority than former director of the FBI Robert S. Mueller III to investigate the league's (mis)handling of this entire circus. On the one hand, what the hell did it matter when the NFL saw that tape? What happened, happened. No one really assumed otherwise and Rice never denied the incident took place. In the resultant fallout, Rice and Janay reconciled and were married while the Ravens released Rice due to his off-the-field conduct. For all intents and purposes, the incident was resolved. Yet none of that preserved the NFL's precious "integrity." That's why Mueller was brought into the fold.

Unsurprisingly to those who follow such league-initiated "investigations," according to a press report summarizing Mueller's findings, "We found no evidence that anyone at the NFL had or saw the in-elevator video before it was publicly shown. We also found no evidence that a woman at the NFL acknowledged receipt of that video in a voicemail message on April 9, 2014."[3] Or, in other words, regardless of what the AP reported—which, if fabricated, could easily have led to a libel suit (but never did)—the NFL told the truth, the whole truth, and nothing but the truth.

The press release regarding Mueller's report also included the following: "We concluded there was substantial information about the incident—even without the in-elevator video—indicating the need for a more thorough investigation. The NFL should have done more with the information it had, and should have taken additional steps to obtain all available information about the February 15 incident."[4]

Excuse me for a moment while I scoff at this.

This was not the behavior of the entity known as NFL Security that I have come to know and loathe. NFL Security is a highly efficient internal league police force reminiscent of the former East German Stasi. It is staffed with former members of the FBI, CIA, DEA, Secret Service and local law enforcement. These are people who know how to investigate criminal activity, and most importantly, do so quietly.

ESPN legal analyst Lester Munson said of NFL Security on the Dan Le Batard radio show, "The most interesting thing to me is to watch how these NFL security people operate. I have encountered them in the course of my reporting. I was bumping into them in the Michael Vick story for about three weeks in Virginia. They are expert investigators, former federal agents, a lot of police chiefs, a lot of detectives—they know exactly what they're doing. And, if they want something, believe me they can get it."[5]

In the case of Ray Rice, Munson believed, "My takeaway is they did not want to see the video of what happened in the elevator, and therefore they didn't get it. They could have had it if they wanted it. If TMZ can get it, the NFL security force can get it....I believe that if they didn't see the video, it's because they did not want to see it. *Somebody* saw it. The Commissioner didn't see it. It gives him a platform now to try to explain what has happened. I think there's some manipulation going on there, and it's not a big surprise if you've seen these guys in operations before. [emphasis in original]"[6]

When Le Batard asked if the NFL was "incompetent, immoral, or ignorant" in this instance, Munson responded with, "My choice among those is that these NFL security agents have been digging up information, spinning it, and hiding it for years. On this occasion, it did not work. Their usual techniques killed them. Now everything has blown up in their face, and there's gonna have to be a scapegoat here, and it's gonna be someone in the security department."[7]

Though no one within the NFL or NFL Security was publicly punished for the Rice "investigation," Munson's point about NFL Security "digging up information, spinning it, and hiding it" should not go unheeded. Just in terms of domestic violence within the league, former Chicago Bears general manager Jerry Angelo told FOX Sports that the NFL "failed to discipline players in 'hundreds and hundreds' of domestic violence cases."[8] He added, "We knew it was wrong....For whatever reason, it just kind of got glossed over....Our business is to win games. We've got to win games, and the commissioner's job is to make sure the credibility of the National Football League is held in the highest esteem. But to start with that, you have to know who's representing the shield....We got our priorities a little out of order."[9]

Angelo was speaking as a 30-year front office veteran, but not as an owner. For the owners, the *only* priority is protecting the shield. It is their money-maker, and in some cases, their lifeblood. To ensure the league's integrity survives all attacks, the NFL has utilized this secret police force in all sorts of quasi-legal maneuvers behind-the-scenes.

In 1946, two members of the New York Giants, fullback Merle Hapes and quarterback Frank Filchock, were accused of taking a bribe to throw the NFL Championship Game against the Chicago Bears. When interviewed beforehand, Hapes admitted to being offered the bribe, but claimed to refuse it. Filchock pleaded innocence. Hapes' confession led to his suspension while Filchock was allowed to play. In the game (which the Bears were reportedly favored by 10 points), Filchock threw two touchdowns and six interceptions, causing the Giants to lose 24-14. Out of this scandal—one of only three attempts to fix an NFL game the league will admit to—NFL Security was born.

"[NFL Commissioner Bert] Bell's action [of suspending Hapes] established in the public's mind the idea that gamblers were ever under his watchful eye and could never hope to influence pro football while he was commissioner," wrote former NFL owner Harry Wismer. "Bell then followed up by hiring an investigating force of former FBI men to concentrate on gamblers and report to him anything that might involve the league. Bell, unlike some baseball magnates, didn't bother to have the players trailed. Instead, he had his staff frequent the haunts of the bookies and gamblers to find out firsthand if any players, coaches, or owners were associating with them...."[10]

Bell's efforts might have gone much further than that. In an FBI memo obtained via the Freedom of Information Act, a Cleveland-based special agent sent an "urgent" radio transmission to headquarters on June 13, 1957. In it, he detailed that an informant (whose name is redacted) believed his telephone had been tapped. The informant and his secretary "had heard unusual noises and sounds on the line while talking or listening over the phone. He described these sounds as a static crackling which possibly could indicate a clicking noise, but also had heard voices as being in a distance."

The informant then told the agent, "Bert Bell commissioner of the National Football League advised him in February last, they had tapped [Washington Redskins quarterback] Sammy Baugh's phone and other National Football League Officials to determine if they were trying to throw any football games." Baugh's phone was allegedly monitored for three weeks. The informant added, "he (Bell) had heard rumors Baugh was throwing football games. Bell did not elaborate any further about that wire tapping, as to when it was put on, where, or whom, but according to [redacted—the informant] Bell did say they obtained no information indicating Baugh was throwing games. [redacted—the informant] further related that Bell also stated he had tapped phones of national football league [sic] officials to see if there were throwing any games, but Bell did not identify these officials or when or where the taps were placed."

At this point, legendary FBI director J. Edgar Hoover chimed in, telling the agent to "thoroughly interview" the informant and that "the statement or statements obtained should contain full specifics regarding Bert Bell and other National Football League Officials as mentioned in rerad." As detailed in my book *Larceny Games: Sports Gambling, Game Fixing and the FBI*, Hoover often took interest in NFL matters, personally writing comments on many of the Bureau's investigations into fixed games.

Unfortunately, this FBI file did not indicate the informant's connection to Commissioner Bell or why Bell would have told him about tapping the phones of NFL officials. The informant did tell the agent that he wasn't sure if Bell told him this information in "jest" or if he truly meant it. Nonetheless, the informant told the agent that the league might be taking a hard look at LA Rams quarterback Norman Van Brocklin, New York Giants wide receiver Kyle Rote, Cleveland Browns quarterback George Ratterman, and NFLPA attorney Creighton Miller, all of whom were scheduled to testify before the House of Representatives Antitrust Subcommittee hearing on professional sports on July 8, 1957. "Informant related that the National Football League and Bert Bell would gain very valuable information if they were aware of the testimony to be given by these individuals at the hearing." For their own, unstated reasons, the FBI did not follow up on any of this information.

Pete Rozelle succeeded Bert Bell as NFL Commissioner shortly thereafter. Investigative journalist Dan Moldea wrote in his 1989 book *Interference* of Rozelle and NFL Security, "[Rozelle] was forced to deal with a gambling problem of one kind or another every year since he was elected the NFL's chief executive officer in 1960. The fact that most fans can't recall much about the NFL's gambling scandals is testimony to his ability to enhance the league's public image while he policed the conduct of its personnel. 'We have a basic rule in the NFL,' says a former law-enforcement official who advises the NFL on security matters. 'It is to keep it upbeat and keep it positive. But, above all, they want to keep everything quiet.'...The security consultant [continued], 'Rozelle's job [was] that of the protector of the appearance of integrity within the NFL. To Rozelle, a problem with a player's gambling or an owner's having some Mafia associations [didn't] really become a major problem until the situation received publicity. Then he [was] forced to act in a public way.'"[11]

Moldea found out firsthand that NFL Security meant business, even if it perhaps bordered on harassment. He claimed that members of NFL Security followed him during his publicity tour for *Interference*. "They would have a tape of every show," he told me. "They would transcribe every show. I mean it was unbelievable what they did. The effort they put into dealing with me."

Legendary sports broadcaster Howard Cosell echoed Moldea's sentiments. "The NFL, you see," wrote Cosell in 1985, "monitors and collects just about everything that is written about it in newspapers and magazines and said about it on radio and television. Apparently, [Joe] Browne [the NFL's director of information] and his troops go so far as to tape my twice-daily radio reports, which I find a particularly frightening aspect of the NFL's never-ending quest to dominate the media. Like the CIA and the FBI, the NFL has its own enemies list—and I got the distinct impression that I was at the top of it."[12]

Lest you get the impression that this sort of behavior is ancient history, consider what happened when former Bills, Panthers, and Colts executive Bill Polian appeared on ESPN's SportsCenter to discuss the Ray Rice case in August 2014. When asked whether someone within the NFL could have obtained a copy of the in-elevator footage of Rice knocking out Palmer and not shown it to Commissioner Goodell as the Associated Press's story alleged, Polian responded:

"It is very puzzling to me. As a matter of fact, I worked as a vice president in the NFL office in 1993, with respect to football operations. I know how the office works, I've physically been there—it was a different building, not the one they're in now—but it's very difficult for me to understand how that could happen. Especially when you're in a situation that is as high-profile as that particular incident is. It's puzzling, and I have as many questions as everyone else. It's outside my area of expertise. For all the years that I was in the NFL, NFL security, and the NFL's ability to protect its integrity, the so-called 'protection of the shield,' was unmatched in American business. Forget about sports—in American business. I mean, you did not step out of line in the NFL, and if you did, there was an unwritten rule that when you were called into the office—and met with someone who was the commissioner or there at the behest of the commissioner—that you better come clean, that you better tell the truth, the whole truth, and nothing but the truth. And if you work in the office, you better be on top of the details. The office was there to make sure that the clubs, the players, the reputation of the NFL remained unsullied. That goes back to the 1960's with the administration of Pete Rozelle. So this is totally, totally out of character for what I know of the NFL office."[13]

A "technical glitch" then cut off Polian. Twenty minutes later, with the connection reestablished, Polian was asked the exact same question again on air, but this time he responded by saying:

"Well it can happen. It's a very large organization, much larger than when I served in the league office, maybe much larger by a factor of 10. When you have a large, bureaucratic organization, which that is, and there are some that think it is too large, very honestly. Things can slip through the cracks. Someone can make a value judgment who has no right to make that judgment. The CEO, who is in effect Roger Goodell, doesn't get all the information he needs all the time. That's a fact of life in bureaucracies. In this case, we'll find out what happened, and they'll absolutely, they being the NFL and Roger, will have to take steps to make sure it never happens again."[14]

His response wasn't just worded differently, the entire tenor changed from a "no" to a "yes." His second answer clearly leaned in the league's favor, and it made some wonder if an entity like NFL Security was behind the sudden change in Polian's attitude.

If you doubt that the NFL could be that much of a Johnny-on-the-spot in such matters, you'd be mistaken. Outside of the 12 or so operatives staffed at league headquarters, NFL Security is comprised mainly of local security representatives. "We had at least two reps in each city," former head of NFL Security Warren Welsh told me. "We had the primary and the alternate. Part of their responsibility had to do with maintaining a liaison with various law enforcement agencies in their particular area."

"It's set up just like the FBI," an anonymous former NFL team official told the *Washington Post*. "Think of the 32 teams as field offices."[15]

If that weren't enough, many franchises hire their own security personnel to protect their interests. These are often local law enforcement officials who moonlight working for a team. It's led to apparent conflicts of interest. On many occasions, these local "fixers" have been on the scene to help a player in trouble prior to the police arriving, or in some cases, even being called.

"There were a whole lot of incidents," wrote former Dallas Cowboys running back Tony Dorsett, "the fight in the bar, my being stopped in my car with a girl who was to have drugs in her purse, a few shouting matches with crazies, people who would bump into me, call me names, challenge me to get into a fight.

And there were some other things that didn't get into the press. Cowboy management found out about them anyway—they had the pipeline."[16] That pipeline was the Cowboys' security department. Dorsett elaborated, "The Cowboy control was everywhere—aimed at where you lived, your social life, who you dated, what kind of friends you had, what you said and how you said it."[17] It wasn't limited to just the players or coaches, either. Dorsett wrote, "Back then the Cowboys had so much clout that the media were afraid of the organization's power. There was an awful lot of control over what the media would say or write about certain individuals or the franchise itself...."[18]

Former undercover FBI agent Larry Wansley has been the security director for the Cowboys since the 1980's. He told the *Washington Post* in 2014 he was lucky to get three hours of sleep a night. "All my professional life," Wansley said, "has basically been on call, responding to situations that take place and addressing them, resolving them."[19] His main job? "Assets protection. It's players, but everyone included in the organization. I hate to put it that simply, but it is. And that includes the integrity of the organization, the business itself, and it's simply that straightforward."[20]

According to an ESPN article written by brothers Steve Fainaru and Mark Fainaru-Wada, the Pittsburgh Steelers' head of security, Allegheny County sheriff's officer Jack Kearney, is "known in some circles as 'The Cleaner.'"[21] They elaborated, "Kearney earned his colorful nickname by using his authority to smooth over and manage a variety of thorny legal issues involving the Steelers, according to an 'Outside the Lines' examination of court documents and police records, and interviews with law enforcement officers, lawyers and players. Sheriff's deputies are prohibited by policy from holding off-duty positions with 'any potential for a conflict-of-interest,' but on numerous occasions, Kearney has acted on the Steelers' behalf: expediting gun permits for players, providing damage control on a domestic violence case and delivering 24-hour assistance that sometimes blurs the lines between law enforcement agent and protector, according to multiple sources in and out of the sheriff's office. In one case, U.S. marshals believed the Steelers, with Kearney as security director, tipped off a player who had been implicated in a Las Vegas prostitution ring, touching off a day-long manhunt that delayed the player's arrest, federal officials told 'Outside the Lines.'"[22]

Dewan Smith-Williams, wife of former Browns, Ravens, and Saints offensive lineman Wally Williams, claims a similar type of "security agent" told her not to call police when her husband became violent during an incident in 2002. "He went and got a baseball bat and was hitting the walls and doors. I ran into a room, shut the door and called his NFL liaison to say I was really afraid," she told the *New York Daily News*. "[The liaison] said, 'Don't call the police, we'll handle it.' They said I should let Wally leave and they'd call me back to check up on me. That never happened."[23] Smith-Williams also claimed that the police also told her not to press charges against her husband in a prior incident. "Smith-Williams has called the NFL the 'good old boys system' which protects their players at any cost—even the cost of violence to their families."[24]

Though the case of domestic violence involving Ray Rice became a national talking-point, a similar 2014 case played out on the opposite side of the country involving San Francisco 49ers defensive end Ray McDonald. Accused of hitting his pregnant fiancée during a fight at a birthday party, McDonald never bothered to call police during the incident. Instead, "he called the 49ers' security director, who put him in direct contact with a San Jose police sergeant [Sean Pritchard] who had done work for the 49ers and who personally went to McDonald's home multiple times that night."[25] Though Pritchard visited McDonald's home three times during the incident—twice while on active duty for the police while also working for the 49ers—it was McDonald's fiancée who finally called 911.

"This wasn't the first time 49ers security got involved in a problem between McDonald and his fiancée. The [district attorney's interoffice closeout] memo also talks about May 24, when McDonald called 911 saying his fiancée had a gun. McDonald said she didn't point it at him or fire it. About the same time, the 49ers' security director called 911 with a different story: 'He reported that McDonald had just called him and told him that his [McDonald's] girlfriend fired a gun,' the memo said. No charges were filed, but prosecutors investigated. They found McDonald changed his story, saying his fiancée 'did fire a gun into the ground as he drove away from his home that day,' the memo said. As for the security director, the memo said he answered with he 'could not recall McDonald's statement.'"[26]

Though charges were not filed in either of these incidents, McDonald was released by the 49ers in December 2014 after San Jose police named him as a suspect in a sexual assault investigation. Believing in "second chances," the Chicago Bears signed McDonald in March 2015 only to release him in May after he was arrested on charges of domestic violence and child endangerment for allegedly assaulting a woman while she was holding a baby.

The NFL's "fixers" can't always make things right. Yet thanks to the "personal conduct policy," players are at the mercy of the league. This often means what NFL Security learns becomes evidence—no matter how they obtained it—and what the NFL determines to be the punishment for this behavior becomes law—even if real-world law enforcement deems no punishment is necessary.

Written 40 years ago, the semi-fictional novel *North Dallas Forty* perfectly described this double standard implemented to protect the league. In the book, wide receiver Phil Elliot stands accused by the league of using marijuana—which was true—which was uncovered not by the police but by a league security agent. In meeting with team and league officials, Elliot is told, "you continually seem to think this is some sort of court proceeding. We are not concerned with semantics or strict interpretation of the law. There is no record being kept. What we are concerned with is conduct unbecoming professional football. That is what you stand accused of, and I might add, pretty well convicted of."[27]

Without being able to properly defend himself, Elliot is informed of the commissioner's pre-determined decision by letter, "As commissioner it is my duty to preside over and guarantee the integrity of the league from attacks from inside as well as outside our structure. This case, as all cases, has been judged solely on its merits. It is not the position of the commissioner's office that criminal action by legal authorities be initiated before we consider a person's behavior detrimental to the well-being of the game. It is, in fact, desirable from the standpoint of the good name of professional football that undesirables be weeded out and removed from our midst with as little public notice...."[28]

Sound like something Roger Goodell has said?

Former chief of NFL Security Warren Welsh told me its number one job was, "In very broad terms, it was the integrity of the sport. If you say, 'what does that entail?' you're looking at things and your major emphasis would be on things that could possibly—not that they are or have been—but that could possibly interfere with the integrity of the sport."

If that statement was completely true, then I doubt the following fact would stand out as much as it does. Despite researching the NFL and its security department for nearly ten years, I cannot find a single instance where a law enforcement agency, be it federal, state, or even local, has praised NFL Security for its assistance or cooperation in a case. Not one.

At the same time, I can report on hundreds of arrests of NFL players and personnel for an assortment of criminal activities. I can cite many more articles and books where NFL players were followed, monitored, and outright spied upon by NFL representatives. I can even show you FBI files in which the Bureau was told to stand down and let NFL Security do their job, despite potential federal crimes being committed.

Something does not add up. But I believe that's the way the league wants it to be.

WEEK 15
@ REFEREES

Officiating for the NFL is not a job I would want. It's a thankless pursuit. When done correctly, officials are invisible, nameless. Yet make a big enough "mistake," and it becomes national news with the implicated official turning into public enemy #1.

As a case in point, look no further than the ending of the Week 3 *Monday Football Game* between the Green Bay Packers and the Seattle Seahawks in 2012. With eight seconds remaining in the fourth quarter, Seahawks quarterback Russell Wilson chucked up a 24-yard Hail Mary pass caught by Golden Tate for the game-winning touchdown. At least, that's how it reads in the box score.

In reality, that final play was a free-for-all. Tate most certainly committed offensive pass interference prior to making the catch—without being assessed a flag—that is, if he actually did haul in Wilson's toss. Packers defensive back M.D. Jennings appeared to catch the ball, yet when he hit the turf with Tate clinging to him, Tate kinda, sorta pulled the ball away. Both players appeared to have possession (with most observers believing Jennings had more possession). One official immediately ruled the play an interception. Another, standing three feet away from the first, ruled it a touchdown. The first official then changed his signal to match the touchdown call. While chaos ensued, the play was booth reviewed and ultimately stood as called on the field: touchdown. Seattle 14, Green Bay 12.

One call created a mushroom cloud of fallout. The closing line was Green Bay -3. So for those who bet the Packers, the game went from a win to a loss in a millisecond, causing an untold shift in millions of dollars. It also cost the Packers a bye and home field advantage in the divisional round of the playoffs (where they lost to the 49ers in San Francisco). At the same time, the bonus win propelled the Seahawks into the playoffs as a wildcard, usurping the Chicago Bears' rightful place.

As this game was played in Seattle, one might be tempted to think the result was a bit of home cookin'. And yes, "home field advantage" is a real phenomenon. In the 2011 book *Scorecasting: The Hidden Influences Behind How Sports Are Played and Games Are Won, authors Tobias J. Moskowitz of the University of Chicago and L. Jon Werthheim of Sports Illustrated reported that* in the last ten years the percentage of home games won in the MLB was 53.9 percent, the NHL 55.7 percent, the NBA 60.5 percent, and the NFL 57.3 percent.

Prior to explaining why this was the case, the authors wrote, "Before considering the causes of the home field advantage, keep this premise in mind: There is considerable economic incentive for home teams to win as often as possible. When the home team wins, the consumers—that is, the ticket-buying fans—leave happy. The better the home team plays, the more likely fans are to buy tickets and hats and T-shirts, renew their luxury suite leases, and drink beer, overpriced and watered down as it might be. The better the home team plays, the more likely businesses and corporations are to buy sponsorships and the more likely local television networks are to bid for rights fees. A lot of sports marketing, after all, is driven by the desire to associate with a winner. In San Antonio, if the fans consistently left disappointed, it's unlikely that AT&T would slather its name and logo on most of the surface area of the arena or that Budweiser Select, Sprite, 'your Texas Ford dealers,' Southwest Airlines, and other sponsors would underwrite T-shirt giveaways, Bobble Head Night, and a halftime shooting contest.

"By extension, the leagues have an incentive for the home teams to win. Although attendance and revenue rise in step with winning percentage for most teams, they rise even more sharply with *home* winning percentage. And healthier individual franchises make for a stronger collective. Does this mean leagues and executives are fixing games in favor of home teams? Of course not. But does it make sense that they would want to take subtle measures to endow the home team with (legal) edges? Sure. It would be irrational if they *didn't*. [emphasis in original]"[1]

After a bit of debate, Moskowitz and Wertheim declared the primary factor in the creation of home field advantage was the referees. "What we've found is that officials are biased, confirming years of fans' conspiracy theories. But they're biased not against the louts screaming unprintable epithets at them. They're biased for them, and the bigger the crowd, the worse the bias. In fact, 'officials' bias' is the most significant contributor to home field advantage."[2]

About the NFL, the authors concluded, "Could referee bias explain a large part of the home field advantage in football? Absolutely....The fact that home teams in football have better offensive stats—such as rushing more successfully and having longer time of possession—could be the result of getting more favorable calls, fewer penalties, and fewer turnovers."[3]

Though a somewhat shocking conclusion, it is all written off by Moskowitz and Wertheim as being simply caused by referees' *unconscious* biases. Officials don't even realize they are doing it because, basically, it's psychological in nature, and there's not much to be done to counter its effects.

What about those economic advantages that go hand-in-hand with home field advantage? Don't worry. Moskowitz and Wertheim wrote, "First, let's be clear: Is there a conspiracy afoot in which officials are somehow instructed to rule in favor of the home team, especially since the league has an economic incentive to boost home team wins? Almost unquestionably no. We're convinced that the vast majority of, if not all, officials are upstanding professionals, ***uncorrupted and incorruptible***, consciously doing their best to ensure fairness. [emphasis added]"[4]

In all honesty, I don't know if I've ever read a more absurd statement in a non-fiction book than that. Referees are human. They are fallible. And as numerous FBI files have shown me, they are certainly corruptible. In fact, the authors almost admitted as much shortly thereafter. Moskowitz and Wertheim wrote: "Remember, too, that on top of the anxiety caused by passionate and sometimes angry fans, the refs receive stress from their supervisors and superiors. In a variety of ways—some subtle, some not—officials must take in cues that the league has an economic incentive for home teams to do well. If your boss sent a subtle but unmistakable message that Outcome A was preferable to Outcome B, when you were forced to make a difficult, uncertain, and quick decision, how would you be inclined to act?"[5]

All of the above may have come into play during that Monday Night game, but what truly made it so memorable was the fact the referees making that deciding call were substitutes. In its never-ending quest for "integrity," the NFL locked out its real officials prior to the 2012 season and filled its officiating ranks with an assortment of unqualified referees mostly queued from the NCAA's division II and III. The league's goal in the lockout? To save a few million dollars in referee pay and benefits.

One of those replacement referees, Jerry Frump , told *Time* Magazine, "We were pawns. This really became a business deal. I told my crew when we first got together, I said, 'Gentlemen, you're now working for probably one of the largest corporations in the country, maybe even the world. We need to keep that in mind, because we need to conduct ourselves professionally and in a way that does not degrade or disrespect what they stand for.' This was [the NFL's] choice. They chose to take this position in the negotiation with the union. Whether I would have [taken the job]—if I hadn't done it, somebody else would have. We did the best we could."[6]

Their best, unfortunately, was nowhere near good enough for football fans or pundits (even though no one stopped watching). The NFLPA posted a letter to the league on its website which stated, "It is lost on us as to how you allow a Commissioner to cavalierly issue suspensions and fines in the name of player health and safety yet permit the wholesale removal of the officials that you trained and entrusted to maintain that very health and safety. It has been reported that the two sides are apart by approximately $60,000 per team. We note that your Commissioner has fined an individual player as much in the name of 'safety.' Your actions are looking more and more like simple greed. As players, we see this game as more than the 'product' you reference at times. You cannot simply switch to a group of cheaper officials and fulfill your legal, moral, and duty obligations to us and our fans. You need to end the lockout and bring back the officials immediately."[7]

The Monday Night debacle did just that, reinstating the NFL's true officiating corps for Week 4. Although some NFL owners didn't see what the big deal was with the replacement refs. While using them in the preseason, Cowboys owner Jerry Jones said, "As long as it's the same for both sides—and it will be—we'll be all right. And they're going to get better as they move along."[8] Texans owner Bob McNair agreed, "We have complaints, it doesn't matter who's officiating. And we look back at it as to those calls that we think were bad calls, and we don't have any more now than we had before. Now, clearly the officials that we have now are not as good professionally as the ones we've had, otherwise we would have had the others all along. But in terms of the impact on the game, I've been watching it and frankly I can't see any difference."[9]

That might have been the case for McNair because in actuality the "real" NFL officials are frequently as off-kilter as their replacements appeared to be.

In 2013, 40-year old Dean Blandino was named the NFL's vice president of officiating. According to the league's press release about his promotion, he joined the NFL fresh out of college as an officiating intern in 1994, served as an instant replay official from 1999-2003, and managed the NFL's instant replay program from 2003-2009. What it failed to mention was that Blandino also worked as a stand-up comic[10] and never once served as an on-the-field official. Nonetheless, Blandino was handed officiating's top spot.

At the 2014 National Association of Sports Officials (NASO) annual convention, Blandino gave the keynote address. One way to improve officiating, he claimed, was through consistency. "We have to make sure that we're checking at each level that the message is clear," he stated. "And how do we do that? How do we achieve consistency in officiating? That's the goal. Coaches, players, administrators—all of our stakeholders—want consistency....But the only way to achieve true consistency is through a consistent evaluation system. Officials must be held to a standard, and that standard should be applied across the board. We need to shrink the gray areas, simplify the rules…effective communication and consistent evaluation will lead to consistent officiating."[11]

It's not easy to be consistent given the state of the NFL's rules. This league reacts in the same way our government often does. As soon as there is a perceived "wrong," no matter how once-in-a-lifetime the play may have been, the NFL attempts to correct it by adding/altering a rule. Instead of clarifying, these adaptations only seem to muddy the waters. Blandino alluded to this in his address when he held up two NFL rulebooks, the current version and one from 1940. He announced that there was only a one page difference between the two; however, "the pre-World War II edition was closer to pocket size."[12] "I can fit four pages of (the older book) onto every page of (the 2014 book)," Blandino told the crowd. "And the 2014 book has 130 pages of casebook plays. Not 130 casebook plays—130 pages. Because as game officials, we need to have every situation accounted for."[13]

Three of the plays/penalties the NFL decided to focus on in 2014 were illegal contact, illegal use of the hands, and defensive holding. In the 2013 preseason, illegal contact was called 18 times, defensive holding 38 times, and illegal use of the hands 28 times. When the 2014 preseason kicked off, yellow flags littered every stadium in the league. Illegal contact was penalized 99 times, defensive holding 172 times, and illegal use of the hands 124 times; a five-fold increase.[14] There were worries NFL officials were becoming too strict as games were noticeably slowing due to penalties.

To the rescue came Blandino. As the preseason wound down, he told NFL Network's NFL Total Access Postgame, "When the regular season rolls around, I think everybody will be on the same page and I think you'll see those foul totals go down."[15] While an average of 23.1 penalties were being called per game during the preseason, Blandino believed that number would drop to around 15 or 16 in the regular season. "That's the level that it's been and I think once everybody gets through this adjustment period I think that's where we'll see the penalties because we certainly don't want to delay the game but we also have to call the violations that are there," Blandino said.[16]

But, wait a second. If those preseason penalties were legitimate—and no one claimed they weren't—what would cause the total number of flags thrown a game to drop by seven or eight as Blandino suggested? Would players wise up? Would referees intentionally scale back? Was Blandino going to employ some Jedi mind tricks? Something had to give because by Week 16 of the 2014 season, Blandino's prediction proved true. The NFL's 17 officiating crews were calling an average of 16.1 penalties per game.[17]

Yet inconsistencies existed within that average. For starters, the range of the average number of penalties called per official varied. According to ESPN, referee Carl Cheffers was issuing 19.1 penalties a game while fellow official Clete Blakeman called a mere 13.[18] Six penalties may not seem like much, but in a game of inches, a 30-yard (or more) swing created by six additional flags could be huge. And it wasn't just the number of calls, but what the referees were penalizing varied, too.

Take offensive holding, the one call that some argue could be made on every down. It's one of many subjective penalties in the NFL; one that's an "I know it when I see it" kind of play for most officials. Through Week 16 of the 2014 season, the officiating crews headed by Carl Cheffers and Jerome Boger each had penalized teams for offensive holding 54 times. Yet working the same number of games, Walt Coleman's crew only threw 26 flags for offensive holding and Bill Vinovich's squad issued a mere 23. Other subjective penalties featured similar discrepancies. Gene Steratore called unnecessary roughness 19 times by Week 16, Clete Blakeman, five. Illegal use of the hands, a preseason focal point, was flagged 27 times by Walt Anderson, but on just four occasions by Walt Coleman.[19]

Was that the type of consistency Blandino demanded? Where one crew will call a particular penalty less than half the time another will?

Punishing a referee for poor work is rare. Every game and play is reviewed to examine each official's performance. The highest graded referees are awarded positions in the playoffs and Super Bowl. If it's felt that a particular official isn't working up to NFL standards, he can be downgraded. It takes a very large consensus of opinion for this to happen. So much so that even when the NFL publicly acknowledges an official made a glaring mistake (which occurs almost weekly), such corrections won't lead to a black mark against the offending referee. "As part of evaluating the performance of our game officials," the NFL stated, "the officiating supervisors recognize that for an incorrect call on a close judgment play the official may have used appropriate reasoning. On such a call, the official is not downgraded."[20]

Fans might be more tolerable of the league's officiating if what are believed to be steadfast rules weren't so apparently open to interpretation. One ref's holding is another's legal block, even though both could point to the same specific rule to justify their decision. As such, the league's best defense against negative perceptions is an increase in transparency. But that word's definition depends on whom you ask.

"If you asked 100 sports fans who were walking down the street what is transparency," said former VP of NFL officiating turned FOX Sports commentator Mike Pereira at the NASO conference, "they would say to you 'admitting that you're wrong.' I mean that's the definition in their mind of transparency. And I think we have to move the needle and bring the officials out from behind the curtain so to speak. I think this: We are now a part of the game. No matter what level we're on we're part of the game. I mean why are we part of the game? Because social media has made us a part of the game, technology has made us part of the game."[21]

NASO president and founder Barry Mano added that sports officials in general have been "forced to lead a cloak and dagger existence. We are forced to always not say something. We're never permitted to comment because I guess we're too stupid, we can't comment. I mean part of that plays out here. If you keep pushing a group of people behind the scenes and under a cloak or a veil what do you think the general public is going to think about us?"[22]

Whether they want to be or not, the NFL has always protected its referees. Rarely are they interviewed, and if they do speak post-game, it is often to an unnamed "pool reporter." At the same time, players and coaches are not allowed to criticize the officiating. Any such talk is almost certainly met with a hefty fine.

Instant replay was supposed to smooth over everything and lead to better and more accurately officiated games. Instead, it has turned into officiating's Achilles heel. Television, especially the advent of HDTV, has warped officiating in ways the league could never have expected. Now anyone sitting at home, in a bar, or even watching the game on their smartphone can see mistakes being committed by referees that affect the outcomes of games, causing knee-jerk reactions within the NFL.

To combat this and aid in transparency, the NFL launched a two-pronged attack in 2014. Blandino laid out the league's plan at the NASO conference. First was the implementation of a "command center" to oversee all instant replay challenges. Based in New York, it allowed communication between Blandino, his staff, and the on-the-field referee involved with the replay. "Digital feeds are being sent all over the country," Blandino said, "and someone in New York is making a decision affecting the outcome of a game in Seattle. It's amazing where we've come."[23]

The goal was obviously to make the right call in each

situation. The more brainpower the league engaged the more likely it was going to get things correct. But the decision to include Blandino and Co. in making in-game rulings led some (like me) to a conspiratorial conclusion. Would the "right" call actually be the correct call, or would it be the one that aided the team the NFL preferred? If the league was already placing its finger on the scales to tip games in favor of the home team more often than not, who's to say the conversations taking place during reviews aren't also predisposed to certain outcomes? If this weren't the case, and the league truly sought more transparency in its officiating, then why aren't the conversations between the stadium referee and NFL HQ broadcast to its television audience? They are just discussing the finer points of the rulebook, right?

Instead, viewers are subjected to announcers' commentary now bolstered by an "officiating expert" such as the aforementioned Mike Pereira. A Big Brother invasion of the broadcast booth is the second part of the NFL's plan. "Blandino said the goal today is to 'communicate accurate and timely officiating information to the largest possible audience.' By monitoring telecasts of games, the officiating department can confirm or correct announcers' comments regarding rules. The department has the ability to speak to the producers or the commentators off the air. Additionally, the network can contact the command center to get an interpretation. 'We're going to proactively explain rules,' he said. 'If we're speaking with one voice, it helps for clarity, consistency.'"[24]

This'll hold true except, you know, in the case of judgment calls where interpretation might actually be needed. "Judgment calls happen every down, every play whatever sport you're in," Blandino said. "And we are not going to go on air talking about judgment calls. It may be correct, it may be incorrect. We'll evaluate that, but that's not what this is about. We'll discuss the relevant rule and what the officials are keying on as part of an educational process. But this is not to second-guess game officials and their judgment."[25] As for truly egregious errors, "Those will be handled on a case-by-case basis," Blandino stated.[26]

All of this came to an ugly head in the one place the NFL didn't want it to: the playoffs. Much to the league's chagrin, wildcard weekend and the divisional round were both marred by questionable calls. These two particular plays act as a perfect microcosm of all the damage the NFL has done to itself when it comes to officiating its games.

Up 20-17 with just over eight minutes remaining in the game, the Detroit Lions had driven from their own 5-yard line to the Dallas Cowboys' 46. On 3rd-and-1, Lions quarterback Matthew Stafford faded back and lofted a pass up to tight-end Brandon Pettigrew. To all in attendance, those watching at home, and even the nearest referee, it appeared that Cowboys linebacker Anthony Hitchens committed pass interference to prevent Pettigrew from making the reception. A flag flew, referee Pete Morelli announced the foul to the disheartened Cowboys' faithful, and the ball was spotted at the new line of scrimmage. It appeared as if the Cowboys playoff run was at an end.

Then, without a word of explanation from Morelli, the penalty was erased. Morelli simply announced, "There is no foul on the play." It was Lions' ball back at the Cowboys' 46-yard line.

The decision caught everyone off-guard. It stunned even FOX's broadcasting crew. No one could explain what just occurred, because, well, nothing like it had happened before.

Despite having cameras covering every inch of the field from multiple angles, NFL rules forbid reviewing penalties either by a coach's challenge or by a call from the replay official. So the play wasn't reviewable, despite the league specifically instituting instant replay to get calls "right." Yet without replay's assistance *something* had to occur to reverse the initial pass interference call. Since NFL referees are now wired to each other to ease communication and since the replay official high above the field has a direct connection to the NFL's command center, methinks all of these entities were involved in overturning that penalty.

"What do you expect when you come to Dallas?" Lions safety Glover Quin said after the game. "Ain't gonna speculate that. But the league likes the story lines and headlines."[27]

Blandino's call for consistency and communication was only heeded after the game when Morelli offered up the official explanation for picking up that flag. "The back judge threw his flag for defensive pass interference," Morelli said. "We got other information from another official from a different angle that thought the contact was minimal and didn't warrant pass interference. He thought it was face guarding [which is not a penalty in the NFL]."[28]

Yet defensive pass interference wasn't the only penalty should have been called on this play. While the referees were assessing the foul (that is, prior to picking up the flag to negate it), Cowboys wide receiver Dez Bryant stormed out onto the field without wearing his helmet to yell at the refs. This was caught on camera and highlighted during the broadcast. However, none of the officials apparently saw Bryant—despite the fact he was verbally abusing them—because if one of them had, it would have resulted in a 15-yard unsportsmanlike conduct penalty. So even when the refs decided not to assess the pass interference call the Lions should've been sitting pretty with 1st-and-10 at the Cowboys' 31.

Only they weren't. It was 4th-and-1.

The Lions subsequently shanked a punt, the Cowboys drove the length of the shortened field, and with just over two minutes remaining, scored game-winning touchdown. Dallas 24, Detroit 20. As Jerry Jones jumped up and down in the arms of

New Jersey governor Chris Christie (who should've been the NFL's sworn enemy for attempting to legalize sports betting in his state), the rest of Cowboys' nation celebrated a tainted victory.

That sumptuous treat would melt into a bitter pill for the Cowboys to swallow the following week in Green Bay. As time ticked down to less than five minutes to play, the Cowboys faced a 4th-and-2 on the Packers' 32-yard line. Instead of running with (my fantasy nemesis) DeMarco Murray, quarterback Tony Romo threw up a bomb for Dez Bryant. Leaping over Packers' defensive back Sam Shields, Bryant caught the ball, took three steps, and stretched out for the end zone. Upon hitting the turf, the ball popped out of Bryant's extended hand, flipped in the air, and was cradled back in his arms. The official positioned at the goal line not six feet from the play signaled it a catch. Cowboys' ball, 1st-and-goal at the Packers' 1-yard line.

Packers' head coach Mike McCarthy quickly issued his red challenge flag. The catch was going to be reviewed. Of course, unlike the subjective penalty call in the Lions-Cowboys game, this subjective ruling of a catch *could* be challenged because the NFL says so.

Referee Gene Steratore went under the hood and conferenced with Blandino back in New York. Though ruled a catch on the field, upon further review the NFL decided this was an incomplete pass. There would be no second round of Jones-on-Christie man-love. Packers' ball, first down. Game, set, match. Green Bay 26, Dallas 21.

"When it happened I did not think for a minute it was not a catch," former Cowboys quarterback turned FOX Sports broadcaster Troy Aikman told *Sports Illustrated*. "When it happened, I'm thinking it is an unbelievable catch. Then when we went to break, [Fox rules analyst] Mike Pereira said he thought the call was going to be overruled. I said, 'Really? It looks to me like if anything is changed to the call it will be ruled a touchdown.' They ruled it the way Mike saw it. I'm not going to argue with Mike. After the game you hear from all sorts of people about the call and 99 percent of my friends who texted me are just fans and most don't know the rules. But I did hear from some coaches and that got my attention. And they felt it was a poor call."[29]

Some NFL fans (like me) saw this as a week-late "make-up" call. The Cowboys won a playoff game on a "bad" call, now they had one taken away on a similar decision. This was done, the thought goes, so the league wouldn't be seen as playing favorites (although both controversial calls and games did go the home team's way. Just sayin').

The NFL had its ways of explaining the non-catch. Blandino tweeted shortly after the call was made, "Bryant going to the ground. By rule he must hold onto it throughout entire process of contacting the ground. He didn't so it is incomplete."[30] Steratore went into more detail post-game, saying, "Although the receiver is possessing the football, he must maintain possession of that football throughout the entire process of the catch. In our judgment he maintained possession but continued to fall and never had another act common to the game. We deemed that by our judgment to be the full process of the catch and at the time he lands and the ball hits the ground it comes loose as it hits the ground, which would make that incomplete. Although he re-possesses it, it does contact the ground when he reaches so the repossession is irrelevant because it was ruled an incomplete pass when he had the ball hit the ground."[31]

Here again is a failing of Blandino's cry for consistency and clarity. Phrases like "process of the catch" and "a move common to the game" can't be deciphered. The Supreme Court would render split decisions on what both terms meant. So what has happened is fans who have watched football their entire lives no longer understand something as simple as what makes for a "catch." I think you'd be hard pressed to find a single football fan who didn't believe Bryant caught that critical 4th down pass as long as those same people didn't then try to interpret the NFL's rule(s) for what a "catch" is. That's how convoluted the NFL has made its rules. What you see with your eyes in beautiful 4K resolution on your 60" LED TV screen can be wrong…if the NFL is making the final decision.

The situation is not about to improve. "The NFL commissioner and all of his henchmen want to have a say in officiating when they know nothing about what they're talking about," Mike Pereira said at the NASO conference. "I mean it's really amazing the phone calls that I used to get from [NFL Commissioner Roger] Goodell during games and he had no idea of what he was talking about, yet he and his guys are setting policy."[32]

WEEK 16
@ TV

"When athletes are no longer heroes to you anymore, it's time to stop writing sports" – Grantland Rice, legendary 1920's sportswriter—and unbeknownst to him—namesake for ESPN's Grantland website

Like Dr. Frankenstein and his monster, television gave life to the modern NFL. Not in the exposure the sport received from being broadcast, though that certainly helped. No, the league's literal debt of gratitude comes from the huge influx of money the networks have thrust upon the league since the 1950's for the rights to its games. The NFL signed its first billion dollar contract with its three television broadcast partners in 1978. Today, ESPN alone pays twice that amount—$1.9 billion—just for the rights to *Monday Night Football*. Or, in other words, the Walt Disney Company (which owns ESPN) forks out over $110 million for each of its 17 primetime *MNF* telecasts a year.

In 2014, each of the NFL's 32 teams received just over

$224 million though the league's revenue sharing program. This is only known because the publicly owned Green Bay Packers must report their yearly earnings (every other team's financial records are secret). The bulk of this income, over $6 billion, came from the sale of the league's television broadcast rights. This money more than covered each team's $133 million salary cap.

If an EMP knocked out America's electronic capabilities tomorrow, the NFL would swiftly die. It could not survive on ticket sales alone (unless it really, really jacked up its prices). It desperately needs television's money to be the biggest, baddest sports league in the nation.

What is more concerning, however, is how television has come to need the NFL. Without football, the major networks would struggle for survival.

"On the walls of 345 Park Avenue, the NFL's headquarters in New York, top executives have a framed copy of a headline that ran in [the *Wall Street Journal*] in 2011. It says 'The League That Runs Television.'"[1] That headline is not far from the truth. Within four months of kicking off its 2014 season, NFL games were 28 of the 30 most-watched television programs for the year.[2] Only Game 7 of the Royals-Giants World Series and an episode of *NICS* managed to crack the NFL's dominance. Hell, the Pro Bowl, the most meaningless of all NFL games, typically garners higher ratings than MLB or NBA playoff games. And believe it or not, in terms of total audience the Super Bowl accounts for the 20 most-watched programs in US history with the 2014 Seahawks-Patriots Super Bowl being #1 all-time, drawing in 168 million viewers.

These numbers are staggering, especially when taken into the context of the season the NFL endured. Though plagued with controversies including two separate player-initiated class-action lawsuits filed against the league, players being arrested for domestic and child abuse as well as other crimes, and incidents such as the New England Patriots' "Deflategate," the NFL welcomed over 202 million unique viewers in 2014, representing 80 percent of all television homes and 68 percent of potential viewers in the U.S.[3]

Not only don't fans appear to care how these scandals mar the NFL's "integrity," it might actually be a draw for some viewers. Just three days after Ray Rice was cut by the Ravens for assaulting his fiancée in that Atlantic City elevator, his former team squared off against the Pittsburgh Steelers on CBS's *Thursday Night Football*. I'll let CBS CEO Les Moonves take it from here:

"Obviously, Baltimore against Pittsburgh is a very good matchup. Obviously, Baltimore and their team were a little bit in the news, you may have heard, other than the football game, so I'm sure that may have attracted a little bit more attention. Possibly in the wrong way, but it did attract attention. And the number was very good. The game wasn't very good. The number could have been even higher if we had a close game, but people started tuning out in the last half hour, 45 minutes."[4]

Moonves was being modest. In fact, the ratings for the Ravens-Steelers *Thursday Night Football* game "were higher than anything CBS has shown on a Thursday in the last eight years."[5]

"This week we have a lesser matchup with Atlanta and Tampa Bay," Moonves continued, "so the numbers will be down, and we expect the other networks to point that out. The advertising is terrific...football is still the best thing on television...the ratings are phenomenal, the advertising rates still go up, there are still certain advertisers that have to have it...we love having those games on Thursday night."[6]

Nothing pulls viewers to their televisions in the way the NFL magically can. In the age of DVRs, on-demand programming, Netflix, and everything else tempting consumers, sporting events are the one show that demand to be watched live.

Never mind that the average three hour NFL game delivers less than 11 minutes of actual action, its in-the-moment consumption has made it mandatory viewing. Even more so when one has money riding on his fantasy team(s) and other such wagers.

The Big Four TV networks of NBC, CBS, ABC/ESPN and FOX (or should I say Comcast, CBS Corporation, Disney, and News Corp, the media conglomerates which own those networks respectively) have taken notice. Unable to retain viewership as they once could through scripted and now "reality" programming, the networks have come to rely on sports—and mainly the NFL—to attract viewers in the key 18-49 demographic range. Grabbing that group's attention is the best way to lure the advertising money needed by the networks to drive profitability.

The networks aligned with the league have passed the massive cost of doing business with the NFL down to the consumer. You don't really think those games you watch on Thursday, Saturday, Sunday, and Monday are *free*, do you? Sure, most are broadcast on "free" TV, but you're paying for it—in more ways than one.

The most obvious cost for consumers has been seen in the rising price of cable and satellite TV. Fans and non-fans alike are shelling out more and more money for sports whether they tune into the games or not. DirectTV was scheduled to raise its monthly rates to all subscribers by six percent in early 2015, mostly to recoup the costs of its multi-billion dollar deal for the exclusive rights to the NFL Sunday Ticket package. Other cable companies such as Time Warner and Cablevision were planning rate hikes from $2 to $5 a month to offset the price increase for carrying channels such as ESPN. The "Worldwide Leader in Sports" demands over $6.50 per subscriber from the cable companies—the most of any non-pay TV channel by nearly $5. At the time of this writing, the second most expensive non-premium cable channel behind ESPN was TNT at $1.61 per subscriber (NFL Network was the second most expensive sports network, costing $1.31). In fact, the average cost-per-channel per cable bill for sports programming has risen from about $.50 in 2000 to over $1 in 2014. During the same time period, the cost for a movie programming dropped from $1.25 to about $.80. And the rise in sports channel prices is expected to exceed $1.40 by 2018.[7]

"How far will consumers go with how much they are willing to pay for sports on cable, even if wildly popular?" said Matt Polka, president of the small cable trade group the American Cable Association, to the *Washington Post*. "In a weird way, the sports programmers are going to harm themselves if they keep going this way."[8]

As the costs of subscription TV rises, more and more people are cutting the cord. Instead of paying for channels and programming they don't watch, consumers are turning to online and other streaming content options. ESPN has been hit hard by this growing trend. Since 2011 the network has lost over seven percent of its subscribers, putting its head honchos in a precarious situation. While the price of doing business with leagues like the NFL refuses to abate, ESPN is in a cost cutting frenzy. It needed to dump $100 million from its 2016 budget, and another $250 million by 2017. This may be why high-priced talent such as Bill Simmons, Colin Cowherd, and Keith Olbermann were all sent packing by the network in early 2015.

This shift in America's viewing habits doesn't sit well with the powers that be at the NFL, either. Although the league launched the NFL Network in 2003, it knows it cannot generate $6 billion in revenue strictly through its own media outlet, even if it broadcast every game. Pay-per-view was an option the league once contemplated, but it realized that sort of distribution would not be as profitable as its current course of business. So the league has begun to get creative, starting with its $1 billion exclusive partnership with the mobile provider Verizon. It has to if it's going to achieve Commissioner Goodell's goal of increasing the NFL's revenue stream to $25 billion by 2027.

This is why gambling may play a significant role in both the NFL's and the TV networks' future plans and profits. If sports gambling were legalized and then embraced by these entities, there is plenty of ways to monetize such connections. FOX Sports has already gotten a jump on this. In 2015, it led a group which invested $300 million in the "non-gambling" daily fantasy website DraftKings, expecting to see that industry's growth tie directly to its sports viewership. ESPN had originally agreed to a similar deal with DraftKings, but Disney backed out as concerns about the "family friendliness" of the site squashed its enthusiasm. Still, ESPN did agree to an ad-only deal with the DFS company.

CBS Sports took a slightly different path into this "non-gambling" foray. Through its highly-rated fantasy sports website SportsLine, CBS had already provided customers with the "CBS Sports Office Pool Manager." It gave players "countless options for customizing your rules: Pick straight up, against the spread or with confidence points, choose pick'em or survivor format, select pro [football] games, college or both." It also offered customers a free NCAA Final Four bracket pool manager.

But in the summer of 2015, CBS Sports revamped SportsLine to make it a full bore gambling-related website. The advertising email I received from the company in August 2015 claimed "The NEW SportsLine combines the power of data with the insight of sports experts to create the ultimate sports picks." It boasted, "Engineered by Science. Perfected by Experts." That's right. The CBS-owned site wasn't just posting odds and betting lines, it was leaning heavily into the tout business by offering supposed "expert" advice and picks (backed by data!) on every game. To top it off, while some advice was free, much of it came with a price: $10 a month or $100 for the year. So I take that back. CBS wasn't leaning into the tout business; the company had officially entered it.

But the real cost to fans does not come in a monetary form. Whether you realize it or not, the price paid for all of this media access is objectivity. The more the networks invest in not just the NFL but all the major leagues, the less adversarial they have become in covering these entities. Let's face it, ESPN isn't about to give the NFL $1.9 billion a year and then turn around and sic a team of investigative reporters on the league to uncover as much dirt as possible about its players, coaches, and owners. That would just be bad business (and may be why the outspoken Simmons and Olbermann were the first victims of ESPN's budget dump). Instead, the two work hand-in-hand, mitigating any potential disasters while merrily tallying their profits.

"When you are sponsoring sports events and generating profits," two-time president of CBS Sports Neal Pilson told the *New York Times*, "you can create conflicts and problems. In CBS Sports, we have major business relationships that are worth billions of dollars and are renewable. You cannot use the people associated with CBS Sports to investigate the morals of the people you do business with."[9]

Comforting thought, isn't it, sports fans?

Pilson's philosophy could be applied across the board at every network because they are the paymasters. Much like players are replaceable cogs in the NFL machine, reporters fill the same role within the media. "Very early in life a newsman must make his decision: Will I sell out my readers?" wrote legendary *New York Daily News* sportswriter Dick Young. "Will I write only nice things, so that the athletes will talk to me? If the answer is no, he becomes a newspaperman. If yes, he becomes a hero worshipper, a house man, a sycophant, a dispenser of pap, and perhaps he goes on to radio and TV."[10]

It is very difficult to be a sportswriter and have the freedom to publish the stories you want *and* get paid a living wage. Beat writers often have to self-censor to maintain access to the locker room, and even nationally syndicated personalities never reveal all they know. While I wrote for the *USA Today* and MLB Advanced Media (MLBAM) outlet SportsonEarth.com, I was allowed tremendous latitude. The SoE editors gave every writer the freedom to cover nearly any topic they felt needed to be discussed. Then, due to a "restructuring," *USA Today* pulled its support of the site. MLBAM took total control. Ninety-five percent of the staff was terminated (technically our contracts were null-and-void with *USA Today*'s departure), and MLBAM decided what direction the site would take. Writers like me were no longer welcome.

The same notion applies to broadcasting. Hall of Fame defensive tackle Art Donovan might have laid it out the best, writing, "The first thing you have to realize about the modern game of football is that it's a television event. Naturally, the networks want to protect their interest, so to the announcers broadcasting these games, everybody's a nice guy. You can be a thief, a murderer, a gangster, you name it, and these guys up in the TV booth can't do anything but sing your praises....Let's try reality, fellas. The guy they're canonizing down on the field is the same guy who tried to run his wife over in the driveway last week. Wonderful fellow, right? The kind of guy you'd like to your daughter to bring home, right? Give me a break! Who needs that crap on television? Just once I'd like to hear the announcer say that so-and-so's a helluva safety, or a goddamn good quarterback, but he also has the nasty habit of kicking the hell out of his wife. Something like that. But that's what television has done to the league. It's all show biz."[11]

Upon the release of the Ray Rice-based Mueller Report, the job of selling it to the football-watching public fell to Al Michaels and Cris Collinsworth during NBC's NFL playoff coverage. Michaels, clearly reading from a script, rattled off the report's findings as the camera lingered on Goodell sitting in the stands, "After interviewing every female employee, after analyzing millions of documents, emails and text messages and searching the computer and the cell phone of the commissioner, the report concluded there is no evidence that Goodell or anyone else in the league received or saw the tape [of Rice punching his then fiancée in the face] prior to it going public."[12]

Collinsworth, sounding slightly more spontaneous, then chimed in, "The decision initially to suspend Ray Rice for two games was a mistake, and the commissioner admitted that. But I never once in all my dealings with the commissioner doubted his integrity. And I think that came out in the report as well."[13]

Many within the world of football punditry lost their shit over the exchange. David Zurawik of the *Baltimore Sun* summed it up by writing, "It had the look of something you might have expected from state-run TV in an Eastern European country in the 1950s: Goodell as Marshall Tito, and Michaels and Collinsworth as his fawning puppet announcers. I'm serious: Seeing the game stopped so that these two could serve as PR operatives to whitewash Goodell's handling of the matter and burnish his image made me as angry as anything I have seen on TV this year."[14]

What Zurawik and the others didn't seem to understand was that Michaels and Collinsworth were simply doing their job. There was no opting out for either. Michaels distaste for the work was palatable, but it didn't stop him. He knew what had to be done if he wanted to sit in that broadcast booth.

"But all sports broadcasters become captives of the club or league that pays them," wrote broadcaster turned NFL and AFL owner Harry Wismer way back in 1965. "This is the way the business operates. I know because I was one of the first of the broadcasting shills and one of the biggest. Objectivity is a luxury that few owners or leagues permit their broadcasters. The last possible hope for more objective sports reporting in radio and television was the networks themselves, but even they have capitulated. They regard sports as entertainment, not news, and have relinquished to the sports writers the burden of objective reporting. But sports *is* news. More newspaper space in this country is given over to sports than to any other single area of news. This may or may not be a laudable circumstance, but it is a fact. The public wants to read about sports and it trusts the reporters who provide the stories. If sports columnists were employed by club owners, honest, critical, objective reporting would vanish and a necessary watchful eye would be removed from the sports scene."[15]

It didn't take NFL owners employing sportswriters to kill objectivity. It merely took the investment of the major media conglomerates into the NFL to do it on their behalf. Look no further than the PBS/Frontline documentary film *League of Denial: The NFL's Concussion Crisis*. Based on the book written by Mark Fainaru-Wada and Steve Fainaru, the film delved into the growing concussion scandal. ESPN, which employs the brother writing team, was a full partner in producing film. Yet weeks prior to its original 2013 airdate, NFL executives secretly met with members of Disney's (not ESPN's) top brass and asked that the network remove its affiliation from the program. Tossing aside all journalistic integrity, ESPN did just that and pulled its promotion and name from the film.

This wasn't the first time the NFL leaned on ESPN to capitulate. Back in 2003, the league was upset with the network's scripted program *Playmakers*. Though the show didn't use the NFL's name or any of its teams or logos, the league felt the dramatic story hit too close to home with its depiction of a fictional football team and needed to go. Since ESPN was in the running to gain control of *Monday Night Football* at the time, the network had to decide which program was more valuable. Guess what ESPN chose?

"'It's our opinion that we're not in the business of antagonizing our partner even though we've done it, and continued to carry [*Playmakers*] over the NFL's objections,' then-ESPN executive vice president Mark Shapiro told the *New York Times*. 'To bring it back would be rubbing it in our partner's face.' The *Times* reported then-NFL Commissioner Paul Tagliabue called Disney Chief Executive Michael Eisner to complain about the show."[16]

John Eisendrath, *Playmaker*'s creator and showrunner, had a different take on the decision. "They were really thugs," he told Sports On Earth. "Terrible thugs."[17]

ESPN isn't the only network capitulating to the NFL's wants and needs. All of the networks affiliated with the league behave in a similar fashion. Whether it's getting clearance for each and every broadcaster hired to cover the NFL (including many of the mealy-mouthed former athletes acting like professional announcers) or it's more overt actions such as the CBS Scene restaurant neighboring Gillette Stadium, a joint venture between Patriots owner Robert Kraft and CBS, the networks are no longer even pretending to be the NFL's adversary.

Even so, it has not stopped the NFL from a practice it began under the leadership of Commissioner Pete Rozelle: monitoring the media. Given his public relations roots, Rozelle recognized the media was the key to the league's success. Strike that. *Manipulating* the media was the key to the league's success. From day one of his tenure, he and his underlings scoured every newspaper, magazine, and television show searching for mentions of the league. When they saw something negative or even just slanted in slightly the wrong direction, Rozelle would make sure a NFL staffer contacted that writer or broadcaster to provide league guidance. Often, that diligence paid off by ushering another converted media member into the NFL's fold.

Though his PR savvy cannot match that of Rozelle's, Goodell hasn't allowed the NFL's media watchdogs to back off. "Behind the scenes," Don Van Natta Jr. wrote for ESPN's *Outside the Lines*, "Goodell and league executives closely monitor reports by the NFL's broadcast partners. With increasing regularity, what they see angers Goodell and league execs, sources say."[18] The problem is the bigger the NFL becomes, more media outlets decide to cover it, leading to less control. TMZ scooping everyone on the Ray Rice video opened up a world the league is not ready to confront.

The fear of losing control over its product's appearance has led the league to drastic measures. According to Van Natta, "In September [2013] the NBC Sports Network planned to run a piece produced by *Sports Illustrated* about spouses and caregivers of retired players. But in an email written a week before the piece was to air, a person involved in the production told a colleague 'the NFL went nuclear and was trying to get it killed.' Sources at both the NFL and NBC say they were not aware of any contact between them about the story. Ultimately, say SI and NBC, they had a disagreement about whether the piece should air. It never did."[19]

It was this coalescence of the sports leagues and the media which caused Howard Cosell to step away from broadcasting. Cosell is one of those names that transcend his profession. Many reading this book might know the name without having ever really seen/heard him perform. Others, like myself, perhaps recall his career too fondly, simply because he was unique. But it is without a doubt that Cosell had a front row seat for the merger of media and sports, and why his take on this subject nearly 30 years later still rings true.

In his book *I Never Played the Game* he wrote, "In the beginning, like most people in America, I had romantic ideas about sports. I found beauty in the contests, and I really believed that the public needed the surcease that spectator sports provided from the daily travail of life. But the past fifteen years have developed vast changes in my thinking and have caused me to reach the conclusion set forth at the top of this prologue.

"In that time, I have walked away from professional

boxing, and I have come to have grave doubts about amateur boxing. I have walked away from professional football because of family pressures and because I no longer believed morally or ethically in the actions of the National Football League. By doing this, I gave up, literally, millions of dollars, and yet I suffered tremendous vilification in print for my action.

"In that time, I came to realize, however reluctantly, that there was an inexorable force working against revelations of truth about sports in America. That force exists in the form of an unholy alliance between the three television networks and the sports print medium. It is the fundamental purpose of both, for their own reasons, to exalt sports, to regale the games, the fights, the races, whatever, to the point where these contests are indoctrinated into the public mind as virtual religious rituals.

"Only rarely does one ever read or hear about how sports in the current era inextricably intertwine with the law, the politics, the sociology, the education, and the medical care of society. It is common practice now for sports franchise owners to rip off great cities in financial distress either by franchise removal or threat of franchise removal. I have seen emphasis upon sports corrupt our higher educational process, and to at least some degree, our secondary educational system....

"I have observed the disgusting extent to which television will go in order to get a rating....I have covered the development of labor unions in sports, lockouts in sports, special-purpose legislation passed by the Congress for sports. And I have seen the birth of a curious new stratum in society, which Robert Lipsyte brilliantly entitled 'the Jockocracy.'...

"The world of sports today is endlessly complex, an ever-spinning spiral of deceit, immorality, absence of ethics, and defiance of the public interest. Yet, somewhere within all that, there continues to lurk the valid notion that there *is* good in sports and that the games themselves provide a necessary respite from the ills and frustrations of life itself.

"It is in that latter notion that the bulk of the American public believes, although the number of such believers decreases almost daily. They believe as they do because they have been taught to do so virtually from birth. They are taught in their homes and by the sports media people....

"....The essential point is that sports are no longer fun and games, that they are everywhere—in people's minds, in conversation, in the importance we attach to it—and that they can affect the basics of our lives (to wit, the part of our taxes that may be directed to supporting a sports franchise, without our ever knowing it). Once I bought the Jimmy Cannon dictum that 'Sports is the Toy Department of life.' I don't now and never will again.

"The task then, as I see it, is to get a fix on sports and put it in its place, in balance with the mainstream of life, and to dispel romantic ideas about sports—ideas that exist only in a fantasy world."[20]

WEEK 17
vs. FIXING

James "The Amazing" Randi said, "No matter how smart or well-educated you are, you *can* be deceived." He should know. Randi began his career as a magician and fooled people for a living. Then, after seeing charlatans use magic tricks to con people out of money, Randi began a crusade to reveal these fakers for what they really were. He took on false mentalists, televangelists, faith healers, and even a couple of college professors and beat them all at their own game. His willingness to use lies to tell the truth won him many fans from all walks of life.

One of his biggest groups of admirers labels themselves as "skeptics." There are magazines, *Skeptic* and *Skeptical Inquirer* to name but two, devoted to this pursuit. But I take umbrage at how these people hijacked the word "skeptic." To them, a skeptic is one who recognizes outlandish claims and sets out to tell the truth about these lies. Their subjects range from mind reading to fortune telling to UFOs to the alternate histories of the JFK assassination, 9/11, and a host of other events.

But here's the problem with the "skeptics": they aren't *at all* skeptical of the mainstream story. They don't doubt what the government or the press has to say about any of these events. They doubt those who dare to question what's put forth by the powers-that-be. They label these deniers "conspiracy theorists." And it doesn't matter if you choose to believe 9/11 was an inside job because of this evidence, or that a secretive cabal of billionaires set out to create a New World Order because of that evidence, or that Bigfoot exists because you saw one; once you declare your belief in any of this subject matter you are a conspiracy theorist. You're ridiculed, mocked, and denounced *even though you are actually the one being skeptical.*

Though the terms now have connotations permanently attached to them—a "skeptic" is a rational person and a "conspiracy theorist" is a whack-a-doo—I don't care what label becomes attached to me for my beliefs. What I attempt to do is look at all the evidence available and reach a conclusion as best as I can. If that puts me in the conspiracy camp, so be it.

That said what should you and I make of the following? According to the NFL, never in the league's 95-year history has a game been fixed. Not once. Should we take such a claim as the "skeptic" would and believe it to be true because the NFL said so? The league does have one hard, undeniable fact on its side: despite untold billions wagered on the sport, no one has ever been convicted of fixing an NFL game. Or should we take the "conspiracy theory" slant and wonder aloud if a multi-billion dollar business such as the NFL might shade the truth in order to protect its integrity on which it believes its entire existence is based?

Well, let's play the devil's advocate for the skeptics and lay out some facts regarding this idea that the NFL's games have been and remain untouchable to any sort of influence.

The NFL will admit there have been three attempts to fix

a game. The first was the 1946 NFL Championship played between the Chicago Bears and New York Giants (as mentioned in Week 13). Twenty-five years passed—supposedly without incident—until retired Denver Broncos running back Donnie Stone phoned his former teammate and then-current Houston Oilers center Jerry Sturm with an offer to shave points in the final three games of the Oilers' 1971 season. It's to Sturm's credit that he rejected the offer. The Oilers' record was 1-9-1 at the time, and the money Stone suggested could be made by shaving points in those three games exceeded Sturm's entire 1971 salary. But Sturm not only held firm, he reported the incident to the proper NFL authorities. As a thank you, the Oilers cut the 11-year veteran after the season ended.

The third fix attempt remains a mystery. It had been assumed that the league only recognized the two incidents mentioned above. However, in late 2012 NFL Commissioner Roger Goodell was deposed as part of New Jersey's case to legalize sports gambling. During his deposition, Goodell "repeatedly stated that he was unsure if there had been any specific incidents of gambling-related game-fixing, yet, curiously, he referenced 'three incidents.'"[1] Goodell refused to elaborate on any of them, saying only, "Those three incidents were involving violations of our policy in association with gambling. And the reason we have those is to make sure that game-fixing doesn't occur. They're preventative, they're to avoid this. That's a serious threat to our game and to the integrity of our game."[2]

In 1989, investigative reporter Dan Moldea wrote *Interference: How Organized Crime Influences Professional Football*. Through the course of his exhaustive research for that tome, Moldea identified 70 allegedly fixed NFL games spanning nearly 30 years (1951-1979), none of which the league acknowledges. Moldea's list included games fixed by bookmaker Donald "Dice" Dawson (who admitted to fixing over

30 games himself), known mob affiliates "Lefty" Rosenthal and Gil Beckley (who may have fixed nearly 20 games in 1966 alone), and a pair of NFL referees (who were investigated by both the FBI and IRS for perhaps fixing eight games in 1979).

Taking a metaphorical hand-off from Moldea, I attempted something no one else had ever done. Utilizing the Freedom of Information Act, I obtained every investigative file the FBI had related to game fixing in American sports. What I received back from the FBI included files on fixed horse races, boxing matches, NCAA football and basketball games, MLB games, NBA games, and yes, NFL games. Those files formed the basis for my book *Larceny Games: Sports Gambling, Game Fixing, and the FBI*.

In piecing together the 400+ files I obtained through FOIA, I learned that even prior to the passage of the Sports Bribery Act of 1964 which made game fixing a federal crime, the FBI set up a nationwide network of sources and informants to monitor illegal sports gambling within the United States. Information constantly flowed to the Bureau's agents from the likes of "top echelon informants" (mostly high level organized crime members) stating that gamblers, bookies, and mobsters were working with players, coaches, and referees to fix games in nearly every sport imaginable.

According to the files, often times the Bureau would learn ahead of time that Player X was working with Bookie Y and were going to fix a particular game. Sure enough, the game's outcome (and Player X's under-performance) would match the information the FBI agent received. But that didn't prove anything. And there was the rub. Though the information came from a reputable source and was strong enough to open a case file, if the FBI couldn't obtain a wiretap to catch the conspirators discussing fixing a game or if they couldn't get the participants to admit to committing the crime, the Bureau had little on which to base a case. In other words, absent of evidence, there was no crime.

To build a case, to warrant an arrest, and to earn a conviction; all of this takes evidence. That's the one thing game fixing lacks. It's often merely a verbal agreement which cinches a fix. If you can't catch that moment on tape, how can one prove a game was truly fixed? Even when alerted beforehand that a player might be involved, his poor performance on the field wouldn't prove a thing. You can't convict a quarterback in the court of law for fixing a game simply because he threw three interceptions. This is why the FBI eventually abandoned ship.

At some undefined point in the 1980's, the FBI ceased investigating the crime of sports bribery. After 20+ years, its network of informants and sources in the gambling underworld had fallen into disrepair. President Reagan had made the Bureau's top priority fighting the War on Drugs. And since all of the time and effort investigating allegations of fixed games rarely ended with a conviction, the FBI decided to stop following these leads. If it did come across strong information relating to a fixed game while investigating another case—which happened in relation to the game fixing scandals at Boston College, Arizona State University, and University of San Diego (among others) as well as in the case of NBA referee Tim Donaghy—the Bureau would pursue it. Otherwise, and this is the frightening part, *the FBI allowed the leagues to investigate themselves.*

Is it no wonder that there hasn't been mention of a fixed game in professional sports in America since the FBI quit the business?

Meanwhile, there is a match fixing cancer spreading throughout the world. Hundreds, if not thousands, of soccer, tennis, cricket, baseball, and rugby matches are known to have been fixed in countries on every continent sans Antarctica. Players, coaches, team owners, gamblers, and members of organized crime have been arrested, tried, and convicted for the crime. The World Anti-Doping Agency (WADA) director general claimed at least a quarter of all sport played today is controlled by organized crime.[3] International organizations have been created to combat the growing epidemic. Businesses designed to monitor sports betting (in the legal markets) have launched with the aims to spot a fix in the making. Corruption upended the international soccer federation FIFA, and soon may cause similar upheavals within the International Olympic Committee.

But here in the United States, our biggest concern was with the PSI of a dozen footballs.

The theory is that today's NFL players make too much money to be susceptible to any sort of fix. On the surface, that sounds pretty reasonable. In reality, it is absurd.

We know that cricket games in the Indian Premier League have been fixed. We know tennis matches at Grand Slam events have been fixed. We know soccer games in the English Premier League have been fixed. We know Olympic events have been fixed. We know that soccer matches in the World Cup—the biggest, most watched sporting event in the world—have been fixed. If all of that was possible, what makes the NFL so sacrosanct?

Not every player makes Ben Roethlisberger or Cam Newton money (two of the highest paid players in 2015). Most don't earn much above the $435,000 league minimum for rookies. Though it's a payday many of us would accept, after taxes, manager/agent fees, etc., the actual take home pay isn't the sort of money with which you can "make it rain" every night. Even for those players who do earn the likes of Russell Wilson's $20+ million a year contract, there's a laundry list of such athletes who have left the game bankrupt. Tack on to that the troubles a player can get into—drugs, gambling, women/men, bad business deals, etc.—and there are many weaknesses available for a would-be fixer to exploit. All that is required is an opening, an in, and a game can be corrupted.

ESPN anonymously polled 83 professional athletes in 2013 about a variety of cheating activities within their respective sports. One question asked was, "Have you ever suspected during a game that a player was on the take?" Astonishingly, 5.5 percent of respondents (none of which came from the NBA, WNBA, or NHL) responded in the affirmative. One NFL All-Pro was quoted as saying, "I won't share details, because I'm not that kind of person. But my answer to this question is hell yes."[4]

Two years later ESPN was back at it, anonymously polling 73 professional athletes about gambling. Asked in this survey was, "Do you ever suspect that games in your sport are fixed?" Even in that relatively small sample size, 3 percent of respondents said "yes" while another 3 percent said "maybe."[5]

While fans want to believe every athlete is "giving 110 percent," "taking it to the next level," and "only thinking about winning a ring," the clichés mask the reality that the NFL is just a job. Most players are simply trying to survive; to last one more game or one more season and hopefully retire with a good-sized nest egg and their health intact. Winning is certainly a benefit, but every NFL player is paid his pre-determined salary whether his team wins or loses (in fact, the lawyers for the Black Sox used this notion in defending their clients against charges of the fixing the 1919 World Series: they were paid to play, not to win).

Since most players fought tooth and nail to reach the pinnacle of the NFL, how hard would that player battle to stay there? Certainly as we've seen, players are more than willing to endure all sorts of pain to play. They consume a variety of drugs, suffer through untold injections, and undergo numerous medical procedures to elongate a career. Some of this circumvents NFL rules. So it is known players are willing to beat the system. To cheat. Well, once this precedent is established, then it's only question of how much cheating would a player accept in order to achieve his goals. Is there a line that goes too far?

Carolina Panthers wide receiver Kelvin Benjamin

intentionally tanked his time in the 40-yard sprint at the 2014 NFL scouting combine. Why did he run slower than he was capable? "Because I wanted to play for the Carolina Panthers," Benjamin said.[6] He knew that his best time in the 40 (4.41 seconds) coupled with his size (6'5" and 240 pounds) would've made him a high draft pick. Too high for the Panthers at 28th overall. So Benjamin ran a 4.61 40-yard sprint at the combine. Lo and behold, he fell to Carolina at that spot.

While that bit of trickery doesn't seem malicious (if anything, it cost Benjamin money), how do you feel about a player faking an injury at a team's request? Former Philadelphia Eagles quarterback Ty Detmer claimed that his brother Koy, also a QB for the Eagles, was told to fake an injury so the team could stash him on injured reserve while clearing roster space for another player.[7] Koy was just a rookie then in 1997, a 7th round draft pick, but the team wanted him in the fold…just not on the roster. So, during a practice with the media present, Koy Detmer laid down as instructed. Running a bootleg fake, Detmer crumbled to the turf, clutching his knee. Later, he was seen on crutches while wearing a knee brace. Only he wasn't really injured. Just a select few Eagles insiders knew the truth to the situation, and all of them kept mum. The ruse ingratiated Koy to the Eagles organization so much so that they kept him on the roster for nine years after the "injury."

Just a bit of roster manipulation, right? But nothing that affected the league's integrity, like, say when a player faked an injury in a game. Or in several games. "We had a guy who was the designated dive guy," former Chicago Bears' All-Pro linebacker Brian Urlacher said during an interview on Fox Sports 1.[8] Urlacher elaborated that in order to slow down certain offenses, one of the Bears defensive players would fake an injury. According to Urlacher, this wasn't coached, yet it was part of the Bears' game-plan. So, without mincing words, he admitted the Bears cheated—often.

Of course, most, if not all, NFL teams practiced a variation of this deception. It used to be especially utilized during the two-minute drill—by both offenses and defenses—in order to preserve the precious game clock, better strategize against the opponent, and give players a quick breather. To combat this cheat, the NFL instituted a rule in which an injured player unable to get off the field after the two-minute warning cost the player's team a time-out.

Again, one could argue that while perhaps not legal by league definition, the "injured player" trick was designed to help a team win. "Everybody in this league is trying to find a way to get away with something that creates an advantage," former NFL quarterback Jeff Garcia once said. "If they get caught doing something, they'll get penalized. But if they don't, they'll keep doing it as long as they can."[9] But isn't cheating still cheating? Who gets to draw the line? At what point is it decided that one cheat is ok and another is reprehensible? Isn't this all added grease on an already slippery slope towards game fixing?

It can get worse. Many NFL stalwarts remember wide receiver Randy Moss's infamous "I play when I want to play" quote. The not-so-subtle subtext was that Moss took plays off. It shouldn't come as a surprise. Focus on one player for an entire game and you'll likely see him not "giving 110 percent" on every down. Who can? But what if such behavior was intentional? Not because of fatigue, but because that player wanted to see another fail?

This was exactly the case for Detroit Lions offensive lineman Lomas Brown. He admitted to not blocking on a play in order to send a message to quarterback Scott Mitchell. Brown told the SVP & Russillo show on ESPN Radio, "We were playing Green Bay in Milwaukee. We were getting beat 24-3 at the time, and [Mitchell] just stunk up the place, throwing interceptions, just everything. I looked at Kevin Glover, our All-Pro center, and I said, 'Glove, that is it.' I said, 'I'm getting him out of the game.' So I gave it the set out, but I got the gator arms on the guy at the last minute. He got around me. He hit Scott Mitchell. He did something to his finger. I don't know what he did to it, but he came out of the game."[10] While Mitchell was "floored" by the revelation and Brown apologized for the incident (20 years too late), none of it excused the fact that Brown's intentional miss wound up injuring Mitchell. Though it resulted in only a broken finger on Mitchell's throwing hand, who's to say under different circumstances it couldn't have been something career-ending?

Certainly similar personality clashes have resulted in players not performing up to their full abilities. My father was a banker in the Chicago-area and related a story to me in which one of the Bears' offensive linemen (who was a customer but shall remain nameless) revealed that the entire offensive line wanted one particular quarterback to play instead of the coach's chosen starter. Since the head coach wouldn't listen to the players, the offensive line took it upon themselves to rectify the situation—by refusing to block for the starting quarterback. This not only led to the Bears losing games, but caused the starting quarterback to underperform and ultimately be replaced by the player the line preferred.

Are you noticing all the integrity?

Players shouldn't be the only ones singled out. Coaches and their staff have been willing to push the limits of league legality as well. In 2012, the New Orleans Saints suffered the indignity of Bountygate in which it was revealed their coaches paid players "bounties" for hits with the intent to injure opposing players. On the heels of that debacle, it was alleged that "Saints general manager Mickey Loomis had an electronic device in his Superdome suite that had been secretly re-wired to enable him to eavesdrop on visiting coaching staffs for nearly three NFL seasons [2002-2004]."[11] Though the bugging of opposing team's coaches bordered on a federal crime, nothing (public) ever came of the investigation.

But eavesdropping and attempting to steal signs isn't a modern invention. "When Marty Schottenheimer coached the Cleveland Browns in the late 1980s, he routinely sent a scout to watch the signals opposing teams used to relay messages from coaches to players. When the scout returned, Schottenheimer's staff would watch the game film and match the signals to the plays that followed."[12] Twenty years later, Kansas City Chiefs head coach Herm Edwards told ESPN not much had changed. He claimed that it was common for coaches to watch a variety of game film, including broadcast television coverage, in an attempt to steal signals.[13]

Of course, in between Schottenheimer and Edward's confessions, the infamous Spygate took place. No one outside of the New England Patriots organization really knows how far and how pervasive the team's videotaping of opposing coaches' signals (and walk-throughs and practices) was because Commissioner Goodell, in his infinite wisdom, ordered all of the evidence tapes destroyed. It's possible the tapes helped the Patriots win three Super Bowls. It's also possible they were of little value. I tend to believe it's closer to the former rather than the latter, otherwise Bill Belichick and his staff wouldn't have wasted the time and effort, nor would the league have punished the team so harshly.

I'm not the only one who continues to question the fallout from Spygate. Former Carolina Panthers general manager Marty Hurney, who oversaw the franchise when it lost to the Patriots in Super Bowl XXXVIII, had this to say about it in 2015, "There isn't a day that goes by since [then] that I haven't questioned...that there were some things done that might have been beyond the rules that may have given them a three-point advantage [Carolina lost 32-29]. And I can't prove anything, and that's why I'm very angry. And the anger has come back over the last couple of days that commissioner Roger Goodell decided to shred all of the evidence after 'Spygate,' because I think there were a lot of things in there that would bring closure to a lot of people."[14]

What had gotten the GM turned radio show host's blood all angered up ten years after the fact? The latest Patriots' scandal, Deflategate. Did Tom Brady tell the team's ball boys to purposefully under inflate the Patriots footballs to his liking prior to the AFC Championship Game against the Colts? Did the ball boys do it without anyone's guidance? Did the balls just deflate on their own due to weather conditions? Did the NFL and its officials screw up measuring the PSI of each ball? Did the footballs make any sort of difference in the 45-7 victory? Was Belichick aware of it? Who knows? All that one can take away from Deflategate is that this scandal has played out over the course of six months while Spygate—a ten-year-long violation of the rules—was settled for all intents and purposes by Commissioner Goodell in *five days*.

"To me, this isn't about deflating balls," Hurney said. "It's about a continuing culture of alleged cheating, and to me, everybody's talking about [coach] Bill Belichick and Tom Brady. When is [Patriots owner] Robert Kraft going to come up and explain why, if they are found guilty of this, why do these things keep happening in this organization?"[15]

Despite Hurney's hostility against the Patriots, most franchises have similar skeletons in their closet. Even during the national talking point of Deflategate a key admission of cheating by former Tampa Bay Buccaneers quarterback Brad Johnson was glossed over. Johnson admitted to the *Tampa Bay Times* that prior to playing in Super Bowl XXXVII, "I paid some guys off to get the balls right. I went and got all 100 footballs, and they took care of all of them."[16] Johnson forked out $7,500 to unidentified people to scuff up the Super Bowl game balls to his liking so he could get a better grip.

Did that cheat help the Buccaneers defeat the Oakland

Raiders 48-21 in Super Bowl XXXVII? Not as much as the fact that the Bucs knew which plays the Raiders' offense was going to run prior to the ball being snapped.

Head coach Jon Gruden had been traded from Oakland to Tampa Bay prior to that season starting, yet he remained in contact with Raiders quarterback Rich Gannon throughout the year—including the week of the Super Bowl. "Tampa Bay defensive players believe Gruden used the friendship to his advantage while preparing for the championship, somehow drilling inside Gannon's head, as he once did when both were with the Raiders, and picking up small, inside details about the Raiders offense, doing so without Gannon ever being aware he was being mentally pickpocketed."[17] This included the realization that not only hadn't the Raiders altered the team's offense since Gruden's departure; it still used the same audibles.

Though Gruden and Gannon may have inadvertently fixed the Super Bowl for the Buccaneers, both now work for the league as broadcasters. All is forgotten. All is forgiven.

In fact, all of these cheats are meaningless to the powers that be in the NFL. If the league was truly concerned about its integrity, none of these "win by any means necessary" schemes would've gone unnoticed. The league has eyes and ears everywhere, yet no one on the inside knew about these deceits until well after the fact? Until the press uncovered them? It seems as though victories should have been stripped, titles abdicated. But the NFL has never done this. Instead, the league shrugs its shoulders as if to say, "What can we do?"

The scary thing is that even if mobsters have fixed countless NFL games for gambling purposes, the league wouldn't really care...unless the public learned about it. Then it would become yet another all-hands-on-deck, full battle stations, damage control situation. Otherwise, the fix only mattered to those in on the swindle. To the rest of us, the outsiders, any fixed game would have appeared to be an undecided contest until the final gun sounded.

That is all the league wants. For fans to believe in the illusion of sports and its supposed random outcomes. This is what they sell, only not for the reasons most fans comprehend. The reality of the NFL was best said by the wife of former New York Jets owner Sonny Werblin who once told to Joe Namath, "Joseph, it's all show business."

"At some point," said Green Bay Packers Hall of Fame general manager Ron Wolf in 2000, "the Super Bowl no longer became a game, but it became a show. And from that, football no longer became a game, it became a business."[18]

NFL games are played for the same reason the circus comes to town: to make money by entertaining people. You can put all the emphasis you choose to when calling the NFL a sport, but the league itself argued before the Supreme Court in 2010 that it was not a collective of 32 individual teams, but one entity known as the National Football League and its business was entertainment.

Teams are set up like ballets. A general manager assembles the talent, coaches direct them how to execute their maneuvers, and the performers exhibit their talents to the audience.

"We sell fantasy," said former Legal Chief Council and then-current President and Chief Operating Officer of MLB, Robert A. Dupuy, Esq. at the 2012 Ninth Circuit Judicial Conference titled "Federal Courts, Federal Law and Professional Sports: Emerging Trends in Antitrust, Labor and Intellectual Property." Dupuy continued, "We don't sell reality. And we have grown men and women in costumes playing for millions of dollars, and more importantly enthralling tens of millions of people. And furthermore, we sell competition. Our teams and our athletes have to be bitter, bitter rivals and competitors on the field of play, but they've got to be partners off the field of play. And we need rules. We sell uncertainty of outcome, and so we need rules, both playing rules and frankly, we need economic rules."

DeMaurice Smith, current chief of the NFL Players' Association, then added, "Isn't the reality that it's a business when owners want it to be a business and it's a sport when they want it to be a sport and for a fan it's—and I agree with you—it's a fantasy."

These aren't quotes taken out of context. You can see the entire exchange on YouTube. Yet such an admission coming from two major league insiders should stop a fan in his or her tracks. The NFL—hell, all professional sports for that matter—is in the business of selling an utter fantasy to their consumers. To hammer this point home, consider that when former NFL wide receiver Nate Jackson traveled to Japan with the Denver Broncos to play in the NFL's American Bowl, his passport was stamped "Entertainer,"[19] not "Athlete."

The NFL has repeatedly been called "the best reality show on television." Most don't stop to think what that really means. I hope I'm not bursting anyone's bubble, but "reality" TV is far from real. It is scripted, re-enacted, heavily edited and produced to draw the desired effect from each scene. *Shark Tank* compresses three hours of negotiations into 15-minutes segments, and many times one side of the "deal" backs out. *Storage Wars* was accused of seeding storage lockers with goods to make certain purchases look better. *The Hills*, called a reality show by MTV, was mostly scripted, going so far as to film their stars "driving" while the cars were actually on the back of trailers. Ashley Simpson famously lip-synced her way through an appearance on *Saturday Night Live*. *The Bachelor* and *The Bachelorette* selectively cast their programs to artificially induce drama. Most of the early judging on *American Idol* was done off-screen by the shows' executives. The list could go on and on, but often times non-disclosure agreements get in the way of revealing the biggest truths.

Of course, all of this manipulation is perfectly legal. In fact, there is only one type of television show not allowed to cheat by federal law: intellectual game shows. This is due to the famous "Quiz Show" scandal of the 1950's. During that time, television networks rigged question-and-answer programs like *Twenty One* and *The $64,000 Challenge* in order to maximize viewer interest. The producers built up certain contestants by providing them with the answers ahead of time. Then, when the drama reached a crescendo, those same winners would take a dive and lose to another paper champion. It was quite effective ratings-wise, and created a national sensation out of one champion, Charles Van Doren. Then a disgruntled former contestant helped blow the lid off the staged events. Congress investigated, and the aftermath spawned what became colloquially known as the "Quiz Show" law.

It is quite specific. The law repeatedly references contests of "intellectual knowledge" or "intellectual skill." The word "intellectual" is the sticking point. Because of that adjective's usage, it allows for programs like *America's Got Talent, The Voice, Chopped,* and *Monday Night Football* to be 100 percent fixed by their producers without violating the law.

Wait, did I just include the NFL in that list? Why, yes, I did.

The fact of the matter is there is no law that exists to prevent the NFL from manipulating the outcome of its own games.

As shown, the "Quiz Show" law is specific for "intellectual" contests, not physical ones. The other law that comes closest is the aforementioned Sports Bribery Act. It's short and sweet, reading: "Whoever carries into effect, attempts to carry into effect, or conspires with any other person to carry into effect any scheme in commerce to influence, in any way, by bribery any sporting contest, with knowledge that the purpose of such scheme is to influence by bribery that contest, shall be fined under this title, or imprisoned not more than 5 years, or both."

Its key word in it is "bribery." If a league instructed one of its employees—be it an official, coach or athlete—to influence and/or manipulate an outcome in a certain manner, such an action does not break this law. It would merely be an employer telling an employee how to do to a job. A paycheck is not a bribe.

The only legal protection remaining for fans is fraud. And that's a tricky one to prove in a court of law. Sports leagues already have a built-in protection against any claims of fraud. This was most recently shown in the lawsuit brought against the New England Patriots over Spygate.

A New York Jets fan who happened to be a lawyer (go figure) sued the Patriots for violating the NFL's rules. The class-action suit sought the Jets ticket holders' money back for 10 years worth of games—the duration of the Patriots alleged cheating.

Senior Judge of the Third Circuit Court of Appeals Robert E. Cowen concluded, "At best, he [Carl Mayer, the plaintive] possessed nothing more than a contractual right to a seat from which to watch an NFL game between the Jets and the Patriots, and this right was clearly honored....Mayer possessed either a license or, at best, a contractual right to enter Giants Stadium and to have a seat from which to watch a professional football game. In the clear language of the ticket stub, '[t]his ticket only grants entry into the stadium and a spectator seat for the specified NFL game.' Mayer actually was allowed to enter the stadium and witnessed the 'specified NFL game[s]' between the Jets and Patriots. He thereby suffered no cognizable injury to a legally protected right or interest."

In truth, the team selling the ticket—actually a license to enter the stadium—holds more rights than the purchaser does. So, when you purchase a ticket to see a game, all the team/league needs to do is put on some sort of physical contest resembling its promoted product. It doesn't mean the game has to feature certain players, that the rules must be strictly enforced, or that the game has to even be legitimate. In essence, you paid to see a game, and be it good, bad, or ugly, you saw one. Contract fulfilled. Case closed.

To add a bit of insult to injury, Judge Cowen added, "We do not condone the conduct on the part of the Patriots and the team's head coach, and we likewise refrain from assessing whether the NFL's sanctions (and its alleged destruction of the videotapes themselves) were otherwise appropriate. We further recognize that professional football, like other professional sports, is a multi-billion dollar business. In turn, ticket-holders and other fans may have legitimate issues with the manner in which they are treated....Significantly, our ruling also does not leave Mayer and other ticket-holders without any recourse. Instead, fans could speak out against the Patriots, their coach, and the NFL itself. In fact, they could even go so far as to refuse to purchase tickets or NFL-related merchandise....However, the one thing they *cannot* do is bring a legal action in a court of law. [emphasis in original]."

If that is the best protection a ticket provides a fan, do you honestly believe watching a game on television grants one *greater* legal rights?

I know, I know. This is all just "conspiracy theory" because I cannot prove the NFL has fixed one of its own games. Same as the FBI couldn't prove that an NFL game was fixed by gamblers. Yet no one doubted the intellect of the contestants on those 1950's game shows until a whistleblower revealed the entire system was corrupt. What I allege is actively occurring in the NFL is the same thing: contest manipulation for television ratings.

I don't believe every game is fixed a la professional wrestling (which is perhaps the most honest sport in the world). What I think happens is when the league sees a storyline develop or a star emerge it is willing to "help" stretch that out as long as possible to profit from the fans' interest in that team or athlete. I don't believe the NFL pre-determines its Super Bowl champion, but if a call here or a tank job there helps a team like the post-Hurricane Katrina New Orleans Saints fulfill a Cinderella story, well, all the better for marketing and ratings.

Even if I am just a crazed conspiracist wrongly accusing the NFL of outright fixing its games, am I wrong to consider that the league might be simply manipulating them? Recall the discussion about "home field advantage" brought about by officiating, and how even the level-headed skeptics admitted that such outcomes benefited the home team, and by extension, the entire league. Now, what if those same referees were instructed to tweak games to keep them closer longer than they should be?

We know television and the NFL are multi-billion dollar industries that need the other to survive. So why does it stretch credulity to think that the NFL might willingly alter its games to create the most dramatic impact possible?

Signs of such manipulation are everywhere, and are even trumpeted by the NFL. In the league's 2014 "Countdown to Kickoff" press release, it stated that 68 percent of its games in 2013 were within one score in the 4th quarter. Because of that, 48 percent of games (123 of 256) were decided by 7 points or less. Through the first nine weeks of the 2013 season, 35 of 133 games (26 percent) featured a fourth-quarter comeback victory while at the same time 30 games saw the winning points scored in the final two minutes of the fourth quarter or in overtime.

These trends continued into 2014. Through Week 10, the NFL had witnessed 23 come-from-behind victories of 10 points or more, on pace to break a league record for a season. Games continued to come down to the two minute warning or the final possession with even the Seahawks-Patriots Super Bowl following this tendency. While all this occurs on the field, off of it TV viewership is at a historic high.

These types of game results are exactly what the TV networks want from their partner, the NFL. Tight, exciting, often high scoring affairs that keep fans glued to their televisions until the final gun. It makes advertisers happy, it makes the networks happy, and it certainly makes the NFL happy. Funny how that just works out for everyone involved, isn't it?

In fact, it's amazing how often supposed "coincidence" benefits the NFL, and by extension, its broadcast partners. Just as an example, here's what happened in Week 16 of the 2014 season...all to the NFL's good fortune:

The playoff-contending Eagles were upset by the sub .500 Redskins to give both the Cowboys and the Packers a guaranteed trip to the playoffs. Of course, because the Lions took care of the Bears, the Detroit-Green Bay game scheduled in Week 17 was important because home-field advantage would be granted to the victor. Meanwhile, the Panthers knocked off the Browns while the Falcons upset the Saints to make the Week 17 Carolina-Atlanta game a "must-win" as the winner moved on to the playoffs while the loser sat home. Noticing a pattern?

But wait, there's more! The much-in-need-of-a-new-stadium Chargers rallied to beat the 49ers, giving them a legitimate playoff hope, yet because the Texans (with a third-string quarterback at the helm) beat the Ravens while the Steelers defeated the Chiefs, the Week 17 games of San Diego-Kansas City, Cleveland-Baltimore, and Jacksonville-Houston all had major playoff implications. Oh, and that Steelers victory coupled with the upset on *Monday Night Football* of the Bengals over the Broncos made the Pittsburgh-Cincinnati game—immediately flexed into the *Sunday Night Football* slot—yet another game with huge playoff implications.

How often does an eight-team parlay hit for a gambler? Never? Amazing then that the NFL managed to land one in Week 16. These "random" outcomes set up three AFC games on CBS with playoff implications in the 1 pm time-slot, two NFC games on FOX with playoff implications at 4 pm, and *Sunday Night Football* on NBC had the all-important Pittsburgh-Cincinnati clash in prime time.

Geez. All of that just *happened*—supposedly without any outside influence—to every business's benefit.

Myself, I don't believe in coincidence. Not on this scale. And not when its supposed occurrence continually benefits a multi-billion dollar corporation whose own commissioner strangely stated that the league doesn't fix its own games.

When asked about playoff expansion by former Associated Press White House correspondent Ben Feller in a sit-down interview, Goodell responded by saying the idea wasn't off the table. Then, without any prompting, Goodell added, "We think it's one of the great things about the NFL, *besides the fact that it's unscripted*, that every team starts, and their fans start, the season with hope."[20]

That hope is brought about thanks to "parity." An idea initiated in the 1960's by Commissioner Rozelle and continued on to today. Basically, parity aimed to create an equal league, one in which any team could beat any other team on any given Sunday. It's a notion that allows a last place team one year to win the division the next and then fall back into the cellar the following year. It's also the perfect cover for manipulating games, if the NFL would decide to do so.

I have made this analogy in radio interviews before, but it bears repeating here. If a company like McDonalds could put something in its hamburgers, some sort of newly FDA-approved food additive, which would make its product taste better while customers are consuming it, wouldn't McDonalds mix it with its beef? Of course it would. Doing so would greatly increase customer satisfaction and sales. They'd be foolish *not* to.

Yet this is exactly what the NFL can do. It *can* legally alter its games while you consume/watch them to make them more exciting and enjoyable. Such actions would inevitably increase ratings, ad revenue, and overall profit. So why doesn't anyone think the league would do so? Integrity?

POSTSEASON

Forty some odd years ago, Peter Gent wrote a famous line about the NFL in which a disenfranchised player exclaimed, "Every time I try and call it a business you say it's a game and every time I say it should be a game you call it a business." The amazing thing about that sentence is that it still holds true to this day. The behind-the-scenes machinations of the NFL have not changed one iota over the decades. If anything, the league has merely honed its practices to a fine point.

Why this business—and don't fool yourself into thinking it is anything but a business—is allowed to get away with what it does is a subject I think only sociologists could unravel. For decades, the NFL (not its individual teams) operated as a non-profit organization. It only recently gave up that benefit because, as Commissioner Goodell announced, it became a "distraction." When Chicago held the 2015 NFL Draft and when cities like Phoenix, San Francisco, Houston, and Minneapolis host the Super Bowl, each municipality is expected to provide a litany of services—from transportation to security protection to hotel room to rounds of golf at the nearest country club—at "no cost to the league." And let's not even open up the can of worms that is the stadium deals cities allow themselves to be hijacked for in order to keep a franchise from fleeing to a more gullible locale. Millions of dollars, mostly taxpayer money, is spent to lay out a rose petal covered red carpet for the NFL while its owners reap all of the financial benefits. Yet no one seems to bat an eye at this discrepancy.

Meanwhile on a micro level, the league's rank-and-file are chewed up and spit out by a system that doesn't appear to care. Players rarely walk away from the game; they hobble. Either forced out by younger, cheaper replacements or left battered and bruised beyond the ability to continue to play. Did multiple concussions leave an athlete with a mental impairment? That's too bad; he knew the risks when he signed his contract. Did week after week of pain-killing injections reduce a player to a junkie-level drug dependency? How awful; it's not our fault.

Fans should be ashamed of the NFL. If any other business operated in such a fashion, citizens would be up in arms with torches and pitchforks. They would not welcome it into their community. But the NFL is cheered. It's celebrated. Its biggest game has become a de facto national holiday. People buy tickets to watch it, they flock to their televisions to consume it, and they train their children to hopefully one day be a part of it.

Why? What is the allure?

It is amazing to watch what these athletes can do. To perform at a level few can achieve in terms of grace, power, and speed. But are those few hours of entertainment on Sunday worth the actual price tag attached to that performance? Is it even a completely honest show? What aren't fans being told about the game they want to believe is pure, despite knowing the corruption that's infused within it?

The NFL isn't deceiving anyone. All of this—the dirty business deals, the criminal athletes, etc.—is public knowledge. If anything, fans are duping themselves into making this league a

Disneyesque fairy tale. And it probably doesn't help that Disney itself along with several other media conglomerates perpetuate this make-believe atmosphere around the sport.

Yet fans can't leave it at that. They can't just be entertained by the spectacle of the NFL. They have to "make it interesting" by wagering on each and every outcome.

It's impossible to determine what percentage of people who label themselves as NFL fans also wager on the league's games either by directly betting on which team wins or else by participating in some form of fantasy football. I suspect the number would be incredibly high. It is the only thing that can explain the huge television ratings the league pulls in week after week, year after year. Fans are watching because they have money riding on the outcome. Why else would anyone care what happens in a Week 14 Jacksonville-Tennessee matchup? The game's just not that interesting otherwise.

While the NFL publicly expresses its want to keep sports gambling illegal, the men and women at the league's New York City headquarters aren't that naïve. They realize gambling fans are engaged fans. Therefore the league hides behind the congressional roadblock known as PASPA to show its resolve while at the same time it slowly but surely eats away at any other impediment to gambling on its sport.

In the course of one season, I was able to bet on the NFL at a Las Vegas sports book, at home with a bookie, at home via an offshore sports book, at church through a charity, at a local gas station with a scratch-off ticket, and with friends and strangers through a variety of fantasy football leagues. How many other ways are there to get action down on an NFL game? And I did all of this without hitting so much as a speed bump. If a person wants to bet on the NFL, they can easily do so—federal anti-gambling laws be damned. So why not legalize it, regulate it, and tax it?

The legalization of all of this activity might be the magic

elixir the NFL needs. Doing so would solve its gambling conundrum without the league looking like a hypocrite. Fans might then be comforted and actually believe the NFL has an ounce of integrity if some form of outside oversight—be it governmental in nature or at the hands of corporate sports books—forced a bit of regulation into the NFL's activities. This wouldn't eradicate corruption from the sport, but it certainly would go a long way in curtailing it.

The bottom line is would any of this change the way the game is played? Not in the least. If the NFL can claim none of the billions of dollars in illegal gambling has altered a single player's performance, then there's no reason to believe legal gambling would change that fact.

But it would have an effect on the way the game is consumed, though many fans might never notice a difference. The only change in television coverage might be that gambling talk takes the forefront of many pre- and post-game programs. Then again, it might not. The consumers' demands would dictate such change. Wagering or not, fans are still going to want to know how the season plays out and who ultimately wins the Super Bowl. Gambling would just be the hot fudge topping on this sundae.

At some point in the near future the NFL's anti-gambling façade will crumble. Not by its own hand; the league has too much "integrity" to go back on decades of rhetoric. But somehow, in some way sports gambling will be legalized in the United States, making this book a relic of a forgotten age. People who stumble upon *A Season in the Abyss* will hardly believe there was a time it was illegal to bet on the NFL, much in the same way some forget a prohibition on alcohol existed or that people could happily enjoy a cigarette in a public area. Though the league will grit its teeth and grumble over sports gambling's legalization, deep in the bowels of the Commissioner's office a cork will pop and champagne will flow.

NOTES

WEEK 1

1 – John Aziz, "How did Americans manage to lose $119 billion gambling last year?" *The Week*, February 5, 2014. http://theweek.com/articles/451623/did-americans-manage-lose-119-billion-gambling-last-year

2 – Mason Levinson and Scott Soshnick, "NBA's Silver Says Legal Sports Gambling in U.S. Is Inevitable," *Bloomberg*, September 4, 2014. http://www.bloomberg.com/news/2014-09-04/nba-s-silver-says-legal-sports-gambling-in-u-s-is-inevitable.html

3 – Ken Belson, "Will Other Leagues Join N.B.A.? Don't Bet on It," *New York Times*, November 14, 2014. http://www.nytimes.com/2014/11/15/sports/not-all-leagues-ready-to-go-all-in-on-legalized-gambling.html?ref=sports&_r=0

4 – Andrew Porter, "Governor Christie On Sports Betting: Leagues Are 'Not In Touch With Reality,'" November 12, 2014. http://philadelphia.cbslocal.com/2014/11/12/governor-christie-on-sports-betting-leagues-are-not-in-touch-with-reality/

5 – Jordan Weissmann, "Big Bucks or Bogus Betting Baloney?" *Slate*,

November 21, 2014.
http://www.slate.com/articles/business/moneybox/2014/11/adam_silver
_says_there_s_400_billion_per_year_of_illegal_sports_betting.html

6 – David Purdum, "Wagers, bettor losses set record," *ESPN*, January
30, 2015. http://espn.go.com/chalk/story/_/id/12253876/nevada-sports-
bettors-wagered-lost-more-ever-2014

7 – "Illegal Super Bowl Bets to Total $3.8 Billion This Year,"
American Gambling Association press release, January 22, 2015.
http://www.americangaming.org/newsroom/press-releases/illegal-
super-bowl-bets-to-total-38-billion-this-year

8 – David Purdum, "Sports betting: 'Until the NFL feels that it can
profit from it, they'll be opposed to it,'" *Betting Talk*, January 27, 2014.
http://www.bettingtalk.com/sports-betting-nfl-feels-can-profit-theyll-
opposed/

9 – David Purdum, "NFL: Stance on sports betting has nothing to do
with money," *SportingNews*, March 6, 2013.
http://linemakers.sportingnews.com/nfl/2013-03-06/new-jersey-sports-
betting-case-nfl-stance-league-lawsuit-roger-goodell

10 – Adam Silver, "Legalize and Regulate Sports Betting," *New York
Times*, November 13, 2014.
http://www.nytimes.com/2014/11/14/opinion/nba-commissioner-adam-
silver-legalize-sports-
betting.html?module=ArrowsNav&contentCollection=Opinion&action
=keypress&region=FixedLeft&pgtype=article&_r=1

WEEK 2

1 – Fantasy Sports Trade Association website. https://fsta.site-
ym.com/?page=Demographics

2 – "41 Million People in the U.S. and Canada Play Fantasy Sports,"
Ipsos press release, June 18, 2014. http://www.ipsos-na.com/news-
polls/pressrelease.aspx?id=6540

3 – Fantasy Sports Trade Association website. https://fsta.site-

ym.com/?page=Demographics

4 – FanDuel website. https://www.fanduel.com/legal

5 – Ibid.

6 – John McDuling, "The bizarre, multibillion-dollar industry of American fantasy sports," December 13, 2014. http://qz.com/298042/the-bizarre-multi-billion-dollar-industry-of-american-fantasy-sports/

7 – "Why Fantasy Sports Is Not Gambling," Fantasy Sports Trade Association website, https://fsta.site-ym.com/?page=FSandGambling

8 – *Outside the Lines* (video), *ESPN*, original airdate August, 2014. https://www.youtube.com/watch?v=xPubMOh_Tw8

9 – Ben Cohen, "How a Full-Time Fantasy Sports Professional Hit the Jackpot," *Wall Street Journal* (blog), December 17, 2014. http://blogs.wsj.com/dailyfix/2014/12/17/how-a-full-time-fantasy-sports-professional-hit-the-jackpot/?mod=WSJBlog

10 – Kirby Garlitos, "NBC increases fantasy sports profile with Rotogrinders deal; Poker pro wins Draftkings Millionaire Maker," *Calvin Ayre*, October 13, 2014. http://calvinayre.com/2014/10/13/sports/nbc-increases-fantasy-sports-profile-with-rotogrinders-deal-poker-pro-wins-draftkings-millionaire-maker

11 – Joe Drape, "Lost a Fantasy Game? Try Again Tomorrow," *New York Times*, July 28, 2014. http://www.nytimes.com/2014/07/29/sports/baseball/daily-fantasy-sports-sites-draw-the-real-worlds-attention.html?smid=tw-share&_r=2

12 – "Welcome bonus," FanDuel website. https://www.fanduel.com/pending-bonus

13 – *Outside the Lines* (video), *ESPN*, original airdate August 2014. https://www.youtube.com/watch?v=xPubMOh_Tw8

14 – Fantasy Sports Trade Association website. https://fsta.site-ym.com/?page=Demographics

15 – *Outside the Lines* (video), *ESPN*, original airdate August 2014. https://www.youtube.com/watch?v=xPubMOh_Tw8

16 – Tony Batt, "Daily Fantasy Sports Surging As NFL Season Begins," September 4, 2014. http://www.gamblingcompliance.com/node/54449?fastlogin=notifications/57E6uc&statmid=2492499

17 – John Kindt interview, July 29, 2013. http://illinois.edu/lb/article/72/76010

18 – John McDuling, "The bizarre, multibillion-dollar industry of American fantasy sports," December 13, 2014. http://qz.com/298042/the-bizarre-multi-billion-dollar-industry-of-american-fantasy-sports/

19 – *Outside the Lines* (video), *ESPN*, original airdate August 2014. https://www.youtube.com/watch?v=xPubMOh_Tw8

WEEK 3

1 – UK Gambling Commission website. http://www.gamblingcommission.gov.uk/Gambling-data-analysis/statistics/Industry-statistics.aspx

2 – Scott Schettler, *We Were Wiseguys and Didn't Know It*. (Self published, 2009), 79.

3 – Douglas S. Looney, "The Line is Pulled Out of a Hat," *Sports Illustrated*, March 10, 1986. http://sportsillustrated.cnn.com/vault/article/magazine/MAG1064579/1/index.htm

4 – Schettler, *We Were Wiseguys and Didn't Know It*, 92.

5 – David Purdum, "Wagers, bettor losses set record," *ESPN*, January 30, 2015. http://espn.go.com/chalk/story/_/id/12253876/nevada-sports-

bettors-wagered-lost-more-ever-2014

WEEK 4

1 – Ihosvani Rodriguez, "'Operation Gotham City' targets illegal gambling, money laundering," *Sun Sentinel*, December 6, 2013. http://articles.sun-sentinel.com/2013-12-06/news/fl-illegal-gambling-operation-20131206_1_money-laundering-adam-green-gambling

2 – Christopher Sheldon and Elaine Van Develde, "Sea Bright, Monmouth Beach Men Charged in $1M-A-Week Gambling Ring Bust," June 25, 2013. http://patch.com/new-jersey/rumson/sea-bright-monmouth-beach-men-charged-in-1-millionaweek-gambling-ring-bust

3 – George Anastasia, "Joe Vito Mastronardo, Gentleman Gambler, Heads To Court," October 31, 2013. http://www.bigtrial.net/2013/10/joe-vito-mastronardo-gentleman-gambler.html

4 – Angela Martin & Stephanie Lucero, "Five Billion Dollar Sports Gambling Ring Busted In North Texas," August 15, 2013. http://dfw.cbslocal.com/2013/08/15/five-billion-dollar-gambling-ring-busted-in-north-texas/

5 – Ibid.

WEEK 5

1 – "BetOnSports Founder Sentenced on Federal Racketeering Charges," U.S. Attorney's Office press release, November 2, 2009. http://www.fbi.gov/stlouis/press-releases/2009/sl110209.htm

2 – Cheryl Wittenauer, "BetOnSports.com founder gets 4-plus years," Associated Press, November 3, 2009. http://usatoday30.usatoday.com/tech/news/2009-11-03-betonsports-founder-prison_N.htm

3 – Ibid.

4 – Matt Richtel, "BetOnSports, After Indictment, Folds Its Hand and

Shifts Focus to Asia," New York Times, August 11, 2006.
http://www.nytimes.com/2006/08/11/technology/11gamble.html?_r=0

5 – Jim Salter, "Three plead guilty in BetOnSports online gambling case," *Associated Press*.
http://abcnews.go.com/Technology/story?id=7912696

6 – "BetonSports.com domain sold to former Gary Kaplan associate," *Calvin Ayre*, December 19, 2013.
http://calvinayre.com/2013/12/19/business/former-gary-kaplan-associate-buys-betonsports-domain/

7 – "BetOnSports Founder Sentenced on Federal Racketeering Charges."

8 – Ibid.

9 – "Three Florida Men and a Corporation Convicted for Running Illegal International Gambling Enterprise," Department of Justice, Office of Public Affairs, March 3, 2015.
http://www.justice.gov/opa/pr/three-florida-men-and-corporation-convicted-running-illegal-international-gambling-enterprise

10 – Ibid.

11 – Marisa Lankester, *Dangerous Odds: My Secret Life Inside an Illegal Billion Dollar Sports Betting Operation.* (Cappuccino Books, Stans, Switzerland, 2014), 299.

WEEK 6

1 - Darren Rovell, "Sports Tout Says He's Out to Change Industry's Reputation," *CNBC*, May 19, 2011. http://www.cnbc.com/id/43082158

2 – Big Al's Sportsline website.
http://www.bigal.com/handicappers.cfm?ID=27

3 – Rick Reilly, "1-900-RIPOFFS," *SportsIllustrated*, November 18, 1991. http://www.si.com/vault/1991/11/18/125398/1-900-ripoffs-the-ads-for-call-in-services-that-offer-sure-thing-betting-advice-on-the-big-

games-couldnt-be-more-tempting-our-own-hot-tip-dont-touch-that-phone

4 – "Who is Brandon Lang?"
http://www.brandonlang.com/Handicapper/BrandonLang#biography

5 – Ibid.

6 – Ibid.

WEEK 7

1 – Gerald Strine and Neil D. Isaacs, *Covering The Spread: How to Bet Pro Football*. (Random House, NY NY, 1978), 4.

2 – Mike Fish, "A Life on the Line," *ESPN the Magazine*, February 6, 2015. http://espn.go.com/espn/feature/story/_/id/12280555/how-billy-walters-became-sports-most-successful-controversial-bettor

3 – Mason Levinson, "Trader Brings NFL Algorithms Back to Defend Betting Title," *Bloomberg*, September 3, 2014.
http://www.bloomberg.com/news/2014-09-04/trader-brings-nfl-algorithms-back-to-defend-betting-title.html

4 – Dave Tuley, "Behind the success of CH Ballers," *ESPN*, December 31, 2014. http://espn.go.com/chalk/story/_/id/12103705/espn-chalk-success-2014-supercontest-winners

5 – Ibid.

6 – David Payne Purdum, "Billy Walters: 'Sports betting requires more skill than poker,'" February 8, 2012.
http://www.covers.com/articles/columns/articles.aspx?theArt=264269

WEEK 8

1 – National Council on Problem Gambling REAP newsletter.

2 – "Deadly Bet: The Jason McGuigan Story" (video), *ESPN E:60*, November 13, 2013.

https://www.youtube.com/watch?v=8YO0mZvPJNg

3 – Ibid.

4 – "Barkley claims gambling problem has cost him $10M," ESPN, May 5, 2006. http://sports.espn.go.com/nba/news/story?id=2432043

5 – Ferris Jabr, "How the Brain Gets Addicted to Gambling," *Scientific American*, October 15, 2013.
http://www.scientificamerican.com/article/how-the-brain-gets-addicted-to-gambling/

6 – "Sports Gamblers Are Delusional About Chances of Winning, Study Finds," Addiction Treatment in Gambling Addiction, July 8, 2013.
http://www.addictiontreatmentmagazine.com/addiction/gambling-addiction/sports-gamblers-are-delusional-about-chances-of-winning-study-finds/

7 – C.D. Carter, "When Fantasy Football Becomes an Addiction," *New York Times* (blog), November 27, 2012.
http://fifthdown.blogs.nytimes.com/2012/11/27/when-fantasy-football-becomes-an-addiction/#more-109106

8 – Ibid.

WEEK 9

1 – Michael Janofsky, "Schlichter: A Pattern of Gambling That Began in His Youth," *New York Times*, July 10, 1983.
http://www.nytimes.com/1983/07/10/sports/schlichter-a-pattern-of-gambling-that-began-in-his-youth.html

2 – Ibid.

3 – Ibid.

4 – Ibid.

5 – "Art Schlichter sentenced to 11 years," *Associated Press*, May 4,

2012. http://espn.go.com/college-football/story/_/id/7890630/ex-ohio-state-buckeyes-indianapolis-colts-qb-art-schlichter-gets-11-years-prison

6 – Corey Nachman, "The 16 Most Legendary Stories of Gambling in Sports," *Business Insider*, April 22, 2011. http://www.businessinsider.com/athletes-gambling-in-sports-2011-4?op=1#ixzz3ZbiRfjIa

7 – Steve Budin with Bob Schaller, *Bets, Drugs, and Rock & Roll: The Rise and Fall of the World's First Offshore Sports Gambling Empire.* (Skyhorse Publishing, 2007), 172-173.

8 – Ibid, 172-173.

9 – Ibid, 174.

10 – Ibid, 174-175.

11 – Patrick Cain, Anna Katherine Clemmons, Craig Custance, Matt Ehalt, Dan Friedell, Hallie Grossman, Doug McIntyre and Matthew Muench, *Gambling Confidential, ESPN The Magazine,* February 3, 2015. http://espn.go.com/chalk/story/_/id/12244334/nfl-nba-nhl-mlb-pros-weigh-sports-gambling

12 – Heather Wardle and Andrew Gibbons, "Gambling among sports people," NatCen Social Research Study.

13 – "NCAA: Men's betting down 9 percent," Associated Press, May 8, 2013. http://espn.go.com/college-sports/story/_/id/9255986/ncaa-study-reports-gambling-athletes

14 – Georgia Council on Problem Gambling website, https://www.georgiagamblinghelp.org/professional-athletes-gambling/

15 – Nachman , "The 16 Most Legendary Stories of Gambling in Sports."

WEEK 10

1 – Jonah Lehrer, "Cracking the Scratch Lottery Code," *Wired*, January 31, 2011. http://www.wired.com/2011/01/ff_lottery/

2 – "Report 13-11," Wisconsin Lottery Department of Revenue, July 2013, 22.

3 – David Broughton, "Lotteries still a scratch and win for sports?" *Sports Business Daily*, February 10, 2014. http://m.sportsbusinessdaily.com/Journal/Issues/2014/02/10/In-Depth/Lottery.aspx

4 – Ibid.

5 – Ibid.

6 – Katie DeLong, "Green Bay Packers…LOTTERY! The Pack teams up with Wisconsin Lottery to offer scratch-off tickets," July 28, 2014. http://fox6now.com/2014/07/28/green-bay-packers-lottery-the-pack-teams-up-with-wisconsin-lottery-to-offer-scratch-off-tickets/

7 – Ibid.

8 – Report 13-11, 23.

9 – "Wisconsin lottery auditors don't like branded scratch games," July 26, 2013. http://www.lotterypost.com/news/264033

10 – Ibid.

11 – Broughton, "Lotteries still a scratch and win for sports?"

12 – Ibid.

WEEK 12

1 – Denis M. Crawford, *Hugh Culverhouse and the Tampa Bay Buccaneers: How a Skinflint Genius with a Losing Team Made the Modern NFL.* (McFarland, 2011), 44.

2 – Joe Drape, "The Official Line vs. the Betting Line," *New York Times*, January 31, 2008. http://www.nytimes.com/2008/01/31/sports/football/31gambling.html?_r=0

3 – Edward James, "Hidden Percentages," *Turf and Sport Digest*, December 1937.

4 – Don Kowet, *The Rich Who Own Sports.*(Random House, NY, 1977), 49-50.

5 –Ibid, 33-34.

6 – Ibid, 36-37.

7 – Don Bauder, "The NFL's Dirty Secret," July 4, 2012. http://www.sandiegoreader.com/news/2012/jul/04/citylights1-nfl-dirty-secret/#

8 – Kowet, *The Rich Who Own Sports*, 50-51.

9 – Ibid, 173.

10 – Ibid, 176.

11 – Jay Busbee, "Colts owner sent $8,500 to a fan who guessed the correct Ravens-Pats score," *Yahoo*, January 24, 2013. http://sports.yahoo.com/blogs/nfl-shutdown-corner/colts-owner-sent-8-500-fan-guessed-correct-145513461--nfl.html

12 – Lindsay H. Jones, "Colts' Jim Irsay suspended six games, fined $500,000 by NFL after DUI plea," *USA Today*, September 2, 2014. http://www.usatoday.com/story/sports/nfl/colts/2014/09/02/jim-irsay-dui-plea-probation-indianapolis/14964761/

13 – "Browns owner's company in trouble," *ESPN*, April 19, 2013. http://espn.go.com/nfl/story/_/id/9187986/cleveland-browns-owner-jimmy-haslam-iii-knew-company-fraud-scheme-documents-say

14 – Matt Wood, "Jimmy Haslam, the FBI & the 158 Pages That Will Cost Him the Browns," April 19, 2013.

http://www.dawgsbynature.com/2013/4/19/4241314/jimmy-haslam-the-fbi-the-158-pages-that-will-cost-him-the-browns

15 – "Pilot Flying J to pay \$92M fine," *ESPN*, July 14,2014. http://espn.go.com/nfl/story/_/id/11214330/jimmy-haslam-company-pilot-flying-j-pay-92m-fine

16 – Ibid.

17 – Jack Bechta, "Five components of an NFL contract that may surprise you," August 1, 2012. http://www.nationalfootballpost.com/5-components-of-an-NFL-contract-that-may-surprise-you.html

18 – Ryan Van Bibber, "Judge rules Vikings owners committed fraud, racketeering," *SBNation*, August 6, 2013. http://www.sbnation.com/nfl/2013/8/6/4594092/minnesota-vikings-zygi-wilf-fraud-lawsuit-new-jersey

19 – Ibid.

20 – Keith Whitmire, "Jerry Jones: Cowboys weren't supposed to beat the Chiefs, Vegas said so," *FS Southwest*, September 17, 2013. http://www.foxsports.com/southwest/story/jerry-jones-cowboys-werent-supposed-to-beat-the-chiefs-vegas-said-so-091713

21 – Ibid.

22 – Drape, "The Official Line vs. the Betting Line."

WEEK 13

1 – "Chris Conte: NFL worth early death," *ESPN*, December 17, 2014. http://espn.go.com/chicago/nfl/story/_/id/12040968/chris-conte-chicago-bears-says-playing-nfl-worth-long-term-health-risk

2 – Nate Jackson, *Slow Getting Up: A Story of NFL Survival From the Bottom of the Pile.* (Harper Collins, NY, 2013). Ebook version, 158-159.

3 – Ashley Dunkak, "Many NFL Players Want Thursday Games To

A SEASON IN THE ABYSS

Disappear; Reggie Bush Says Games Are 'Like A Car Crash,'"
December 4, 2013. http://detroit.cbslocal.com/2013/12/04/many-nfl-
players-want-thursday-games-to-disappear-reggie-bush-says-its-like-a-
car-crash/

4 – Bob Kravitz, "Pain! Lifelong Companion of Many NFL Alumni,"
The Pittsburgh Press, December 23, 1984.

5 –Peter Gent, *North Dallas Forty*. (Open Road Integrated Media, NY,
1973, 2003) Ebook version, 2568.

6 – Dave Meggysey, *Out of their League*. (Ramparts Press Inc., NY,
1971), 72.

7 – Kravitz, "Pain! Lifelong Companion of Many NFL Alumni."

8 – Ibid.

9 – Dan Pastorini with John P. Lopez, *Taking Flak*. (AuthorHouse,
Bloomington IN, 2011), 35.

10 – Ibid, 87.

11 – Ibid, 137.

12 – Clare Farnsworth, "Kam Chancellor, Richard Sherman and Earl
Thomas played with, and through, serious injuries," February 4, 2015.
http://www.seahawks.com/news/articles/article-1/Kam-Chancellor-
Richard-Sherman-and-Earl-Thomas-played-with-and-through-serious-
injuries/f35b464e-b6a3-42eb-a5a1-2f6418c5fe53

13 – Ibid.

14 – Ibid.

15 – Dan Wiederer, "NFL and pain: League zeros in on one pain
medication," *Star Tribune*, August 22, 2012.
http://www.startribune.com/sports/vikings/166712256.html?refer=y&re
fer=y

16 – Ibid.

17 – Ibid.

18 – Ibid.

19 – Ibid.

20 – Ibid.

21 – Larry Getlen, "How the NFL leaves players broken — and broke," *New York Post*, December 14, 2014. http://nypost.com/2014/12/14/how-the-nfl-leaves-players-broken-and-broke/

22 - John Keim, "Most would play SB with concussion," ESPN, January 28, 2014. http://espn.go.com/nfl/story/_/id/10358874/majority-nfl-players-play-super-bowl-concussion-espn-survey

23 – Ibid.

24 – Ibid.

25 – Meggysey, Out of their League, 108.

26 – Eric Kesteroct, "What I Saw as an N.F.L. Ball Boy," *New York Times*, November 10, 2014. http://www.nytimes.com/2014/10/11/opinion/what-i-saw-as-an-nfl-ball-boy.html?ref=sports&_r=2

27 – Ashley Dunkak, "NFL Explains Why Players Not Fined For Violating Concussion Protocol," January 14, 2014. http://detroit.cbslocal.com/2014/01/14/nfl-explains-why-players-not-fined-for-violating-concussion-protocol/

28 – Ibid.

29 – Dunkak, "Many NFL Players Want Thursday Games To Disappear; Reggie Bush Says Games Are 'Like A Car Crash.'" http://detroit.cbslocal.com/2013/12/04/many-nfl-players-want-thursday-games-to-disappear-reggie-bush-says-its-like-a-car-crash/

30 – Mike Florio, "League of Denial fails to tell the whole story

on concussions," *Pro Football Talk*, October 9, 2013.
http://profootballtalk.nbcsports.com/2013/10/09/league-of-denial-fails-
to-tell-the-whole-story-on-concussions/

31 – Meggysey, Out of their League, 73.

32 – Ed Werder, "Player: NFL treats us 'like criminals,'" *ESPN*,
January 29, 2015.
http://espn.go.com/nfl/playoffs/2014/story/_/id/12248954/seattle-
seahawks-miffed-hgh-tests

33 – "NFL will begin testing for human growth hormone on Monday,"
October 3, 2014.
http://www.nfl.com/news/story/0ap3000000404929/article/nfl-will-
begin-testing-for-human-growth-hormone-on-monday

34 – Jackson, Slow Getting Up, 71.

35 – Ibid, 100-101.

36 – Ibid, 217.

37 – Jim Litke, "DEA agents raid NFL medical staffs after games,"
Associated Press, November, 16, 2014.

38 – Sally Jenkins and Rick Maese, "Federal drug agents launch
surprise inspections of NFL teams following games," *Washington Post*,
November 16, 2014.
http://www.washingtonpost.com/sports/redskins/federal-drug-agents-
launch-surprise-inspections-of-nfl-teams-following-
games/2014/11/16/5545c84e-6da5-11e4-8808-afaa1e3a33ef_story.html

39 – Ibid.

40 – Elizabeth Murray, "Is Medical Weed Possible For NFL Players?"
January 14, 2014. http://fusion.net/story/4651/is-medical-weed-
possible-for-nfl-players/

41 – Ibid.

42 – Getlen, "How the NFL leaves players broken — and broke."

43 – Kevin McSpadden, "NFL Hall of Famer Mike Ditka Wouldn't Let His Son Play Football Today," *Time*, January 20, 2015. http://time.com/3673997/nfl-painkillers-mike-ditka-1985-chicago-bears/

44 – Don Reese with John Underwood, "I'm Not Worth a Damn," *Sports Illustrated*, June 14, 1982.

WEEK 14

1 – Kevin Draper, "According To The NFL, NFL Security Is Incompetent," *Deadspin*, October 6, 2014. http://deadspin.com/according-to-the-nfl-nfl-security-is-incompetent-1643195208

2 – Rob Maaddi, "AP Newsbreak: Source says Rice video sent to NFL," *Associated Press*, September 11, 2014. http://bigstory.ap.org/article/ap-newsbreak-source-says-rice-video-sent-nfl

3 – Tom Ley, "NFL-Backed Investigation: NFL Didn't Lie About Seeing Ray Rice Tape," *Deadspin*, January 8, 2015. http://deadspin.com/nfl-backed-investigation-nfl-didnt-lie-about-seeing-ra-1678291973

4 – Ibid.

5 – Ryan Glasspiegel, "ESPN Legal Analyst: NFL Security Has Been Digging Up Information and Hiding it For Years," September 10, 2014. http://thebiglead.com/2014/09/10/espn-legal-analyst-nfl-security-has-been-digging-up-information-and-hiding-it-for-years/

6 – Ibid.

7 – Ibid.

8 – "NFL ignored 'hundreds' of domestic violence cases: former exec," *New York Post*, October 9, 2014. http://nypost.com/2014/10/09/nfl-ignored-hundreds-of-domestic-violence-cases-former-exec/

9 – Ibid.

10 – Harry Wismer, *The Public Calls It Sport*. (Prentice-Hall, Inc., Englewood Cliffs NJ, 1965), 53-54.

11 – Dan E. Moldea, *Interference: How Organized Crime Influences Professional Football*. (William Morrow & Co, NY, 1989), 33.

12 – Howard Cosell with Peter Bonventre, *I Never Played the Game*. (William Morrow and Company, Inc. NY 1985), 110.

13 – Tom Ley, "Something Very Weird Happened During ESPN's Interview With Bill Polian," *Deadspin*, September 11, 2014. http://deadspin.com/bill-polian-disagrees-with-bill-polians-insider-opinion-1633593081

14 – Ibid.

15 – Kent Babb and Adam Goldman, "NFL's elaborate security network is supposed to protect league from trouble," *Washington Post*, September 13, 2014. http://www.washingtonpost.com/sports/redskins/nfls-elaborate-security-network-is-supposed-to-protect-league-from-trouble/2014/09/13/795949aa-3b4a-11e4-8601-97ba88884ffd_story.html

16 – Tony Dorsett & Harvey Frommer, *Running Tough: Memoirs of a Football Maverick*. (Doubleday, NY, 1989), 70-71.

17 – Ibid, 83.

18 – Ibid, 147.

19 – Babb and Goldman, "NFL's elaborate security network is supposed to protect league from trouble."

20 – Ibid.

21 – Steve Fainaru and Mark Fainaru-Wada, "Deputy also Steelers' security fixer," *ESPN*, January 22, 2015. http://espn.go.com/espn/otl/story/_/id/12210027/pittsburgh-steelers-

security-chief-dual-role-sheriff-officer-questioned

22 – Ibid.

23 – Polly Mosendz, "Wife of Former Player Says NFL Told Her Not to Call Cops During Violent Incident," September 17, 2014. http://www.thewire.com/business/2014/09/wife-of-football-player-says-nfl-told-her-not-to-contact-authorities-for-help/380325/

24 – Ibid.

25 – Diana Moskovitz, "DA Memo In Ray McDonald Case Shows How Cop Worked As 49ers Lackey," *Deadspin*, November 10, 2014. http://deadspin.com/da-memo-in-ray-mcdonald-case-shows-how-cop-worked-as-49-1656872780

26 – Ibid.

27 – Gent, *North Dallas Forty*, 4571.

28 – Ibid, 4608.

WEEK 15

1 – Tobias J. Moskowitz and L. Jon Werthheim, *Scorecasting: The Hidden Influences Behind How Sports Are Played and Games Are Won. (Three Rivers Press, 2011)*, 115-116.

2 – Ibid, 138.

3 – Ibid, 152.

4 – Ibid, 157.

5 – Ibid, 160.

6 – Sean Gregory, "I Was a Replacement Ref: Inside the NFL's 7 Weirdest Weeks," *Time* (blog), September 28, 2012. http://keepingscore.blogs.time.com/2012/09/28/a-replacement-ref-reflects-did-the-nfl-overlook-an-obvious-experience-gap/?sct=hp_t2_a5

7 – Michael David Smith, "NFLPA accuses owners of 'greed' for locking out referees," *Pro Football Talk*, September 23, 2012. http://profootballtalk.nbcsports.com/2012/09/23/nflpa-accuses-owners-of-greed-for-locking-out-referees/

8 – Michael David Smith, "Jerry Jones can't see a difference with replacement refs," *Pro Football Talk*, August 23, 2012. http://profootballtalk.nbcsports.com/2012/08/23/jerry-jones-cant-see-a-difference-with-replacement-refs/

9 – Michael David Smith, "Bob McNair on replacement refs: 'I can't see any difference,'" *Pro Football Talk*, August 20, 2012. http://profootballtalk.nbcsports.com/2012/08/20/bob-mcnair-on-replacement-refs-i-cant-see-any-difference/

10 – Elizabeth Merrill, "Dean Blandino keeps refs in check," ESPN, January 28, 2015. http://espn.go.com/nfl/playoffs/2014/story/_/id/12243782/former-comedian-dean-blandino-one-most-powerful-men-nfl

11 – Jeffrey Stern, Tood Korth, Rick Woelfel, and edited by Jerry Tapp, *Whole New Ballgame: Safe, Secure, by the Rules*. (The National Association of Sports Officials and *Referee* Magazine, Racine WI, 2014), 13-14.

12 – Ibid, 13.

13 – Ibid, 13.

14 – Kevin Seifert, "Inside Slant: Penalties begin to regulate," *ESPN*, August 29, 2014. http://espn.go.com/blog/nflnation/post/_/id/137844/inside-slant-nfl-penalties-begin-to-regulate

15 – Matt Birch, "Dean Blandino: Number of penalties will decrease in regular season," *Yardbarker*, August 22, 2014. http://network.yardbarker.com/nfl/article_external/dean_blandino_number_of_penalties_will_decrease_in_regular_season/17107259?mb_edition=3647&linksrc=mb_story_related_6_17126978

16 – Ibid.

17 – Kevin Seifert, "Inside Slant: Most penalty types sorted by referees," *ESPN*, December 19, 2014. http://espn.go.com/blog/nflnation/tag/_/name/officiating-report-2014

18 – Ibid.

19 – Ibid.

20 – Kevin Seifert, "Inside Slant: In NFL officiating, 'right' or 'wrong' aren't only options," *ESPN*, October, 3, 2014. http://espn.go.com/blog/nflnation/post/_/id/143210/inside-slant-in-nfl-officiating-right-or-wrong-arent-only-options

21 – Stern et al., *Whole New Ballgame*, 25.

22 – Ibid, 26.

23 – Ibid, 14.

24 – Ibid, 15-16.

25 – Ibid, 15-16.

26 – Ibid, 15-16.

27 – Rick Maese, "Fans throw conspiracy flag at NFL," *Washington Post*, January 5, 2015. http://www.washingtonpost.com/sports/fans-throw-conspiracy-flag-at-nfl/2015/01/05/a8ec224c-952b-11e4-8385-866293322c2f_story.html?tid=pm_sports_pop

28 – Todd Archer, "Pete Morelli: Penalty not warranted," *ESPN*, January 5, 2015. http://espn.go.com/dallas/nfl/story/_/id/12121292/referee-pete-morelli-explains-overturned-pass-interference-call-dallas-cowboys-detroit-lions-wild-card-game

29 – Richard Deitsch, "Man behind the mic: Fox NFL analyst Troy Aikman on broadcasting, more," *SportsIllustrated*, January 14, 2015. http://www.si.com/nfl/2015/01/13/troy-aikman-fox-nfl-analyst-qa

30 – Todd Archer, "Dez catch reversal dooms Cowboys," *ESPN*, January 12, 2015.

31 – Ibid.

32 – Stern et al., *Whole New Ballgame*, 30.

WEEK 16

1 – Kevin Clark, "The League That Runs Everything," *Wall Street Journal*, September 15, 2014. http://online.wsj.com/articles/the-league-that-runs-everything-1410736053

2 – Darren Rovell, "NFL: Fans still watching in droves," *ESPN*, November 20, 2014. http://espn.go.com/nfl/story/_/id/11909048/nfl-games-comprise-28-30-most-watched-television-shows-fall

3 – Sara Bibel, "NFL 2014 TV Recap: 202 Million Viewers, Game Viewership Nearly Triples Broadcast Primetime," January 9, 2015. http://tvbythenumbers.zap2it.com/2015/01/09/nfl-2014-tv-recap-202-million-viewers-game-viewership-nearly-triples-broadcast-primetime/348433/

4 – Paul Bond, "CBS CEO Leslie Moonves: 'Football Is Still the Best Thing on Television,'" *Hollywood Reporter*, September 17, 2014. http://www.hollywoodreporter.com/news/cbs-ceo-leslie-moonves-football-733822

5 – Clark, "The League That Runs Everything."

6 – Bond, "CBS CEO Leslie Moonves: 'Football Is Still the Best Thing on Television.'"

7 – Cecilia Kang, "Bidding war between networks, sports leagues will increase price of cable TV," *Washington Post*, January 23, 2015. http://www.washingtonpost.com/business/economy/bidding-war-between-networks-sports-leagues-will-increase-price-of-cable-tv/2015/01/23/d0cb19f4-9db8-11e4-a7ee-526210d665b4_story.html

8 – Ibid.

9 – Cosell with Bonventre, *I Never Played the Game*, 311-312.

10 – Mark Kriegel, *Namath: A Biography*. (Viking: The Penguin Group, NY, 2004) 319.

11 – Arthur J. Donovan, Jr. and Bob Drury, *Fatso: Football When Mean Were Really Men*. (William Morrow and Company, Inc, NY, 1987), 155-156.

12 – Cindy Boren, "Bill Simmons rips NBC's Al Michaels, Cris Collinsworth for lauding Roger Goodell during NFL playoffs," *Washington Post*, January 11, 2015.
http://www.washingtonpost.com/blogs/early-lead/wp/2015/01/11/bill-simmons-rips-nbcs-al-michaels-cris-collinsworth-for-lauding-roger-goodell-during-nfl-playoffs/

13 – Ibid.

14 – Ibid.

15 – Wismer, *The Public Calls It Sport*, 129-130.

16 – Aaron Gordon, "Playmakers, the Show the NFL Killed for Being Too Real," *Vice*, April 22, 2015.
https://sports.vice.com/en_us/article/playmakers-the-show-the-nfl-killed-for-being-too-real

17 – Ibid.

18 – Don Van Natta Jr., "OTL: His Game, His Rules," *ESPN*, April 18, 2013. http://espn.go.com/espn/story/_/page/RogerGoodell/game-rules

19 – Ibid.

20 –Cosell with Bonventre, *I Never Played the Game*, 13-16.

WEEK 17

1 – Ryan M. Rodenberg and L. Jon Wertheim, "Gambling fills the coffers of all major sports, but at what price?" *SportsIllustrated*, May 7, 2014. http://www.si.com/more-sports/2014/05/07/sports-gambling

2 – Ibid.

3 – "WADA director general: 25 percent of sport is controlled by organised crime," *Sports Business News*, October 11, 2014. http://sportsbusinessnews.com/content/wada-director-general-25-cent-sport-controlled-organised-crime

4 – "Cheating confidential," *ESPN*, May 30, 2013. http://espn.go.com/espn/story/_/id/9305464/confidential-survey-shows-how-athletes-define-cheating-espn-magazine

5 – "Gambling Confidential," *ESPN*, February 3, 2015. http://espn.go.com/chalk/story/_/id/12244334/nfl-nba-nhl-mlb-pros-weigh-sports-gambling

6 – Eric Edholm, "Kelvin Benjamin said he purposely ran slow 40 so Panthers would draft him," *Yahoo*, October 29, 2014. http://sports.yahoo.com/blogs/nfl-shutdown-corner/kelvin-benjamin-said-he-purposely-ran-slow-40-so-panthers-would-draft-him-135822941.html

7 – Frank Schwab, "Ty Detmer says brother Koy and Eagles faked knee injury," *Yahoo*, November 12, 2014. http://sports.yahoo.com/blogs/nfl-shutdown-corner/ty-detmer-says-brother-koy-and-eagles-faked-knee-injury-001153536.html

8 – Michael C. Wright, "Brian Urlacher: Bears had 'dive guy,'" *ESPN*, September 4, 2013. http://espn.go.com/chicago/nfl/story/_/id/9634085/brian-urlacher-admits-chicago-bears-faked-some-injuries

9 – Jeffri Chadiha, "NFL players look for any edge they can get," *ESPN*, August 9, 2007. http://sports.espn.go.com/espn/cheat/news/story?id=2957893

10 – "Lomas Brown regrets whiffed block," *ESPN*, December 27, 2012. http://espn.go.com/nfl/story/_/id/8783859/lomas-brown-former-detroit-lions-offensive-lineman-current-espn-analyst-regrets-allowing-injury-scott-mitchell

11 – John Barr, "Sources: Saints' GM could eavesdrop," ESPN, April 24, 2012. http://espn.go.com/espn/otl/story/_/id/7846290/new-orleans-saints-mickey-loomis-eavesdrop-opposing-coaches-home-games

12 – Chadiha, "NFL players look for any edge they can get."

13 – Ibid.

14 – David Newton, "Ex-GM on Pats: Culture of cheating," *ESPN*, January 23, 2015. http://espn.go.com/nfl/story/_/id/12216634/former-carolina-panthers-gm-marty-hurney-angry-spygate-amid-new-england-patriots-controversy

15 – Ibid.

16 – Michael David Smith, "Brad Johnson paid a bribe to tamper with footballs at the Super Bowl," *Pro Football Talk*, January 21, 2015. http://profootballtalk.nbcsports.com/2015/01/21/brad-johnson-paid-a-bribe-to-tamper-with-footballs-at-the-super-bowl/

17 – Mike Freeman, *Bloody Sundays*. (William Morrow and Company, Inc., NY, 2003), 60.

18 – Michael MacCambridge, *America's Game*. (Random House, NY, 2004), 430.

19 – Jackson, *Slow Getting Up*, 18.

20 – Kevin Patra, "Roger Goodell: No momentum for playoff reseeding (video)," January 8, 2014. http://www.nfl.com/news/story/0ap2000000310694/article/roger-goodell-says-nfl-considering-playoff-expansion

ABOUT THE AUTHOR

Brian Tuohy is America's leading expert on game fixing in sports. He is the author *The Fix Is In: The Showbiz Manipulations of the NFL, MLB, NBA, NHL, and NASCAR*; *Larceny Games: Sports Gambling, Game Fixing, and the FBI*; and *Disaster Government: National Emergencies, Continuity of Government, and You*. He has been published in *Sports Illustrated, Vice Sports, Sports On Earth*, and *Bleacher Report*, and has appeared as a guest on the Dan Patrick Show, Coast to Coast AM, the Steve Czaban Show, the Artie Lange Show, Boomer & Carton, Chris Myers Interviews, JT the Brick, the Brian Kenny Show, and Alex Jones among many, many others.

Brian can be contacted through his website: thefixisin.net

Made in the USA
Lexington, KY
28 March 2017